BLUNT
INSTRUMENTS

BLUNT
INSTRUMENTS

RECOGNIZING RACIST CULTURAL
INFRASTRUCTURE
IN MEMORIALS, MUSEUMS,
AND PATRIOTIC PRACTICES

KRISTIN ANN HASS

BEACON PRESS,
Boston

BEACON PRESS
Boston, Massachusetts
www.beacon.org

Beacon Press books
are published under the auspices of
the Unitarian Universalist Association of Congregations.

© 2022 by Kristin Ann Hass

25 24 23 22   8 7 6 5 4 3 2 1

This book is printed on acid-free paper that meets the uncoated paper
ANSI/NISO specifications for permanence as revised in 1992.

Composition by BookMatters, Berkeley

Library of Congress Cataloging-in-Publication Data
is available for this title.

Hardcover ISBN: 978-0-8070-0671-9
Ebook ISBN: 978-0-8070-0672-6

For Cameron and Finn and Cole and Hazel

For K

*And for my teachers and classmates
at Columbus School in 1974 and 1975*

CONTENTS

INTRODUCTION

White Lies Matter

IN MARCH 2021, A group of activists calling themselves "White Lies Matter, Inc." stole a heavy stone chair from a cemetery in Selma, Alabama. It was a memorial to Jefferson Davis. The group emailed local media with ransom terms for the memorial's owners, the United Daughters of the Confederacy (UDC). They included photographs of a hole being cut into the seat (of a clever replica) of the chair and promised to use it as a toilet unless the women of the UDC hung a banner on the front of their headquarters in Richmond, Virginia, quoting Assata Shakur: "The rulers of this country have always considered their property more important than our lives." The group asked for the banner to hang for twenty-four hours on Friday, April 9, 2021—the anniversary of the Confederacy's surrender in the Civil War. Unsurprisingly, the savvy UDC did not take the bait. (See Figure 1.)

But "White Lies Matter, Inc." was on to something, and the group's wit should not mask its cunning. Its name could hardly be smarter, and it captured something crucial about cultural infrastructure in the United States. The activists successfully called out the power of the ordinary—memorials in parks, museums visited by school kids, and routine practices of patriotism, for instance—to naturalize simple untruths. In other words, "White Lies Matter, Inc." helps us see, in a quick, vivid snapshot, that these lies are all around and that they really do matter.

Jefferson Davis was the president of the Confederate States for the duration of the war. He was a man who said things like, "African slavery, as

FIGURE 1 Jefferson Davis Memorial Chair replica

it exists in the United States, is a moral, a social, and a political blessing."[1] And yet the plaque that stood beside the stolen memorial read, "He was the most honest, truest, gentlest, bravest, tenderest, manliest man." There is an undeniable contradiction between believing slavery to be "a moral blessing" and being the "most honest, truest, gentlest, bravest, tenderest, manliest man"—unless you believe in white supremacy. The lie that is implicit in this memorial, and hundreds like it, is that *it is not* an emblem of inequity or violence. The lie is that it is neutral "heritage"—something the UDC has maintained it can proudly protect in 2021 *without being actively racist.* The lie is that these memorials are innocent relics of the past. Pat Godwin, the president of the Selma chapter of the Daughters, claimed to be "absolutely devastated" by the theft, and in 2021 she had good reason to be worried.[2]

In the days and weeks after George Floyd was murdered on May 25, 2020 on the street in front of Cup Foods in Minneapolis, people across the United States and across the world took to the streets to protest. They chanted his name and called for an end to police brutality—and they toppled monuments and memorials. This may have seemed incongruous, initially. By the end of the summer, more than 150 memorials had been knocked down by protesters or unceremoniously removed by municipal governments. Almost none of them were memorials to police officers. They were memorials and monuments of all kinds—mostly in the United States but also in India, Columbia, South Africa, and the UK. In the United States, most were memorials that had stood quietly in local parks and on the grounds of government buildings for at least a century, and most were memorials to Confederate soldiers or Christopher Columbus. They had stood mute, but it seemed to become clear, quite suddenly, that they had been doing the serious cultural work of maintaining racial hierarchies. The protesters tore them down in an effort to reject these everyday affirmations of profound inequities.

And while there is plenty of room for subtlety and nuance in understanding and representing even the most fraught heritage, most cultural infrastructure is like the Davis chair—not made for the expression of subtlety or nuance.

Like the "White Lies Matter" folks, the protestors pulling down monuments were refusing to tolerate lies embedded in the landscape. They were right that these monuments are an important part of the cultural infrastructure, a system of meaning-making, that enabled a brutal murder—which took more than nine minutes and was witnessed by as many as a *billion* people—to be committed by one police officer in front of three others. But these monuments, and the thousands that still stand across the United States, are only one part of the cultural infrastructure—the blunt instruments—that work to maintain basic untruths about race (for instance, that white people are better, more worthy, matter more than Black and brown people).

Blunt Instruments is a field guide of sorts to racist cultural infrastructure in the United States. It is intended to be a tool to help readers identify, contextualize, and name elements of our everyday landscapes and cultural practices that are designed to seem benign or natural but that, in fact, work tirelessly to tell vital stories about who we are, how we came to be, and who belongs. These are stories about who has power in the culture and who doesn't. They are also almost always stories about race.

Blunt Instruments looks at three categories of cultural infrastructure: memorials, museums, and everyday patriotic practices. Each of these has been very much in the news for most of the twenty-first century. In fact, more intense, riotous, fraught attention has been paid to them in the last twenty years than in most of the first two hundred years of American life. And yet they are seldom looked at together or understood explicitly as tools used by particular people in particular times and places to shape the culture in particular ways. This book responds to this gap. *Understanding what cultural infrastructure is and the deep and broad impact that it has is crucial to understanding how structures of inequity are maintained and how they might be dismantled.*

This book is shaped by a few basic observations. The first is that it takes a tremendous amount of work to make fictional ideas about race seem natural. (For instance, the bold, insistent assertion that Confederate soldiers gave their lives to preserve an innocent, race-neutral American heritage.) The second is that cultural infrastructures are powerful tools. (The same people who describe monuments as benign or neutral will go to extraordinary lengths to prevent their removal.) The third is that all infrastructure is cultural. (It is always shaped by the values of the culture.) The fourth observation builds on these. It is that we are surrounded by cultural objects that don't necessarily seem to have anything to do with culture or values or ideology (like a science museum) but that work every day to tell us who we are—and, crucially, that much of this telling, in the obviously cultural infrastructure and the less obviously cultural infrastructure, has been about racial hierarchies and has been effective in maintaining structures of inequity.

This short book does not try to be a comprehensive guide to all cultural infrastructure or to engage with every contemporary debate. Instead, it offers a brief history of three forms of cultural infrastructure—memorials, museums, and everyday patriotic practices—and close readings of a few particularly important examples of each to make it easy for readers to understand the cultural infrastructure they encounter in their daily lives.

STARTING WITH COLIN KAEPERNICK

It began in the preseason and was, initially, such a modest gesture that it went largely unnoticed. San Francisco 49ers quarterback Colin Kaepernick was not in uniform for the first game the team played. He was sitting on the bench—and when the national anthem was played on August 14, 2016, he stayed seated.[3]

Four years earlier, in 2012, teenage Trayvon Martin was murdered in Florida because he seemed threatening to the man who killed him with impunity. In 2014, 18-year-old Michael Brown Jr., who was unarmed, was murdered in broad daylight in front of witnesses. His hands were raised above his head, and he was saying, "Don't shoot."[4] A few months later, Eric Garner was murdered in Staten Island in front of a crowd of witnesses. He told the police officer who had him in a chokehold "I can't breathe" eleven times before he died.[5] Garner's murder, like George Floyd's, was witnessed by millions of people across the United States and around the world who watched a video of the murder that was recorded as it was happening. His death was determined to be a homicide, but the officer who killed him was not indicted.[6] The Black Lives Matter movement emerged, led by Alicia Garza, Patrisse Cullors, and Opal Tometi, and then exploded.

Murders like this were not new in 2012 or 2014 or 2016; they are one of the worst examples in US culture of basic, everyday lies about race that we all live with. We are surrounded by rhetoric about freedom and equality and American ideals. We often share the thrill of those aspirations, *and* we live in a culture in which unarmed Black men, women, boys, and girls are regularly killed by police officers who are not held responsible for their violence. (Eric Garner is not even the only E. Garner to be killed by police in New York City.) We can elect a Black president and still allow Black people—on a regular basis—to be murdered with impunity. We can witness every minute of the murders; we can all watch them over and over and then watch the perpetrators of the violence walk free.

As Kaepernick tells it, he simply hit a breaking point with these contradictions. His act of protest was first noticed on August 26, 2016. After the game, he told reporters, "I am not going to stand up to show pride in a flag for a country that oppresses Black people and people of color. To me, this is bigger than football, and it would be selfish on my part to look the other way. There are bodies in the street and people getting paid leave and getting away with murder."[7] The NFL responded in a bold statement that read, "The national anthem is and always will be a special part of the pre-game ceremony. It is an opportunity to honor our country and reflect on the great liberties we are afforded as its citizens. In respecting such American principles as freedom of religion and freedom of expression, we recognize the right of an individual to choose to participate, or not, in our celebration of the national anthem."[8] This statement implies that the national anthem has always been part of football games, and this is simply not true. It does, however, convey a sense of what Kaepernick was messing with. It insists with quiet authority that "this is how we do things"; and it asserts, with remarkable tone-deafness, that the point of the anthem is to "reflect on the great liberties we are afforded as...citizens" without seeming to understand how ridiculous this might sound to people frustrated by living in a culture in which some people seem to be empowered to kill Black people—in front of millions of witnesses—at will. For the NFL in 2016, the only options were flag or no flag, celebrating liberties or not celebrating liberties. There was no acknowledgment that there might be a bigger problem, no conception that those liberties might be inequitably distributed, no awareness that the anthem and the act of standing for it were part of the system that enables some Americans to believe they live in an egalitarian society despite the obvious fact of the deaths of Martin, Brown, Garner, Floyd and many more, including Breonna Taylor, Sandra Bland, and Michelle Cusseaux.

Kaepernick is an important starting place for this book because he refused to participate in cultural infrastructure in which there has been a huge investment. He refused cultural infrastructure that is built to deny inequality and to make an *invented* story about who we are in the United States seem to be an untouchable, eternal truth. This may seem like an overreach—and that is why this book is useful, because it is actually fairly easy to make the case that it is not. The fifth and sixth chapters on patriotic practices show that the national anthem was made official relatively late in the short life of the nation and was intended, in part, to build a particular kind of race-based national unity to claim freedom for all that was, in fact, freedom for some. They show that practices around standing to salute the flag were invented in the 1890s by people who were anxious about immigration. And they explore how the NFL, when it was up in arms about Kaepernick, was being paid tens of millions of dollars by the Department of Defense to deliver patriotic pageantry. (The league was cynically defending patriotism, for which it was getting paid, while Kaepernick was paying dearly for his deeply patriotic act.)

These patriotic practices, and our museums and historic sites and the memorials and monuments that shape our shared landscapes, are all made things. They are made in particular places by particular people to do particular work in the culture. They have been remarkably effective at simultaneously reinforcing and denying inequity, and that is why they need to be transformed.

Kaepernick's refusal to participate in the anthem's cultural project both threatened the social order it maintains and revealed its mechanisms. His refusal was a personal act, but it provoked an enormous reaction because he dared to deny a big, powerful lie by refusing to be a part of its daily maintenance. In doing so, he had a profound and lasting impact. He asked us all to think about how obvious, crushing inequities are maintained; he asked us all to think about the work that our cultural infrastructure does and what we can do about it.

It is also worth noting that Kaepernick's refusal wasn't a rejection of the country or the anthem. (He got down on his knee.) It was a call for all of us to do better: to live up to our shared desire to be a free and brave people.

WHAT IS CULTURAL INFRASTRUCTURE? WHY DOES IT MATTER?

A simple definition of *infrastructures* goes something like this: "Infrastructures are the systems that enable circulation of goods, knowledge, meaning, people, and power."[9] This is nearly all we need for the purposes of this book. Infrastructures are systems that enable the circulation of knowledge, meaning, and power. Most people are likely to associate infrastructure with physical infrastructure, like bridges and highways and electrical grids, and most people are likely *not* to associate this physical infrastructure with ideology. Infrastructure seems like the practical bedrock of a functioning society. But it is a mistake to imagine either that the bedrock of a functioning society is based only on physical properties and material considerations or that the only infrastructure that keeps a society functioning is the most obviously physical kind. All of the structures we build are shaped by principles of engineering *and* ideas about what and who a given society values.

Seen in this light, the term *cultural infrastructure* is redundant. If all infrastructure is made by culture, why bother with the modifier? *Blunt Instruments* relies on the redundancy of the modifier to make the point, repeatedly, that while all infrastructure is cultural, some infrastructure is explicitly cultural—built with the explicit intent of shaping the culture with the expression of a particular set of ideas about who we are. To track and understand this, we must be aware of the "shifting boundaries between material and immaterial structures," and we must recognize the active intentions of those who designed and built them. In other words, a power grid is designed to move electricity to enable a society to function. This is, in itself, a reflection of cultural values. At the same time, the power grid further reflects cultural values in the decisions it requires about, for instance, which neighborhoods get transmission towers. (Highways have also had an enormous cultural imprint for many reasons, the most painful of which is that in many cities, it was decided that middle-class African American business districts would be bulldozed to make room for them.) A museum or a monument, or a less material bit of infrastructure like standing for the playing of the national anthem, is also a piece of infrastructure that is *designed and built to convey ideas* that are intended to enable a society to function. The emphasis needs to be on *infrastructure* rather than *cultural* to keep the explicit work they were intended to do—to enable the society to function—always present in our understanding.

Cultural infrastructure is, in other words, a fairly straightforward concept that requires some clarification and careful thinking because we are not accustomed to thinking about either culture or infrastructure in this way. Both are ubiquitous, and both come with an unspoken assumption of neutrality. Understanding how the patently untrue is made to seem natural—how clear, basic, obvious untruths like the supremacy of white people or men are sustained in a culture as unspoken givens—is vital to creating a more just society. "Naturalizing" obviously wrong foundational values takes work as does understanding the process through which this happens.

Donald Trump's 2020 executive order requiring "traditional" architecture for all federal buildings is a useful example of seriously intentionally cultural infrastructure in the making. It is striking that in a moment defined by a raging global pandemic, the deaths of five hundred thousand

Americans, staggering economic challenges, and a violently contested election, one of the last official acts of the Trump presidency was the signing of an executive order mandating architectural style. If nothing else, this executive order—informally called "Making Federal Buildings Beautiful Again"—is evidence of an ongoing and deliberate investment in cultural infrastructure to do big, important work in the culture.[10]

The language of the order is instructive. It states that post–World War II federal architecture has been unpopular and reads, "It is time to update the policies guiding Federal architecture to address these problems and ensure that architects designing Federal buildings serve their clients, the American people." It goes on: "New Federal building designs should, like America's beloved landmark buildings, uplift and beautify public spaces, inspire the human spirit, ennoble the United States, command respect from the general public, and, as appropriate, respect the architectural heritage of a region."[11] All of this is interesting—uplift, inspire, ennoble, and then "command respect." This last goal seems a bit out of place, or at least out of fashion. (Architecture made to command respect has long been associated with monarchies and fascism.) When Pierre L'Enfant was designing the US capital city in 1791, to uplift, inspire, and ennoble would surely have been among his goals, but he was more cautious about the idea of commanding respect. There was considerable tension around how grand (how commanding) Washington D.C. should be. If it was too grand, it risked seeming to imitate Europe—to be using architecture and the layout of the city to make monarchical-era statements about where power lies in the culture. If it was too modest, it risked failing to express the dignity and importance of the nascent democracy.

In the Trump model, there is an inherent contradiction in the need for architects to serve their client, the American people, and to command the respect of those same people. Trump sought to do this by requiring tradition, and this is worth thinking through.

The architectural style the order mandates is explicitly classical or traditional. (Think of the Lincoln Memorial or any government building with white pillars.) The order states, "'Classical architecture' means the architectural tradition derived from the forms, principles, and vocabulary of the architecture of Greek and Roman antiquity, and as later developed and expanded upon by such Renaissance architects as Alberti, Brunelleschi, Michelangelo, and Palladio; such Enlightenment masters as Robert Adam, John Soane, and Christopher Wren; such 19th-century architects as Benjamin Henry Latrobe, Robert Mills, and Thomas U. Walter; and such 20th-century practitioners as Julian Abele, Daniel Burnham, Charles F. McKim, John Russell Pope, Julia Morgan, and the firm of Delano and Aldrich. Classical architecture encompasses such styles as Neoclassical, Georgian, Federal, Greek Revival, Beaux-Arts, and Art Deco."[12] This is actually a fairly broad list of styles. (Federal style architecture tried to avoid the excesses that monarchies inscribed into landscapes and to work at a human scale. Beaux-Arts architecture held to the Federal focus on symmetry and classical elements but let in a little more decorative play on its surfaces.) And most of these people were great artists.

What is odd here, especially in the context of the urgency of so many other matters of state in 2020, is the *requirement*. With a few possible exceptions, the order mandates that federal buildings be classical or traditional. (No other president has ever done this.) Why might this be so important to Trump and his supporters? Why does federal architecture have to be traditional? The order quotes architect Sir Christopher Wren declaring that architecture "establishes a nation," "makes the people love their native country," and "aims at eternity."[13] So, it makes the point that architecture does important cultural work. It is less explicit about why this power needs to be expressed in "classical or traditional" terms.

The American Institute of Architects (AIA) offered a modest, but still pointed, critique of the order, writing, "Architecture should be designed for the specific communities that it serves, reflecting our rich nation's diverse places, thought, culture, and climates."[14] It is suggesting that a reflection of diversity better serves a diverse nation. This seems as though it should be relatively uncontroversial. The extent to which the AIA's careful phrasing is actually fraught begins to emerge when it is set in contrast with the gleeful pronouncements of support that came from neo-Nazis following the signing of the order.

Pharos is a website dedicated to documenting appropriations of Greco-Roman culture by hate groups. (Apparently there is a need for such a thing.) It explains, "White supremacist and xenophobic sites immediately expressed support for the executive order. Writing for *American Renaissance*, Gregory Hood called the order 'one small step toward reuniting white Americans with our civilizational tradition' and argued that 'if people feel connected to their heritage and history, they are more willing to fight for it.' Other forms of architecture, Hood continued, 'reinforce an idea of racial deracination' and 'alienate white people from their past' in order to 'make them feel helpless, rootless, and weak.'"[15]

Hood is not a particularly compelling thinker; he is only worth taking up here, and in *Pharos*, because he is overtly stating what is often left unsaid: that for some (maybe many), what matters about the architecture is its *relationship to the past*. In the history of white civilization in the United States—which is full of every kind of good thing *and* also scarred by a long, seemingly intractable investment in white supremacy—calls for "tradition" and "heritage" are often calls for the maintenance of a social order that always put white people at the center. As Hood uses them here, "tradition" and "heritage" are dog-whistle terms for the explicitly racist. They are code words for communicating ideas that are just beyond the borders of acceptable public speech.

Heritage is a particularly loaded term—so loaded that it becomes hard to think about cultural infrastructure linked to "heritage" as any but the bluntest of racial instruments. Hood is thrilled by "Making Federal Buildings Beautiful Again" because he understands the mandating of classical architecture as not only an explicit effort to assert the supremacy of *white* heritage but also a valuable tool in recruiting people to "fight for" the maintenance of that white heritage. His vision of what the architecture could inspire—curing the alienation white people may feel about their past and empowering them to fight for a continuing white ideal—may seem like a lot to ask of a few white columns, but it is a bold statement about why actors across the political spectrum continue to be so deeply invested in cultural infrastructure.

Classical architecture is, of course, not necessarily racist; but *mandating* it begs the question of why—in a world full of beautiful and inspiring architectural styles—this one style was so important that it required a presidential executive order when the federal government was quite literally in an all-out state of emergency. Hood's glee at the announcement is key to seeing why it was so important to Trump and his supporters and why it is vital to understand cultural infrastructure that may seem like window dressing. The mandate promotes cultural infrastructure that is intended to do a specific kind of ideological work that relies on a spurious notion of tradition to take a stand for a white social order.

In other words, the order demonstrates that neoclassical architecture is *perceived* to be a useful tool in the maintenance of a white social order. (Again, this is the work that gleaming white pillars across the landscape are *understood* to be doing.) This does not mean the form itself is inherently racist; it means it is valued as a tool for the preservation of a particular social order.

If the executive order itself does not make this clear enough, two days after it was issued, Trump reshuffled the membership of the body charged with making the final decisions about federal architectural designs, the Commission on Fine Arts (CFA). Trump appointed new members of the commission so that "Taken together with the three current commissioners, who were also appointed by Trump, all seven members of the Commission on Fine Arts are now white men—a departure for a commission that, in 2019, included three women and two African Americans. Like their predecessors, they were appointed for four-year terms, with the first replacement up in 2022. Trump's fully staffed commission is the first to include only men since 1963 and the first all-white one in a decade."[16] The CFA was intentionally all white and all male for the first time in *fifty-eight years*. (Of course, an all-white and all-male commission could make great decisions about architecture; what matters is that this was a requirement from Trump in 2020.) So, even though President Biden undid the executive order and appointed four new members, the plan had been for the next decade of federal architecture to be shaped by men for whom architecture that "commands respect" is a clear expression of "traditional" values and would ensure the "stability of America's system of self-government" as the key criteria for decision making.

"Making Federal Buildings Beautiful Again" was, in part, a response to a lively debate about cultural infrastructure that has taken place unevenly and with great intensity over the last forty years. These debates about monuments and memorials started with the building of the Vietnam Veterans Memorial in 1979 and have had dramatic peaks and valleys, resulting first in a great push to build new memorials and then in an even more dramatic push to bring them down. A push to transform museums has a similar trajectory; it started slowly in the 1980s and has ebbed and flowed without ever really reaching a fever pitch until the post-Floyd moment. And while Kaepernick is absolutely not alone in pushing back against less material cultural infrastructure, he was certainly the first highly visible and influential voice bringing those practices back into this longer, ongoing national conversation.

It is also important to say here that all of this infrastructure is complicated, always. Museums, for instance, are in no way simple expressions of one racist ideology. The impulses that drive them are complicated—and condemning them all as bastions of power dedicated to the maintenance of white supremacy would be a mistake. Doing this would miss the enormous good they have done—teaching, celebrating beauty, inspiring all kinds of wonder. It would be a ridiculous mistake, as would neglecting the inequitable distribution of all of these good things. In other words, thinking about museums or monuments as blunt instruments of social power requires holding two contradictory thoughts at the same time. It requires understanding that all infrastructure is cultural—and that cultural infrastructures like museums and historic sites are built with the explicit intent of shaping cultural life—*and* that in the United States, this has been both marvelous and dangerous.

Each of these infrastructures is a system that enables the circulation of knowledge, meaning, and power. And they do so in a national context. In fact, it is the circulation of knowledge, meaning, and power they enable that creates the nation itself. Understanding this is crucial for understanding how cultural infrastructure works.

HOW DO NATIONS WORK? (THEY ARE MADE AND REQUIRE MAINTENANCE)

Ensuring the "stability of America's system of self-government"—the work "Making Federal Buildings Beautiful Again" promises to do and that Kaepernick is accused of trying to undo—surely cannot rest in the hands of federal architects and a handful of football players. Can it? Law, government, and the military come to mind as more obvious agents of protecting and maintaining our system of government. But while these are certainly important elements of the maintenance of any social order, it is useful to remember that our social order—our nation—is actually relatively fragile. Like all nations, it has always required law and governance and a military to sustain itself *and* has also always required cultural infrastructure.

Nations have been the primary form of human social organization over the last two centuries, but nations do not exist in nature. They are not a form of social organization that was somehow destined to emerge from the natural evolution of human societies. Nations are an invention: therefore they are not "natural." They are made and they have been made by particular people in particular times and places and in particular forms. And, as it turns out, across place and time, they are made not only by the sharing of place and language and religion and ethnicity and geography but also by the sharing of fictions and untruths. Nations are made by the evocative, invented stories people tell about themselves.

The first, and one of the most brilliant, theorists of nations and nationalism put this idea at the center of his work. At the Sorbonne in Paris in the 1890s, Ernest Renan argued that nations are "spiritual principles" defined by shared pasts. The key to his thinking is that shared pasts are collectively invented or "misremembered." He wrote, "A nation is a soul, a spiritual principle. Two things, which in truth are but one, constitute this soul or spiritual principle. One lies in the past, one in the present. One is the possession in common of a rich legacy of memories; the other is present-day consent, the desire to live together, the will to perpetuate the value of the heritage that one has received in an undivided form."[17]

This is a simple and powerful idea. Nations, as they are understood by those who study them, are very much made by culture. They are made by "the will to perpetuate the value of the heritage that one has received in an undivided form." They are made by feelings created by cultural objects that help us tell each other a story of who we are. (They are made by cultural infrastructure.)

People writing about these cultural objects return again and again to museums and memorials and patriotic practices. These are the cultural objects that seem to be at the center of the nation-making process. This is in part because they are invented objects that evoke, even rely on, a sense of timelessness and permanence. They are also focused on the past for the purposes of the present. It is fair, in fact, to say they purport to be about a knowable, discrete shared past but are actually very much about the future. So, culture about shared culture is vital, and culture about the past is at the heart of the matter.

There is another shared element to much of this culture: loss. Memorials are at the epicenter of this process. Renan defines nations as not only "spiritual principles" made by culture but also shaped by shared loss. He argues that collectively *misremembered* shared losses are the center of nations. He writes, "Forgetting, I would even go so far as to say historical error is a crucial factor in the creation of a nation."[18] This misremembering is key, and it underscores the role that invention plays in the process. The nation is not defined by just any version of the past. People pick particular versions in particular moments to do particular cultural work.

So, misremembered losses have been very effective in the process of making nations. It is hard to imagine a more vivid and specific demonstration of this point than the avalanche of references to and quotations from Abraham Lincoln that we witnessed in the weeks following the January 6, 2021 attack on the US Capitol by enraged Trump supporters. In speech after speech, on the Senate floor and CNN and Fox News and to crowds of reporters in freshly cleared hallways, congressional representatives and senators turned to Lincoln for language about that moment of acute crisis. And while there were some references to the "angels of our better nature" from his first inaugural address, I don't recall any references to the powerful written-in-the-midst-of-an-actual-civil-war second inaugural address. Instead, reference after reference was pulled from Lincoln's address at Gettysburg.

This is fascinating from the perspective of thinking about how nations work. At Gettysburg, Lincoln was nearly a century into this vast human experiment of making nations, and he was trying to figure out how to manage the potent and unwieldy beast. His speech is a notable effort in this process. He used the loss of American soldiers, for the first time, in a way that would become ubiquitous. He stood over the graves of soldiers, who were buried in individual marked graves and honored for the first time, and tried to use their loss to bring unity. He made the speech about the sacrifice of the soldiers, arguing that what would enable a "government of the people, by the people, and for the people" was loyalty to their memory.

In that speech, Lincoln was writing a nationalism playbook—one that relied heavily on cultural infrastructure—that is still very much in use. Two phrases used in the weeks after the January 6 attack, and especially during the subsequent impeachment process, were "government of the people, by the people, and for the people," and his phrase "testing whether that nation, or any nation so conceived and so dedicated, can long endure."

Lincoln's answer to this question about how the nation might survive the test was cultural infrastructure—a cemetery for the war dead at Gettysburg. He achieved unity through loss, and his language was what leaders grasped for when they were briefly under siege in 2021.

President Biden, it is worth noting, took a slightly different tack than many of his fellow politicians in that moment. He also quoted Lincoln, but he turned to the 1862 address to Congress delivered in the days before Lincoln signed the Emancipation Proclamation, in which he concluded, "We shall nobly save, or meanly lose, the last, best hope on earth....The way is plain, peaceful, generous, just—a way, which if followed, the world will forever applaud and God must forever bless."[19] I doubt that Biden assumed that most people would get that this was a direct reference to how white supremacy, then expressed in the form of human bondage, has always threatened the American nation. For those not familiar with the context in which Lincoln spoke, it probably sounds like a simple prayer that we are able to maintain the "last, best hope on earth." But Biden was quoting Lincoln lamenting the damage violent racial hierarchies had done and were doing to the nation.

So the flash of violent disruption of national feeling at the Capitol on January 6, 2021 inspired a turn to Lincoln that reveals two useful things. First, nations rely on cultural infrastructure that relies on loss. This may not have been immediately obvious in the language of Lincoln that was used to respond to and recover from the attack on the Capitol, but it was very much present, and it is crucial to how nations work. Deep feelings are relatively easily stirred by the specter of collective, shared loss. Second, the threat posed by basic lies about race, like but not limited to the capacity of some Americans to hold other Americans in bondage, was very much present. It was most obvious in the Confederate flags waving across the National Mall and most stunning in the images of the Confederate flag inside the Capitol building itself. But it was also there in the language of Lincoln.

The Carhartt-wearing insurrectionist who broke into the Capitol and roamed the halls with apparent impunity, carrying a Confederate flag on a long flagpole, got almost as much press in the days after the attack as the shirtless guy wearing a fur cape and Viking horns. The *New York Times* quoted noted historians expressing their disgust and contending that "the sight of a man casually carrying the Confederate battle flag outside the

Senate floor was a piercing reminder of the persistence of white suprem-acism more than 150 years after the end of the Civil War."[20] The shock of this sight makes perfect sense—the flag of the nation formed to wage war on the US government, a war that resulted in six hundred thousand deaths, being paraded through the Capitol of the victorious nation is al-ways going to be startling—but this shock and all the press the flag re-ceived were also somewhat surprising given that the flag has been flown in all kinds official contexts across the southern United States until very, very recently. And also given that, as many observers noted, this flag bearer was photographed walking by an elegant oil portrait of John Calhoun, a slave holder famous for his declarations that slavery was a positive good for the United States, which has hung in a place of honor in the Capitol for more than a century. In the end, the shock is probably more instructive than anything else. How can we be shocked to see the flag hang, however momentarily, next to the portrait? The shock makes the implicit lie ex-plicit—it reveals the contours of the untruths that we have so successfully told ourselves.

But as the struggles of both Lincoln and American leadership in early 2021 make plain, managing the unwieldy process of nation-making and nation-maintaining is not simple. The fundamental problem is that nations require some form of nationalism. And this is where things get tricky: the nation requires the stirring of national feeling. In the twenti-eth century, nothing was more dangerous or deadly than national feeling, especially national feeling in Europe (causing twenty million deaths be-tween 1914 and 1918 and sixty million deaths between 1939 and 1945).

So, nationalism has been a force to fear for most of the last cen-tury. And it is experiencing something of a startling reemergence in the United States. Trump-era conservatives have embraced "nationalism" in full-throated ways that we have rarely seen in the mainstream since the end of World War II. Heritage Foundation scholar Kim Holmes tries to take this on when he urges fellow conservatives to understand the "prob-lem of nationalism." For Holmes, the problem is that the new rhetoric, like Rich Lowry's in *The Case for Nationalism* or Yoram Hazony's *The Virtue of Nationalism*, which defines "nationalism as flowing from a people's 'natural devotion to their home and to their country'" and asserts that "'the world is governed best when nations agree to cultivate their own traditions, free from interference by other nations,'"[21] fail to take this history seriously.

Holmes writes, "Defined in these terms, it sounds like little more than simply defending nationality or national sovereignty, which is why Lowry, Hazony, and others insist their definition of nationalism has nothing to do with the most virulent forms involving ethnicity, race, militarism, or fascism."[22] He continues, urging conservatives to recognize the historical specificity of nationalism and its violent advocates, to argue that exceptionalism is a better bet than nationalism because it is not freighted with fascism. Either way, he is grasping for language to describe and encourage a "muscular" national pride without ringing fascist alarm bells. And while being on alert for surges in fascism seems like a good idea, always, and as even-handed as Holmes may seem to be trying to be, he seems to have no interest in the particular terms through which national feeling in the United States has been stirred, manipulated, and put to use. You can't usefully think about nationalism in the US context without thinking about race, specifically anti-Black racism. The guy with the Confederate flag and senators quoting the Gettysburg Address and Biden quoting Lincoln's 1862 address to Congress are all negotiating tensions between national feeling and anti-Black racism. Like Kaepernick and the NFL and the advocates of "Making Federal Buildings Beautiful Again," Biden and the guy with the flag are negotiating the white supremacy at the heart, to paraphrase Renan, of the American "soul."

WHAT DOES THIS MAINTENANCE LOOK LIKE? (THE AWFUL INHERITANCE)

"Negotiating white supremacy" might, in fact, be a useful way to describe the long process of maintaining national feeling in the United States. This phrasing is useful because it is hard to avoid ideas about Black/white racial hierarchy in the context of US national feeling and because it is inaccurate to plot those negotiations as totalizing, definite, or absolute. They seem always to be present, in play, and shifting.

Understanding this requires, of course, understanding white supremacy. *White supremacy* is a term that has experienced a fairly dramatic shift in popular use in recent years. Five years ago, it was largely used by academics in American studies and by people in or describing explicitly racist groups like the Klan or the Proud Boys. This is no longer the case. Likely in response to the success of the Black Lives Matter movement and the increasingly explicit racism of prominent, mainstream right organizations, *white supremacy* is no longer reserved for descriptions of well-organized but largely covert fraternal organizations.[23] Even as the FBI has publicly stated that these "white supremacists posed a 'persistent threat of lethal violence' that has produced more fatalities than any other category of domestic terrorists since 2000," less explicit racism has come to be understood more broadly as part of white supremacy.[24] This is, of course, linked to Donald Trump.

In 2017, when ESPN anchor Jemele Hill tweeted, "Donald Trump is a white supremacist who has largely surrounded himself w/ other white supremacists,"[25] she stirred up a small firestorm. She was responding to an article in *The Atlantic* by Ta-Nehisi Coates in which Coates writes that Trump's "ideology is white supremacy, in all its truculent and sanctimonious power."[26] As Coates explains, "With one immediate exception, Trump's predecessors made their way to high office through the passive power of whiteness." He builds on this, writing, "Their individual triumphs made this exclusive party seem above America's founding sins, and it was forgotten that the former was in fact bound to the latter, that all their victories had transpired on cleared grounds."[27] He states quite simply, "No such elegant detachment can be attributed to Donald Trump—a president who, more than any other, has made the awful inheritance explicit." Perhaps making the awful inheritance explicit is a great gift that he has given us all. (That and the MeToo movement.)

"To Trump," Coates explains, "whiteness is neither notional nor symbolic but is the very core of his power."[28] Coates's most salient observation—and the one that his own work participates in undoing—is that "the scope of Trump's commitment to whiteness is matched only by the depth of popular disbelief in the power of whiteness." Coates concludes that "Trump's legacy will be exposing the patina of decency for what it is and revealing just how much a demagogue can get away with."[29] That was true in 2017. In 2022 it is both more true and more complicated. In 2017, George Floyd was still alive, the Confederate flag had not been paraded through the Capitol, and "white supremacy" did not roll nearly as easily off the tongues of commentators of all stripes. I am making no claim for a sudden and radical transformation, but *Blunt Instruments* argues that, to borrow from Coates, the thin patina—always easy for all to see through and impossible for some to avoid—of our awful inheritance is more transparent and more visible and more fragile in this historical moment than it has been in a long time.

One of the challenges in understanding our "awful inheritance," and the patinas that mask it, is that it has been centuries in building and is highly decentralized. The sharing of this inheritance has *not* been undertaken or controlled by a few powerful individuals or interests. It is not straightforward governing work, nor is it five guys in New York controlling everything. This book does not see twenty women in Richmond (in the United Daughters of the Confederacy headquarters) wielding absolute power to direct national feeling, although the ladies of Richmond are highly relevant, and it is certainly tempting given the power those women have exerted. In other words, this understanding of how nations work is not a tightly bound, hermetically sealed, top-down model of social control and the exercise of power. *Blunt Instruments* takes a broader, more nuanced view of how power operates.

It does not see the war memorial, for instance, as issuing a direct and precise command to which citizens must respond in specific ways. This doesn't mean that it sees the war memorial as subtle. A Confederate memorial, for instance, has the power to articulate a vision of racial hierarchy using a heartfelt celebration of a young man, figured as innocent and tragic, who was willing to die in defense of his right to own, enslave, rape, murder, and otherwise torture other human beings. Figuring these young men as heroic in our public parks and other places of shared civic communion sends a very, very powerful message about who we are and who matters in the United States. There is no getting around this. These memorials have never been innocent or just about individual loss or only about the past—not for one minute. They were built to matter. They were built because they would matter. (They have also been resisted at every turn.) And they have been shockingly effective. So effective that they have set the foundation for other parts of our infrastructure. They have worked hard to naturalize and make the patently untrue, the profoundly unfair, and the meanly conceived seem not only logical but benign. This is a great magic trick. And it has worked. It allows outrageous racism to define our fundamental social organization without any one person ever having to say or do anything that is explicitly racist.

Blunt Instruments, this guide, is intended to show how this process works. It is driven by the four observations I began with: that it takes a tremendous amount of work to make the patently untrue seem natural, that cultural infrastructure is powerful, that all infrastructure is cultural, and that we are surrounded by cultural objects that don't necessarily seem to have anything to do with culture or values or ideology but that work every day to tell us who we are. As legal scholar john powell has noted, the scale of discrimination in the United States cannot have been achieved simply on the basis of personal animus—it has required hard and fast structural mechanisms to ensure its long, bitter reign.[30]

Like the blocks in a Roman arch, each of these elements is a heavy potential weapon on its own; and when fitted together using only unseen forces (gravity, in the case of the arch), they become a formidable tool that enables the expansion of a vast empire. To indulge this metaphor just a bit more, cultural infrastructure not only maintains nations by directing national feeling but also always makes that feeling seem natural and obvious and benign. This infrastructure is the product of the imaginations of a group of individuals in a particular historical moment, *and* it is built to feel as if it has existed for all time. So, even though it is by its very nature invented, it is understood to be whatever the opposite of *invented* is—*natural?* Antonyms for *invented* are *true, genuine, actual, authentic,* and *correct.* This is a pretty fancy party trick for these pieces of infrastructure, and it is precisely what makes memorials and museums and patriotic practices such powerful tools. They enable an easy articulation of patently untrue ideas that come to seem to be eternal truths.

This magic quality has not escaped the attention of memorial and museum builders and advocates for the national anthem or the Pledge of Allegiance. In the United States, they emerged as popular additions to the landscape of small towns and big cities and as part of the daily routines of children in school at about the same time. From 1890 to 1920, there was a memorial and museum building boom, and simultaneously, a flurry of new patriotic traditions were invented. These efforts were broadly viewed by the many and varied participants as opportunities to literally concretize ideas they felt were threatened or needed reinforcement without requiring explicit statements of those ideas.

"Making Federal Buildings Beautiful Again" never mentions guidelines for building memorials or taking them down. This is both an inconsequential omission—federal architecture includes federal memorials but also involves much more—and is telling. What could possibly have evoked more anxiety about the dominance of "heritage" in the American landscape than the toppling of hundreds of Confederate memorials in a period of a few months before the issuing of the executive order? There was no federal building boom marked by any notable controversy in 2020. There was no particular controversy raging about architecture in the capital. In fact, the most recent significant new building in the memorial core of Washington was completed in 2016. David Adjaye's National Museum of African American History and Culture is a radical departure from the sea of neoclassicism in which it sits, and it was met with nearly universal public acclaim.[31] Inspired by a range of African and African American forms, the building is—to the informed observer—a melding of neoclassical elements and forms from the African diaspora, but the big hit of it is that it is definitely not business as usual. Standing between the White House and the Washington Monument and wrapped entirely in a deep, bronze-colored reflective metal lattice, Adjaye's building makes a blunt point in no uncertain terms: the neoclassical version of who we are as a nation, as a people, is not the only story to be told. The brilliance of the design is the way in which it both rejects neoclassical homogeneity and includes the neoclassical. This suggests a different way to think about *heritage* that is quite profound.

WHAT IS HERITAGE? (A THIN PATINA OF DECENCY?)

All of the above requires a careful discussion of the concept of *heritage*. Like infrastructure, *heritage* has come to have an oddly neutral cast. It has come to signify a proud, finite, and definite past. *Heritage* has come to mean a specific closed version of the past to which we can refer and to which we might owe some kind of allegiance. But it is crucial to understand that heritage is entirely invented. This is not necessarily a bad thing. It is just a fact. People who have studied the long history of heritage nearly all end up focusing on the "invention of tradition." Historian Eric Hobsbawm has been arguing for decades that "the national phenomenon cannot be adequately investigated without careful attention to the 'invention of tradition.'"[32] This is another obvious point you might not necessarily see if it is not pointed out, but it is crucial. All traditions begin someplace for some reason. Those reasons are always deeply cultural and of a particular time and a particular place. Perhaps the most famous example of this, among historians, is the invention of the Scottish tartans. Generations of Scots, and more Scottish Americans, have proudly worn their clan tartans and kilts with a sense that these plaids connect them to an ancient heritage, a long line of people to whom they are allied and with whom they share admirable qualities about which they feel real pride. There is some truth to this. The plaids do make people feel connected to a time before themselves and to a place and people they could never know. They create a sense of belonging and collectivity that many of us deeply crave. But what is most authentic, most real about the connection they feel, is the connection itself. The tartans were invented by a wild Scottish population struggling to develop an identity distinct from the Irish in the context of British colonial rule. The tartans, and the plaid kilts in particular, encouraged in them an allegiance and sense of a largely fabricated (literally) Highland past—or heritage.[33] As Hugh Trevor-Roper writes, "Before the later years of the seventeenth century, the Highlanders of Scotland did not form a distinct people." But the tartan kilts helped them form a shared identity by the end of the eighteenth century. So, it turns out that this ancient heritage is a relatively modern invention. In other words, heritage is evoked as discrete and timeless—as culture beyond the influence of the culture of the moment. But this is simply not true. Heritage is and always has been a tool.

The Proud Boys wearing neon yellow and black plaid kilts in a Make America Great Again march in December 2020, a march to defend President Trump's false claims of election fraud, at which four people were killed, were not so much explicitly claiming a proud Scottish heritage as a proud Scottish-is-very-white heritage.[34] They are unlikely to have been reading Hobsbawm and Trevor-Roper or to be aware the tartan kilt is a favorite example among scholars of a tradition that was invented nearly from whole cloth. It is probably enough for them that the kilts are an easy shorthand for "white," but it matters that they are also a shorthand for "heritage." (They made this point at the December rally and then again inside that Capitol Building on January 6, 2021.)

The word *heritage* comes from the Old French, *eritage*, and from the Latin, *heres*. Both mean some form of inheritance, and this is key. *Heritage* might be defined as a condition or state transmitted from ancestors. Heritage is a reference to the expectation of transmission from ancestors. Most definitions also have a vaguely genetic cast. This is a much more salient definition than the more popular and slightly less finely tuned definitions described earlier. Heritage is about what the owner of that heritage expects to receive; and when you understand the use of *heritage* in contemporary debates about history and heritage in this context, the hyperracialization and weaponizing of heritage by those seeking to maintain a postbellum racial order makes sense. It is pretty simple. Heritage is what they *expect* to inherit—a culture in which white supremacy, for instance, is an unspoken expectation. White supremacy, then, becomes what the users of this tool expect to inherit. Countless Confederate monuments and implicitly racist museum exhibitions and other patriotic practices have been protected from the accountability that a direct statement of Black inferiority might require with "heritage" held up as a badge of honor and a shield. Heritage masquerades as a neutral, benign gesture toward a clearly defined and understood past. It is, instead, a powerful tool in the work to maintain counterfactual social inequity.

There are endless explicit examples of the use of heritage to cover for white supremacy. In the summer of 2020, as George Floyd's murder was roiling cities, the *Columbus Dispatch* ran a story about locals who continued to proudly fly the Confederate flag. It quotes Herman Nelson saying, "It ain't got a thing to do with racism or race....To me, it just represents part of American history," and Caroline Holiman, an Arkansas native, saying the flag is all about "heritage, not hate."[35] Holiman tells the reporter, "Don't judge me by the flag I fly, but how I treat you and your friends."[36] This local story is remarkable mostly for how unremarkable it is. Both Nelson and Holiman deny any interest in race and are quite confident that the "heritage" defense protects them from the suggestion that flying the flag is making a point about race. The sleight of hand that erases, for them, the contradiction between celebrating the nation formed to protect the right of white people to enslave Black people and expressing racist views is the magic of "heritage." It is the long game of cultural infrastructure making the patently untrue seem natural. In what way could the history Nelson refers to *not* be about race *and* racism? How is this fundamental disconnect maintained? Remember the flag bearer in the Capitol parading past the portrait of John Calhoun, and the outrage? (It takes a tremendous amount of work to make the patently untrue seem natural.)

So, "heritage" is a weapon and needs to be understood as such. It is part of the system that makes the instruments that this book explores both so powerful and so blunt. Understanding these blunt instruments empowers us to remake the truths they tell.

To return to the, perhaps wobbly, metaphor of the Roman arch, it is important to note that "heritage" is produced and maintained by cultural infrastructures but that these don't work alone—they are supported, structurally, by all of the other building blocks of the society. This book does not try to be totalizing or make any claims about a tightly sealed system of meaning-making. Other crucial kinds of infrastructure work to tell Americans the story of who they are and who belongs.

Housing policy in the United States is perhaps the most consequential tool for race-making in the twentieth century. (There have been decades of scholarship demonstrating this point—Thomas Sugrue's *The Origins of the Urban Crisis*, Richard Rothstein's *The Color of Law*, and Keeanga-Yamahtta Taylor's *Race for Profit* jump to mind—but this scholarship has not successfully reached the broad audience it deserves.) *Redlining*, the devastating practice of drawing race-based maps over 239 American cities to determine home loan eligibility, was a profoundly impactful federal practice that lasted from the late 1930s into the 1970s, and its imprint is still very much alive in cities and families and individuals. Its continued impact on public education, for instance, is substantial and has been sustained for nearly one hundred years. You can't understand race in the United States without understanding redlining. This is incontrovertible. The same is true for the carceral system. More than two million people in the United States are in more than six thousand prisons. Black people are imprisoned at higher rates than any other population. The ripple effects of incarceration are a constant force in the lives of millions of Black Americans. The US military is and has always been another determinative racial structure. As historian Khary Polk writes, "Black bodies have been central subjects and objects in American citizenship projects like national military service, whereby the corporeal reality of Black life is the medium through which discourses of inclusion and exclusion find their practice."[37] Redlining, the carceral state, and the military are key elements of American "heritage," and they do crucial cultural work. *Blunt Instruments* attends to the more obviously cultural elements of cultural infrastructure with the understanding that they are part of a larger system—perhaps the more decorative, more carefully shaped stones at the top of the Roman arch, if the metaphor holds.

As introduced here, *Blunt Instruments* frames race in the United States in Black and white terms. This framing reflects the fact that so much cultural infrastructure has been built to protect a white ideal in the context of the legacies of slavery. But it isn't sustained across the book because that wouldn't accurately reflect the complexity of our cultural infrastructure. Infrastructure created to keep a lie of white supremacy alive has had broad impacts across all kinds of thinking about race and all kinds of experiences of being American. All of this is alive in the stories of the infrastructures that follow.

A ROAD MAP FOR THE BOOK

Blunt Instruments works a bit like a field guide. A *field guide* is associated with natural history—it aids in identifying elements of the natural world—and this book is about how racist infrastructure makes the artificial *seem* natural. The structure of a field guide is useful here because a field guide is written to be read through *and* used as a reference in which a reader might make a deep dive into one topic or another. To achieve some of the structure of a field guide, each section of the book is organized by a series of principles for understanding cultural infrastructure and by a series of questions raised by those principles. Each chapter is shaped by a timeline through which these principles are demonstrated and these questions are answered. The repetitions built into this structure are designed to enable easy access and to emphasize the similarities in these forms of infrastructure. Identifying blunt instruments that are designed to seem like anything other than blunt instruments requires pointed, consistent frameworks. (These practices have been enabling real inequities for at least a century, so a little repetition seems like a small price to pay for their careful identification.)

Each of the book's three sections—"Memorials," "Museums," and "Patriotic Practices"—begins with a short introduction to thinking about the form and then is split into two chronological chapters that move through a series of linked, sequential close readings of important and telling examples.

Chapter One, "The Lost Cause Won," takes up early memorial impulses and the ubiquitous Confederate memorials. Chapter Two, "The Lost Cause Keeps Winning," walks readers through the equally powerful monuments that have received less attention—living memorials built in the 1950s, like the highways that replaced Black neighborhoods in hundreds of American cities; war memorials built after the Vietnam War, designed to emphasize white male military service while recruiting young people of color; and the new wave of engagement with memorials now.

Chapters Three and Four turn to similarly powerful sites that have received considerably less attention in this context: museums. Chapter Three, "White Temples Emerged," explores the racial logics that drove the building of most of our major museums—art and history and natural science—and the plantation sites that have long been overseen by determined, often explicitly racist ladies' societies. Chapter Four, "White Temples Reshaped?" looks at how these logics have been maintained and challenged—from the blockbuster King Tut exhibit at the Metropolitan Museum of Art in the 1970s, to the decades-long tug-of-war at the Smithsonian over whose stories to include, to a close look at a "radical restoration" project at Montpelier, James Madison's plantation.

Chapters Five and Six move from physical sites to everyday practices. They look at invented patriotic rites that have wielded a great deal of cultural power by coming to seem both eternal and sacred. Chapter Five, "Allegiance Got Pledged," explores the creation of American traditions by somewhat disparate, ground-up patriotic organizations. These practices include the Pledge of Allegiance, treatment of the American flag, and the singing of the national anthem. Chapter Six, "Allegiance Got Paid For," reveals how the increasing involvement of the federal government in producing patriotism across the twentieth century led to a post-9/11 frenzy of paid patriotism that stands in serious tension with both the reaction of many to Colin Kaepernick's refusal to be a part of it and the aspirations expressed in the practices themselves.

Blunt Instruments ends with a very short conclusion that uses one new bit of cultural infrastructure—a statue on the streets of Richmond, Virginia called *Rumors of War*, which puts a young Black man on a horse on a plinth—to reveal and subvert the conventions explored in this book and make a powerful argument for new uses to which this infrastructure might be put.

MEMORIALS

MONUMENTAL BASICS

A photograph of the Strom Thurmond Monument on the grounds of the state capital in South Carolina shows a figure of a man caught mid-stride, still in action. A photograph of the inscription on one of the panels on the memorial's base shows how hard it is to change the logics we inscribe in our landscapes. These photographs are a useful place to start an exploration of memorials and monuments because they evoke a compelling set of questions about our shared public landscapes across the United States. (See Figures 2 and 3.)

As you look at these photographs, you see a very familiar form in which something is not quite right. In the background of the first image, the neoclassical architecture of the South Carolina state house and its white pillars, stone steps, and domed rotunda are all familiar elements of traditional civic architecture. (Exactly the elements that the "Making Federal Buildings Beautiful Again" executive order sought to require going forward.) The figure in the foreground is also familiar: a man on a stone plinth. In this case, the man is Strom Thurmond, the longest-serving member of the United States Congress and a life-long full-throated segregationist. It is in the close-up of the plinth that something appears to be wrong. The word *five* is a mess, a rough disruption of the clean and controlled text. The engravers had the difficult task of turning *four* into *five* when Essie Mae Washington-Williams asked the state of South Carolina to add her to the monument. She was the mixed-race daughter of Thurmond and Carrie Butler, a young domestic worker in his parents'

FIGURE 2 Strom Thurmond Memorial

house. While he was alive, Thurmond kept secret the fact that he had a mixed-race child.[1] After his death, she came forward and asked to be added to the monument. She put herself into the landscape, but it was not easy to do. First she had to ask the state, and approval from the state senate was required to make the change. But, more significantly, she had to insert herself into a visual and symbolic vocabulary that was organized to exclude her: to keep the very idea of her, the possibility of her, hidden. This is a big claim to make, but a little information about memorials and monuments in the United States should make it pretty easy to support. The jagged *five* raises a question about how we fit a carefully repressed perspective into an existing landscape—an existing symbolic vocabulary. The *five* also demonstrates how powerful messing with that vocabulary can be. The effect is kind of breathtaking, yes? Certainly it helps to elicit a visceral feeling of the work memorials and monuments do.

A few basic principles, to build on this feeling, will make understanding memorials and monuments easy.[2] First, *they are powerful.* Second, *they are doing their best work when they seem to fit seamlessly into the landscape; when they stop being noticeable, their job is done.* Third, *they are more about the time they are made than the time they memorialize.* Fourth, *they are made by people*

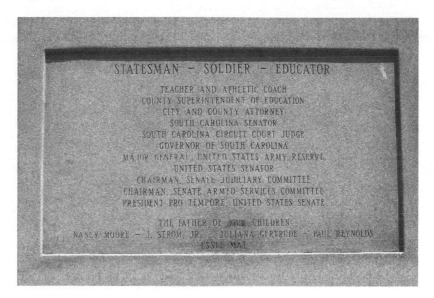

STATESMAN ~ SOLDIER ~ EDUCATOR

TEACHER AND ATHLETIC COACH
COUNTY SUPERINTENDENT OF EDUCATION
CITY AND COUNTY ATTORNEY
SOUTH CAROLINA SENATOR
SOUTH CAROLINA CIRCUIT COURT JUDGE
GOVERNOR OF SOUTH CAROLINA
MAJOR GENERAL, UNITED STATES ARMY RESERVE
UNITED STATES SENATOR
CHAIRMAN, SENATE JUDICIARY COMMITTEE
CHAIRMAN, SENATE ARMED SERVICES COMMITTEE
PRESIDENT PRO TEMPORE, UNITED STATES SENATE

THE FATHER OF FIVE CHILDREN:
NANCY MOORE ~ J. STROM, JR. ~ JULIANA GERTRUDE ~ PAUL REYNOLDS
ESSIE MAE

FIGURE 3   Strom Thurmond detail

who feel strongly that they have something very important to say. Fifth, *they are not neutral. Ever.* Sixth, *they don't innocently remember a discrete event; they invent a particular past that they worry will not be recognized without a memorial.* Seventh, *they are often inspired by anxiety, not the confidence the bronze and limestone might seem to project; they come from an unsettled moment.* And, eighth, *memorials use a few basic and familiar conventions to make their points.*

Each of these principles deserves a little fleshing out.

First, they are powerful. This may seem obvious, but it is not necessarily always explicit. They are built to convey power: the power of a particular group in a particular time and place. They claim shared public space with authority, and they claim their ideas for all who share that public space—or who aspire to. In the case of the Thurmond memorial, which was built after his death in 2013, he stands in broad daylight representing the ideas he stood for across his political career: an explicit, repeated, unrepentant insistence on "white supremacy." And here, this term is used in its simplest form; it is neither hyperbolic nor a reference to racist white fraternal organizations. Thurmond fought for segregation and repeatedly expressed his belief in the need to protect white spaces from Black people. So, that is what he claims as he stands on the lawn of the capitol in Columbia in 2021. He doesn't need to wear a Klan robe or be shown enacting violence to express the ongoing power of his ideas in South Carolina. In a state with a population of nearly 1.5 million African Americans, a celebration of a figure with his ideas is a blunt expression of power. (There are also many college and university buildings named for him in the state, as well as high schools—and even a lake.)

Thus, to say that memorials are powerful is to say two things: (1) that they convey power, and (2) that they are effective—they really matter. A useful shorthand for this is the specter of protesters pulling down monuments and protesters fighting to protect them. (Think Charlottesville in May 2017.)

Second, they are doing their best work when they seem to fit seamlessly into the landscape; when they stop being noticeable, their job is done. Or maybe it is more accurate to say that when they stop being noticeable, they maintain the power they express. In other words, they never stop working, but the less noticeable they are, the more effectively they have conveyed their message. For example, the memorial in a small town to soldiers killed in the First World War is likely to be a figure of a doughboy, a soldier on a plinth, in a public place. Standing there, season after season, the soldier probably does not figure explicitly in the thinking of teenagers who gather in the park to smoke and drink. They are not likely to think about it much at all, except maybe as a place to duck various authorities. But it is still doing its work, sending the message that they could be called up, could be asked to fight and die, and the world would keep spinning—the town would return to business as usual. It conveys that military sacrifice is such a fundamental part of the culture that it doesn't need to be made explicit.

Third, they are more about the time in which they are made than the time they memorialize. This idea is quite logical once you stop to think about it. A Confederate memorial built in 1920, or in 1960 for that matter, tells us more about 1920 than 1865. In fact, the assumption that this is not the case gives many memorials their greatest power. One of the enduring myths about Confederate monuments is that they celebrate young men whose families deserve to remember them as noble and heroic. They are framed as emblems of local and personal "heritage." They are understood as being about lost sons. Who could deny grieving mothers this? The problem with this logic is that most Confederate memorials were built between 1890 and 1920. This was decades after the war, at a time when life expectancy in the United States was forty-four years. So the chances that mothers who were forty in 1865 were leading the memorial charge at age seventy in 1895 are not great. Some were, absolutely, but most were not. But this has been a powerful and sustaining fallacy. The memorials built to the Confederacy were largely initiated and brought to fruition by women's groups, but the women who participated were not grieving mothers in the immediate wake of the war. They were women who, after Reconstruction, were anxious about threats to the racial order they wanted to maintain. (Much more on this to come.) The young man on the plinth in the park remembering the Civil War was likely not put there by his mother, and to understand him, we need to start with that fact.

Fourth, they are made by people who feel strongly that they have something very important to say. Again, this may seem obvious, but it is an important point. Even in periods in which memorials were popping up all over the place, building a memorial—in any public space—was not easy and required all kinds of stakeholders to unite, exert pressure, and keep their eyes on the prize. One organization, The Ronald Reagan Legacy Project, is currently working to get a memorial of Reagan built in every county in the United States. Founded in 1997 by Grover Norquist, the project "is committed to preserving the legacy of one of America's greatest presidents throughout the nation and abroad."[3] It claims, "Each one of these dedications serve (sic) as a teaching moment for those who were not yet alive during his presidency or to grant those who remember him with (sic) the opportunity to reflect on his accomplishments."[4] The schools and airports and roads named in his honor and the figure of Reagan that stands in the California statehouse were all created by a desire to teach future generations that Reagan's ideas—about everything, including race—are the ideas that we, collectively, value: the ideas that matter. The Ronald Reagan Legacy Project wants to make his values, his ideas, seem to be shared values, shared ideas. Its creators want to build him into the landscape to ensure his legacy, not just celebrate it.

Fifth, they are not neutral. Ever. If memorials were neutral, no one would ever bother to build one. Their magic is that they seem to be neutral—seem to be benign expressions of shared foundational truths. But this is simply not true. One of the most interesting things about memorials is the collective investment many have in the idea of their neutrality. A few years ago, at a conference in Washington D.C., two panelists—both men in their sixties or seventies, both highly educated, and both students of memorials—spoke with real fondness for the *Silent Sam* memorial on the campus of their shared alma mater, the University of North Carolina. (*Silent Sam* is a figure of a Confederate soldier, gun raised to his shoulder, on a stone plinth.) One described it as "harmless." The other used the word "benign." This was shocking twice. First, they were professional historians who studied memorials, so if anyone should know better, it should be them. Second, *Silent Sam* was very much in the news that week. The day before, a story in the *Washington Post* quoted from the speech given at the 1913 dedication of the memorial by the biggest donor to the memorial effort, Ku Klux Klan supporter Julian Carr.[5] Carr said that Confederate soldiers saved "the very life of the Anglo Saxon race in the South…to-day, as a consequence the purest strain of the Anglo Saxon is to be found in the 13 Southern States—Praise God," and,

> One hundred yards from where we stand, less than ninety days perhaps after my return from Appomattox, I horse-whipped a negro wench until her skirts hung in shreds, because upon the streets of this quiet village she had publicly insulted and maligned a Southern lady, and then rushed for protection to these University buildings where was stationed a garrison of 100 Federal soldiers. I performed the pleasing duty in the immediate presence of the entire garrison, and for thirty nights afterwards slept with a double-barrel shot gun under my head.[6]

If her skirts hung in shreds, imagine what happened to her flesh. How could this violence—in response to insulting a Southern lady—be understood as benign? How does that possibly work? It works because masking the monstrous as neutral is a special power of monuments.

Another useful example of masking the monstrous as neutral is the Little Bighorn memorial. Few things seem more inert than a wind-whipped stone obelisk (think short, boxy stone pillar) on an open prairie. And it would be easy to be fooled by the Little Bighorn Battlefield National Monument. It is modest in scale and sits adjacent to the Custer National Cemetery just off I-90 in rural southeastern Montana. Despite its remote location, it quietly draws a crowd. In 2016, more than three hundred thousand visitors, more than a quarter of the state's population, showed up to see it.[7] Like the Alamo memorial in Texas, the Little Bighorn Battlefield National Monument remembers a defeat, but that was unlikely to be the takeaway from a visit during the first century it sat at the site of General George Custer's famous last stand. It took decades of work on the part of local Indigenous people to add their version of the story to the site. As *Smithsonian Magazine* tells the story, "In 1991, Barbara Sutteer, the first Native American superintendent of the site, oversaw the name change, long requested by Indians, from Custer Battlefield to Little Bighorn Battlefield National Monument." She also got an "Indian Memorial" approved.[8] Twelve years later, the first line in a newspaper article read, "After 127 years of waiting, the memorial to the Indian warriors who fought at the June 25, 1876, Battle of Little Bighorn was dedicated on Wednesday."[9] But none of this was easy. Sutteer received death threats in response to her efforts to include the story of Lakotas and Cheyennes at the site.[10] If the decades-long resistance to a name change and an additional memorial don't make the point that the original memorial was quietly doing cultural work that mattered—that it was not neutral—then the death threats certainly do.

Sixth, they don't innocently remember a discrete event; they invent a particular past that they worry will not be recognized without a memorial. The past is not only unfinished but also not a set of discrete, fully known events. In fact, part of the work that memorials do is to make the past tidy and manageable in ways that it rarely actually is. The Alamo Cenotaph, for instance, recognizes the "heroes" of the siege at the Alamo. (A cenotaph is usually a single boxy pillar.) This event should be fairly discrete—it happened in one place over a period of a few days, at the end of which the key actors were all killed. The inscription on the cenotaph reads, "Erected in memory of the heroes who sacrificed their lives at the Alamo, March 6, 1836, in the defense of Texas. They chose never to surrender nor retreat; these brave hearts, with flag still proudly waving, perished in the flames of immortality that their high sacrifice might lead to the founding of this Texas."[11] Dedicated in 1939, this memorial celebrates the Texas centennial in pretty dramatic terms. Flames of immortality. High sacrifice. Certainly it expresses no ambivalence. It also soars above the modest Alamo structure, which might not quite live up to almost two centuries' worth of overwrought rhetoric. This rhetoric has mostly told a story of good versus evil in which white rebels were good and Mexicans defending their homeland were evil. But even this event, which would seem to be easy to capture in stone, has proven to be more complicated.[12] Since the days after the siege and the burning of the bodies of the rebels by the triumphant Mexican authorities, there have been shifting ideas about the names and status of the fighters as Mexicans, Texians, and Americans. Finally, there has been disagreement about the ideas for which they died—the word *heroes* appears on the monument, but the word *slavery* does not, even though many historians are confident that defending the Alamo was linked to defending slavery in Texas. The link to both slavery and anti-Mexican racism has led to questions about the extent to which the soldiers were heroic. At the very least, unless you already know the story of the Alamo, it would be hard to walk away with the impression that the "defenders" lost—a very basic fact of the event.

Seventh, memorials are often inspired by anxiety, not the confidence the bronze and limestone might seem to project; they come from an unsettled moment. These last few basic ideas about memorials might seem to be similar or to blur together, but they are distinct. Memorials invent the past they seek to remember; they are always actively working, no matter how still they stand; *and* they nearly always come from anxiety, not confidence. You need to invent a particular past to remember in perpetuity because you are not confident that the version of who we are in the United States will prevail or continue to dominate without the work the memorial can do. The Japanese American Memorial to Patriotism During World War II is a fascinating, multifaceted example of anxiety about how boundaries of national inclusion are drawn.[13] The idea for the memorial came from veterans of the 442nd Regimental Combat Team who, inspired by recent additions to the National Mall, wanted a memorial to recognize their contributions in the Second World War and their achievements as "the most decorated unit for its size and length of service, in the entire history of the US Military."[14] The short version of a very long story is that Congress rejected their claim that the history of the 442nd was of enough national significance to merit a site on the National Mall but agreed, after some strange negotiations, to give them Mall-adjacent space if they made the memorial about the patriotism of Japanese Americans during the war—despite their "relocation" to internment camps. This is, of course, a far cry from a celebration of the military heroism of Japanese American men, although these men are referenced in the memorial. The memorial as it now stands highlights Ronald Reagan's apology, "Here we admit a wrong," to those who were put in internment camps, and their peaceful participation in the process. For visitors, it is a somewhat confusing monument, and this reflects the competing anxieties that produced it. As the federal act authorizing it states, it was intended to "commemorate the experience of American citizens of Japanese ancestry and their parents who patriotically supported this country despite their unjust treatment during World War II."[15] Both the veterans who were anxious that their contributions be remembered, especially given the fact that many of them left internment camps to serve, and the officials in Congress who wanted an affirmation of patriotism from people who had been badly mistreated got a bit of what they wanted, but ultimately conflicting anxieties are also quite literally concretized. The center of the memorial is a crane, a symbol of good luck in Japan, wrapped in barbed wire; this snarl of mixed metaphors reflects unresolved anxiety more than anything else.[16]

And, finally, eighth, memorials use a few basic and familiar conventions to make their points. The most basic of these conventions involve things like height and scale. This could hardly be simpler, but a big memorial makes a big statement. (The Washington Monument was designed to be the tallest structure in the world, to reflect Washington's stature.) They also involve straightforward visual clues conveyed by clothing—it is nearly universally the case that a barely dressed female figure with an ample breast is allegorical. A nearly naked woman is a regular part of the conventions of memorials, but the women whose bodies are on display are rarely representations of individual women. Rather, the more naked they are, the more likely they are intended to represent, in their beauty and the fullness of their breasts, abstract ideals. (Think "Liberty," "Justice," and "Peace.") Half-dressed or nearly naked men are almost always racialized figures or powerless in some way. The relationships between figures are also often key, an easy way to establish a hierarchy. (The Emancipation Memorial in Washington D.C., which features a formerly enslaved man—nearly naked—kneeling at Lincoln's feet is a pretty vivid example of this.) Military figures are usually marked by the weapons they carry, generally not drawn but idly standing at the ready, or by the horses they ride; and explorers are often figured holding maps. (Think of almost any figure of Columbus with a scroll.)

Taken together, these principles make the work of understanding monuments and memorials relatively straightforward. They set up a clear set of questions to ask of any memorial: (1) When was it built? (2) By whom was it built? (3) What was unsettled about the time in which it was made? (Ideas about racial hierarchy after Reconstruction? Military service after the Vietnam War?) (4) What point did the builders want to make, and what past did they invent to make it? (Victory at the Alamo? Grieving Civil War widows?) (5) How, in what forms, did they try to make their point? (Cenotaph? Soldier on a plinth? Crane wrapped in barbed wire?) (6) And, finally, what happened to the memorial in the summer of 2020? (Has there been any pushback?)

Because the first question—"When was the memorial built?"—is so key and leads to the answers to the other questions, a timeline for the building of war memorials in the United States is a crucial tool. And, while this timeline does not try to be absolute or definitive, it is possible to characterize the impulses that drove the building of monuments and memorials in a given period, and these characterizations can offer a useful shorthand for understanding the work that a given memorial was intended to do.

The two chapters in this section take up key periods in the building of memorials, as follows. Chapter One takes up the periods 1776–1890 and 1890–1920. 1776–1890 is, of course, the first whole century of American life, during which there was a struggle to figure out what an American monument might be. 1890–1920 saw the first memorial boom, when most Confederate memorials were built. Chapter Two takes up the periods 1920–1980, 1980–2010, and 2010-present, 1920–1980 was a period of building infrastructure as living memorials, which also witnessed the emergence of a second wave of white ethnic memorials and civil rights memorials. 1980–2010 was a robust period of war memorial building—the second great memorial boom—and 2010–present was a see-saw period of Confederate and Columbus memorials coming down and new anti-racist memorials going up.

1

THE LOST CAUSE WON

1776–1890: FITS AND STARTS

The first thing to know about memorial and monument building in this early period is that Americans were inventing both *their nation* and *the idea of a nation* as a concept. The nation, as a form of human social organization, emerged from particular historical circumstances in the eighteenth century. Again, nations were not, and are not now, natural or necessarily logical or linguistically simple or theologically straightforward. They are, however, enormously powerful social inventions—produced by ideas that emerged outside of long-established religious and monarchical structures. Nations required new, and at least partially secular, mechanisms for inspiring and maintaining social cohesion, feelings of community, and devotion—emotional connections that drive individual investment in the invented nation. And this process, these mechanisms, developed in fits and starts.

In the United States, this context was complicated in a few ways. People weren't just inventing this nation, they were developing the whole concept of a form of social organization that was made by men and women rather than mandated by God as the monarchies to which they were responding were once believed to be. They were also forging a contradictory identity—liberty seekers "settling" on the land of people with their own complex forms of social organization. They were leery of too much adulation of any kind of centralized power. They did not want to repeat the baroque practices of monarchies. (In fact, one of the acts of rebellion that set off the revolution was pulling down and beheading a memorial to King George III in New York City.) And finally, they had very mixed feelings about the military, which is so often central to shared memorial culture. Until the Civil War, the American military was more of a collection of local militias than the kind of single standing army we think of today. This was because so many Americans were suspicious of the power a federal military could wield. As surprising and even un-American as it might seem, eighteenth-century Americans would find our contemporary pro-military-or-anti-American flag-waving not just unseemly but frightening, a potential threat to their hard-earned liberty from tyranny. All of which is to say, memorial building in this period wasn't yet part of the nascent cultural infrastructure; memorials were not yet an important part of the national tool kit.

However, a few consequential and easily identified patterns emerged early. A small number of memorials to military leaders were built in the immediate Revolutionary War period. George Washington emerged as the first "icon" of the new nation, and the back and forth over memorializing him is telling and important to track, especially between 1790 and the mid-1800s. Ideas about how the dead, civilian and military, should be treated were evolving. And the centennial celebrations—an obvious opportunity for mechanisms for inspiring and maintaining social cohesion—stirred some patriotic activities and led to the formation of patriotic organizations that would shape the American landscape for the next one hundred years.

Revolutionary War memorials were almost all built during the first memorial boom, between 1890 and 1920, or around the American bicentennial in 1976. They were not built just after the war. As the following chart, borrowed from Kieran J. O'Keefe's study of Revolutionary War memorials, vividly demonstrates, interest in building memorials to the revolution did not pick up until nearly a century after the war.[1] (See Figure 4.)

There is a very straightforward and important explanation. Most memorials of any kind in the United States were built by two women's patriotic organizations: the Daughters of the American Revolution and the United Daughters of the Confederacy. Both of these came into existence in the 1890s—hence the memorial boom.

American Revolution Monuments by Date of Dedication

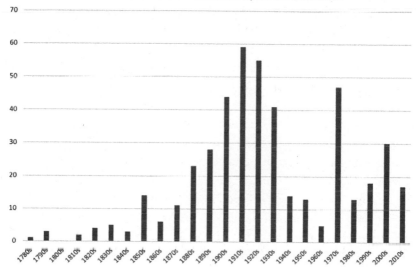

FIGURE 4 American Revolution monuments

Without these organizations, and without much in the way of veterans' organizations, the typical mechanisms for memorial building didn't yet exist. But, of course, they didn't exist because *there was not a need* for them—building memorials was not yet part of the culture.

The first memorial for the Revolutionary War was approved by Congress in 1776 to honor the memory of General Richard Montgomery. It was completed in 1787.[2] But this was much more the exception than the rule. There were others, like a state-funded memorial in Lexington, Massachusetts, the Revolutionary War Monument, a granite obelisk erected in 1799 on the town green. (It was so modest that a century later, the Daughters of the American Revolution would be inspired to add to and embellish it.) There was also, especially starting in the 1830s, a flourishing production of statues of George Washington for civic buildings. But, again, the number of these and the scale at which they were made, life-sized rather than out-sized, demonstrate the modesty of most of these early efforts.

The Washington Monument in Washington D.C. was the first truly ambitious national monument. The structure and the impulses that drove it are likely to be much more recognizable to most Americans now. Its advocates, the Washington National Monument Society, wanted to throw off the humility that had guided previous memorial attempts. They wanted the biggest, tallest, most centrally located monument that engineering and political will could build.[3] It took them more than four decades, but it is hard to deny their success. When it was dedicated in 1884, it was the tallest building in the world, and it held that title for five years, until the Eiffel Tower was completed. And certainly, as it slowly rose across the decades, it matched a changing sense of the importance of big national symbols. The early hesitancy to do anything that might look like a familiar, European celebration of centralized power was fast disappearing as new concerns occupied the young nation.

Beyond the breakout gesture of the Washington Monument, this early period saw the emergence of two new memorial practices related to the burial of the dead. They are worth noting, even though they lack the drama of Washington on the Mall, because they laid a foundation for much of what was to come.

The rural cemetery movement, the most well-known example of which is the Mount Auburn Cemetery in Cambridge, Massachusetts, emerged in the 1830s in response to new levels of urban density, an increased interest in landscape architecture, and evolving ideas about the meaning of death.[4] These cemeteries were intended to be public spaces, civic institutions for communing with nature and honoring the memory of the dead. They reflected an uptick in interest in memorial culture and venerating the dead as a civic activity.

Most early Americans had had a grimmer, more no-nonsense approach to death and burial. Quakers were not allowed to mark graves, and this was not wildly out of step with other practices. Historians like James Hijiya have noted that early Americans were guided by "the theological tenet that what is important in a human being is not the body, but the soul; that once the soul has departed, the body is trivial."[5] So, the afterlife of the body was not a major priority. In this context, the emergence of these new cemeteries was a significant shift. As historian Colleen McDannell writes, it was thought that "Picturesque landscapes purified the sentiments of visitors while monuments to the dead evoked a sense of history, continuity, and patriotism."[6] So, forty years into national life, these American deaths were understood a little less as grim evidence of a wrathful god and a little more as new occasions for patriotism. This led to more changes.

The burial of American soldiers shifted dramatically in the 1860s. (These changes would reshape everything about American memorial culture.) This is a surprising story that is ultimately, in the context of memorials, hugely significant. As hard as it is to believe from the perspective of 2022, before 1863, American soldiers killed in battle were buried in mass graves into which they were unceremoniously tossed. They did not wear dog tags, because there was no need—there was no expectation that anyone would identify their bodies in the event of their deaths. There simply was no expectation that their bodies would be tended to in any way. This changed with the building of Gettysburg National Cemetery in 1863.[7] The site, which created the occasion for the Gettysburg Address to which so many in Congress clung in the days after the January 2021 attack on the US Capitol, is one of the first places American soldiers killed in battle were buried together in marked graves.

Lincoln's Gettysburg Address is not only one of the most famous and admired American speeches and a stabilizing force in a moment of crisis, it is also a guide for two crucial things: defining a nation and remembering a war. It may seem odd to readers now that when Lincoln says, "It is altogether fitting and proper that we should do this," he is talking about providing honorable, individual burials for fallen soldiers. It is hard to imagine a twentieth- or twenty-first-century president explaining that it is appropriate to bury our war dead. But Lincoln is introducing a new and vital idea: that each soldier is owed a burial that will honor his service and sacrifice. (This is work that the ladies' patriotic organizations would take up after the Civil War; it wasn't common practice before Gettysburg.)

Lincoln, in part of the speech that is a guide for defining the nation, goes so far as to say that the fallen soldier is actually at the center of the nation—that citizen-soldiers are powerful beyond his own "poor power" and that a great, sacred debt is owed to them. In this short speech, he proposes that the project of the nation is to forge and protect their memory. From the twenty-first century perspective, the absurdity of the idea that our soldiers might be thrown into shallow graves and abandoned is evidence of how completely Lincoln's ideas at Gettysburg have been accepted. They are the backdrop against which the story of subsequent memorials in the United States must be told.

A few other developments in this period are worth noting. Patriotic ladies' associations began to form before Gettysburg but took off after the cemetery was dedicated there. They came first from an impulse to preserve the plantations of the founding fathers. These were being passed down through the generations and sold off. Ladies' associations formed to buy, preserve, and protect them. This started in 1853 when the Mount Vernon Ladies' Association was founded to prevent Washington's plantation from being sold out of the family.[8] We will return to these ladies' societies in the next chapter, but they are important to note here as an emerging and powerful force.

The Centennial International Exhibition of 1876 was a modest affair, but it did stir some commemorative activity that would have a couple of specific and lasting cultural infrastructure effects. The first will be important to return to when we are thinking about museums, because the museums at the exhibition cast a long shadow on the development of American museums. The second is that the fair, which was attended by a shocking one in five Americans and came during a frightening economic downturn, stirred enthusiasm for patriotic activities, inspiring interest that would lead to the founding of new patriotic organizations that would fundamentally transform American cultural infrastructure.

So, the pre-1890 period is a mixed bag. During this time, the initial hesitancy of Americans to indulge in grand patriotic gestures—to embrace a full-throated celebration of federal power—gives way to an eagerness to make big, bold statements in our shared landscape. Interest in shared memorial culture and shared mourning starts to rise. And, most significantly, the role of the soldier in the culture shifts from one marked by suspicion to the beloved, heroic citizen sacrificing for an indebted nation that is, in part, defined by his near-sacred sacrifice. This last bit is a very powerful cultural tool that was taken up by emergent patriotic societies and used in the years that followed with stunning efficacy—and not necessarily for the purposes for which it was developed.

1890–1920: THE FIRST MEMORIAL BOOM

Scores of historians have written about American memorial and patriotic practices in this period. It is difficult to understand American life in the twentieth century without understanding the cultural work that the memorials built in this period have done and are doing. Really. There was a push in this period to create, define, and manage national culture, especially national patriotic culture, that is both crucial to understand and not yet fully part of the public conversation about monuments and memorials or other forms of cultural infrastructure. (If there were a place to embed flashing neon lights in this book, this would be it.)

The 1890s were shaped by dramatic and punishing volatility in the emerging industrial economy; the largest wave of immigration to the United States to date in response to the need for cheap labor in this new economy; a resultant consolidation of wealth on a scale not previously seen in the this country; surging urbanization and the transformation of American cities; the brutal end of the Indian Wars and a new level of resource extraction in the American West; and a decisive new phase in the struggles to establish a new, post–Civil War racial order that included the solidification of the structures that enabled Jim Crow laws across the country. This is a lot for one decade. These developments created anxiety and left many feeling unsettled and determined to find order. One of the ways they did this was to form all kinds of patriotic organizations. These organizations determinedly made grand emphatic pronouncements, in many forms, that continue to powerfully shape national culture and how we understand it 130 years later.

Two familiar and significant markers that might help as a shorthand for this decade are the panic of 1893 and the Supreme Court decision on *Plessy v. Ferguson* in 1896. The panic of 1893 saw the bottom drop out of just about every aspect of American economic life. A long boom—especially in railroads, banking, and international trade—came to a screeching halt. Hundreds of banks closed, tens of thousands of businesses were shuttered, mortgage foreclosures spiked, stocks plummeted. Cities were suddenly full of jobless and penniless immigrants from all over Europe and migrants from rural states. Three years later, the Supreme Court decided, in one of its most consequential rulings, that segregation was not a violation of a constitutionally mandated right to equality. This set the template for the "separate but equal" racial order in the United States for much of the century to follow, in which segregation of races was a legal imperative supported at the highest levels. The bottom was falling out, and racial fault lines were being fortified in deeply fictionalized ways. For most people in the United States standing before a memorial in

2022 these bits of history may be familiar and understood as unfortunate, but are unlikely to seem directly connected to the memorial—either a Confederate memorial or a Revolutionary War memorial—but they are. The churning turmoil, economic and racial, of the 1890s fueled a boom in patriotic organizations that led to a public landscape transformed by monuments of all kinds.

Patriotic organizations are the most crucial element of the memorial story in the United States. Most of the significant patriotic organizations were also, tellingly, hereditary organizations. This means that their membership was determined by blood: by lineal heritage. In other words, membership was limited to people who could claim, and sometimes prove, to be a direct descendant of a "patriot" from either the Revolutionary War or the Confederacy. And while it is hardly a surprise to think that a hereditary organization celebrating the Confederacy would be dedicated to policing boundaries of national belonging, it is somewhat less immediately obvious that this same goal of defining national belonging in tightly defined, virtually all-white terms would be centrally important to other hereditary organizations. But understanding cultural infrastructure in the United States requires understanding that this was very much the case—almost all of these organizations were deeply invested in policing boundaries of national inclusion, which meant defining true patriots, true Americans, as white. This may seem overwrought or like a presentist view of the past, but it is neither. Even a cursory look at any of these organizations, especially at a moment when their rules of membership or their racial logics were challenged, reveals that they were dedicated to protecting a kind of patriotism that put whiteness first. These organizations include the Daughters of the American Revolution (DAR), the Colonial Dames of America, the Mary Washington Monument Association, Preservation of Virginia Antiquities, the United Daughters of the Confederacy, and the Sons of Confederate Veterans. They were very dedicated to ideas about race—specifically, racial purity—and they worked hard to inscribe these ideas on the American landscape. (For instance, you can join the DAR if your relative paid a slave to fight for him; you will have a much harder time joining if you are a relative of the slave who fought.)

Southern ladies' memorial associations were initially formed for a very practical purpose in the post–Civil War years. Following Lincoln's lead at Gettysburg, these ladies took up the rather gruesome task of giving their Confederate dead proper burials. Two factors had mitigated against the burial of the Confederate dead. First, as already noted, prior to the Civil War, most soldiers in the United States and most of Europe were not given individual marked graves or ceremonial burials. The second difficulty was a lack of interest in the burial of Confederate dead on the part of the War Department. So, voluntary organizations sprang up near battlefield sites, and the women of ladies' memorial associations saw to the burial of the dead.[9] These women worked mostly in the late 1860s and 1870s, and they deserve credit for beginning the memorial boom that was to come in the 1890s. Most of their work, however, was more private and directly related to grief for individual soldiers. The "Ladies' Memorial Associations were...organized," according to their members, "...for the purpose of collecting the bodies of fallen heroes...so that the grass should be kept green and flowers lovingly placed upon them."[10]

The Daughters of the American Revolution was founded in 1890 and was part of a loose network of organizations that required bloodlines for membership and that long excluded Black Americans, Indigenous people, and immigrants who arrived after 1780. These organizations built a huge swath of American cultural infrastructure and were dedicated to maintaining an ideal of a white nation. In the case of the DAR, its most significant nineteenth- and early twentieth-century contribution to cultural infrastructure came in the form of Americanization programs for recent immigrants. The memorial work of their sister organization, the United Daughters of the Confederacy (UDC), is a different story entirely.

The United Daughters of the Confederacy was founded in 1894. They are at the very center of the story of this book and they are why the Lost Cause won. The Lost Cause, the idea that the cause of the Confederacy was just, honorable and not at all about slavery, was partly their invention and was surely a defense of white supremacy. It has always been at the heart of the work they have been doing for more than 100 years. The UDC was founded in the same movement as the DAR, and there was plenty of overlap in their membership.[11] As the organization tells it, "The UDC is the outgrowth of numerous ladies' hospital associations, sewing societies, and knitting circles that worked throughout the South during the War Between the States to supply the needs of the soldiers."[12] This is important to note. The UDC's website says that the UDC is an outgrowth of organizations that formed during the Civil War. This suggests that they find it very important to assert that they are *of the period of the war*, despite the thirty-year gap between the war and the formation of the UDC in a time in which life expectancy was, as I've said, around forty-four years.[13] In other words, the women who founded the UDC were not necessarily the same women who contributed to the war effort.

The UDC claims that it was founded with seven goals:

> 1. To honor the memory of those who served and those who fell in the service of the Confederate States. 2. To protect, preserve and mark the places made historic by Confederate valor. 3. To collect and preserve the material for a truthful history of the War Between the States. 4. To record the part taken by Southern women in patient endurance of hardship and patriotic devotion during the struggle and in untiring efforts after the War during the reconstruction of the South. 5. To fulfill the sacred duty of benevolence toward the survivors and toward those dependent upon them. 6. To assist descendants of worthy Confederates in securing proper education. 7. To cherish the ties of friendship among the members of the Organization.[14]

The UDC wanted to honor memory, protect historic places, preserve a truthful history, give women their due, fulfill a duty to the fallen, educate, and cherish friendships. This is all pretty benign language, and it stands in stark contrast to a statement that consumed the organization's homepage in 2021.

The 2021 statement issued by UDC President General Mrs. Linda Edwards begins, "The United Daughters of the Confederacy appreciates the feelings of citizens across the country currently being expressed concerning Confederate memorial statues and monuments that were erected by our members in decades past."[15] It frames the problem with Confederate memorials as "feelings" and continues, "To some, these memorial statues and markers are viewed as divisive and thus unworthy of being allowed to remain in public places. To others, they simply represent a memorial to our forefathers who fought bravely during four years of war. These memorial statues and markers have been a part of the Southern landscape for decades." Edwards identifies the problem that so many now have with these memorials as a possible "view" that they are "divisive" but claims that others see them as "simply" representing "forefathers" who fought in an unnamed war. She goes on to defend the memorials as "part of the Southern landscape for decades," as if they are somehow a natural outgrowth of that landscape, like trees or hills. And then the statement starts to get really crazy.

The president general continues, boldly and in outrageous if polite defiance of facts,

> We are grieved that certain hate groups have taken the Confederate flag and other symbols as their own. We are the descendants of Confederate soldiers, sailors, and patriots. Our members are the ones who have spent 126 years honoring their memory by various activities in the fields of education, history and charity, promoting patriotism and good citizenship. Our members are the ones who, like our statues, have stayed quietly in the background, never engaging in public controversy.[16]

This is a stunning series of statements. First, Edwards manages to disavow the Confederate flag and protect it in the same sentence. The problem in this formulation is not the flag or the six hundred thousand dead its advocates produced, or the four million enslaved people and their descendants whom they sought to keep in bondage, but certain hate groups who would dare abuse it. Is this a direct reference to Dylan Roof, who murdered nine people as they worshiped in their church in South Carolina in the summer of 2015? Roof, enraged by the protests after the murders of Trayvon Martin and Freddie Grey, had been trying to spark a race war because he feared "blacks taking over," and his affinity for the Confederate flag stirred up a volley in a 150-year conversation about it.[17] Or is it a reference to the neo-Nazis who carried the flag at the Unite the Right rally in Charlottesville in the spring of 2017? Or the insurrectionists carrying the flag in the Capitol building in January 2021? Or is it just a more general reference to the myriad hate groups who use the flag?[18] And might the fact that so many use the flag in this way suggest something about the flag itself? But Edwards actually uses the current pushback against the flag as an affront against her organization; she is "grieved," thrown into what has been a very powerful position—that of the grieving Southern woman.

When she goes on to say "Our members are the ones who, like our statues, have stayed quietly in the background, never engaging in public controversy," she is revealing an awful lot.[19] Stating boldly that more than a century of building and protecting memorials to explicitly and avowedly racist historical actors who sought to maintain white supremacy (and put an end to the United States) is the same as staying quietly in the background and "never" engaging in controversy is a master class in making the patently untrue seem natural. It is a vivid demonstration of how well the UDC has met its goal of honoring and protecting its fictionalized history of the war. The confidence of the statement might be the most important thing to note.

But the statement gets worse. Edwards continues, "The United Daughters of the Confederacy totally denounces any individual or group that promotes racial divisiveness or white supremacy." Really? Fighting tooth and nail to keep Robert E. Lee statues standing? (Or refusing African American members? Essie Mae Washington-Williams, with whom this chapter began, tried—for years—to join the UDC but was never admitted, despite the fact that her white sisters were members.)[20] Edwards goes on, "We are saddened that some people find anything connected with the Confederacy to be offensive. Our Confederate ancestors were and are Americans. We as an Organization do not sit in judgment of them nor do we impose the standards of the 19th century on Americans of the 21st century."[21] So, Confederates are important to honor simply because they were American? (Never mind that they waged war against America.) They should not be judged? Or, if they are judged, they should be judged by nineteenth-century rather than twenty-first century standards? They were never offensive? *And* they should be honored in perpetuity?

Edwards is working hard here to claim a kind of racial innocence, and her confidence in this argument is notable. Even the most basic facts categorically undermine every single thing she says. And yet, she continues, "It is our sincere wish that our great nation and its citizens will continue to let its fellow Americans, the descendants of Confederate soldiers, honor the memory of their ancestors. Indeed, we urge all Americans to honor their ancestors' contributions to our country as well." And as if this isn't enough, she concludes, "This diversity is what makes our nation stronger."[22] Lest a reader begin to wonder about the sincerity of the UDC's commitment to diversity or the honoring of all Americans's ancestors, the final element of the statement on the homepage casts the rest of Edwards's statement in a new and important light. Edwards follows this startling proclamation on the value of diversity with a "Reaffirmation of the Objectives of the United Daughters of the Confederacy,®"[23] which begins, "WHEREAS, The United Daughters of the Confederacy is a tax-exempt, non-profit Organization whose objectives are Historical, Benevolent, Educational, Memorial and Patriotic..."[24] What follows is a legalistic anti-discrimination statement that seems very much designed to protect the UDC's tax-exempt status as a non-profit organization. It can be difficult, although not impossible, to maintain tax-exempt status if an organization breaks federal anti-discrimination laws. So even for the unlikely few for whom the arguments Edwards is making about the UDC are not clearly full of outrageous falsehoods and dog whistles, the relationship between her statement and the legal statement is pretty clear evidence of what inspired this new interest in diversity and other people's ancestors.

There is one more thing to note here before turning to the work of the UDC. It is the *assumed* distinction between erecting a memorial and taking one down. This is another opportunity to see the magic of memorials as potent cultural infrastructure. Edwards positions the work of putting up a memorial as something entirely different from taking one down, when both are, in fact, the work of groups seeking to shape our cultural infrastructure. In her framing, creating a memorial is a "sacred duty," and taking one down is an impertinent, blasphemous disruption. Of course, neither is true, as *Silent Sam* tells us quite emphatically.

Silent Sam wasn't silent. But he is a typical UDC memorial, and returning to him here is useful. *Silent Sam* stood at the entrance to the University of North Carolina for one hundred and five years, from 1913 to 2018. He is a bronze figure standing on a stone plinth. The plinth has three plaques. The first is a bas-relief figure of a woman appealing to a young student to join the fight. The other two read, "To the sons of the university who entered the War of 1861–65 in answer to the call of their country and whose lives taught the lesson of their great commander that duty is the sublimest word in the English language," and "Erected under the auspices of the North Carolina division of the United Daughters of the Confederacy aided by the alumni of the university." The language of these inscriptions is both very straightforward and a little confusing. First, the war is not named as the Civil War or the War Between the States. It is simply the War of 1861–65. Another name might create some confusion about the next phrase: "the call of their country." It would beg the question—which country? Not, in a civil war or a war between states, the country of which North Carolina was a part before 1861, yes? This gentle language avoids the problems of insurrection and rebellion and the soldier on the plinth as a traitor to the nation in which he stands. This is a simple but important point. It is underscored by the second half of the sentence in which readers learn that *Silent Sam*'s and other such soldiers' "lives taught the lesson of their great commander that duty is the sublimest word in the English language." It is pretty safe to assume that readers in 1913 would have understood the great commander to be a figure larger than Robert E. Lee: that the reference was to God, rather than the commander of the Confederate troops. So, Sam is answering a call from God, and his duty to God is sublime. It is not impossible to see how this might be moving to generations of students entering the campus of the University of North Carolina. Sam is introduced as an innocent who was called and answered that call. Certainly his place of honor on the campus immediately communicates the great value the university and the community place on his willingness to sacrifice and his respect for his duty. (See Figure 5.)

There is an implication, because it is a memorial, that Sam gave his life for this cause, that visitors to the monument are casting their eyes on a young man who made the ultimate sacrifice out of a sense of duty to his country. But this is not the case. The memorial is for the sons of the university who served, not specifically for those who died. This may seem like an odd point to make, but it is worth making because it undermines the twenty-first century (and the twentieth-century) defense of these memorials as the work of mothers grieving their lost sons and wives grieving their lost husbands. That claim is made over and over again.[25] But in this case and most others, the soldier is remembered for his service—the dead are not specifically remembered for their sacrifices.[26] This memorial is more about responding when duty called than about loss. (The bas-relief is of a woman urging the young man to fight—not a grieving mother or wife.) All of this undercuts the argument that the memorials were intended to remember personal losses that constitute the shared, sacred heritage that Edwards and the UDC still seek to defend.

So, *Silent Sam* wasn't a lost son. He was a son of the university. And this, it is worth noting, gives us a fair bit of information about him. He was probably not an "everyman" of North Carolina; he was much more likely to belong to the planter class or the gentry. In 1860, this meant that he

FIGURE 5 *Silent Sam*, Chapel Hill, North Carolina

probably came from people who owned a significant number of slaves.[27] The simply dressed young man on the plinth was in all likelihood fighting for his own economic interests—and that matters.

The figure earned the name *Silent Sam* because the sculptor, John A. Wilson, was one of many northern sculptors whose work, cast in northern foundries, featured generic young men (as opposed to distinct individuals) who were holding a rifle—or had one leaning against their legs—without a cartridge box for ammunition, so that their weapons were silent.[28] But *Silent Sam* wasn't silent in 1913, and he hasn't been silent since.

After *Silent Sam* was toppled by protesters in 2018, a lot of attention was paid, appropriately, to the language of the speech made at the dedication of the monument by Julian Shakespeare Carr, a university trustee and supporter of the Ku Klux Klan.[29] Carr's rhetoric soared. He claimed, "The whole Southland is sanctified by the precious blood of the student Confederate soldier."[30] He continued, "Their sublime courage has thrown upon the sky of Dixie a picture so bright and beautiful that neither defeat, nor disaster, nor oppression, nor smoke, nor fire, nor devastation, nor desolation, dire and calamitous, and I might with truth add, the world, the flesh nor the Devil has been able to mar or blemish it."[31] He compares them to the "Knights of the Holy Grail" and refers to the war as the "Sacred Cause." And he gives the women of the South the credit the UDC felt they were due, claiming, "The war between the states was fought, really, by the women who stayed at home. Had they uttered a cry, had they complained, the morale of Lee's army would have been dissipated in a day."[32] But what got the most attention in 2018 was the language he used at the end of his speech to tell the personal story I have already drawn from.

Recall that he asked permission to relate that "One hundred yards from where we stand, less than ninety days perhaps after my return from Appomattox, I horse-whipped a negro wench until her skirts hung in shreds, because upon the streets of this quiet village she had publicly insulted and maligned a Southern lady, and then rushed for protection to these University buildings where was stationed a garrison of 100 Federal soldiers. I performed the pleasing duty in the immediate presence of the entire garrison, and for thirty nights afterwards slept with a double-barrel shot gun under my head."[33] The shock of the violence of the whipping and the pleasure he expressed in this "duty" certainly makes the "heritage" argument tricky to sustain. It also raises a question about the sacredness of the duty at the heart of the whole enterprise.

It is hard not to draw a line between this easy, shared, even celebrated violence against Black bodies in 1913 with the easy, shared violence against Black bodies that student Maya Little sought to connect to the memorial when she read aloud from Carr's speech and splashed her own blood and red ink on the memorial in 2018. As Little describes it, "All we wanted to do was show that, within this monument's history and within its current representation, it represents white supremacy, and it has no place on this campus."[34] Her argument that the memorial represents white supremacy is hard to refute in the face of Carr's speech, and her remarkable actions led to the eventual removal of the memorial—first by students who top-pled the statue and then by the University, which determined that the location of the memorial was "unsafe."

University Chancellor Carol Folt issued a statement in 2019 that tried to avoid the issue of white supremacy, claiming, "*Silent Sam* has a place in our history and on our campus where its history can be taught…but not at the front door of a safe, welcoming, proudly public research uni-versity."[35] She continues, perhaps referring obliquely to Carr's remarks, "I hope we can agree that there is a difference between those who commem-orate their fallen and people who want a restoration of white rule."[36] This statement is fascinating. In 2019, Folt is saying that the memorial is not just about the "fallen" but about "those who commemorate their fallen" and that we should be able to distinguish between white supremacy and commemoration of the Confederacy. It begs the questions: Did she read any of the speeches given at the dedication? And does she realize that she is participating in exactly the logic that the UDC hoped to naturalize despite its obviously untrue nature?

Carol Folt is a highly trained scholar and has been a leader of three great universities, but before she resigned her position at the University of North Carolina, she played right into the hands of the UDC. She was willing to state publicly that while the university rejected white suprem-acy, it did not reject the memorial—as if it was possible to disaggregate the two. And, to be clear, *it is not possible to disaggregate the two*. The memorial was very clearly built for those who served, not just for the fallen, and the point of the commemoration was to remember a shared "duty" that enabled Carr the "pleasure" of horse-whipping a Black woman "until her skirts hung in shreds." (Again, can you imagine what happened to her flesh if her skirts hung in shreds?)

How could a smart woman like Folt miss this? Her response to the memorial is a vivid testament to the success of the UDC in its extraordi-narily effective campaign to use the fallen as a foil in a very thinly veiled effort to protect the racial logic, the white supremacy, that was so central to the organization's mission. The woman of the UDC were not "people who want a restoration of white rule," as Folt sees the worst-case sce-nario, but people who fought—with hugely consequential ambition and success—to *maintain* white rule. Folt could miss it because the UDC was very good at what it was doing.

The description of the horse-whipping in Carr's speech is disturbing. But the most terrifying thing he said came toward the end: "And the people of all sections of our great Republic, moved by the impulse of sincere and zealous loyalty, of fervent and exalted patriotism may say: 'All is well that ends well.'"[37] He is claiming, rightly, a kind of victory for the Lost Cause; the Confederates may not have won on the battlefield, but "In the knowledge of subsequent developments, the progress, peace and prosperity of our united, common country, victor and vanquished now alike believe that in the Providence of God it was right and well that the issue was determined as it was."[38] He can offer the assurance that "all is well" because the loss was limited enough that he could, fifty years after the war was over, stand in front of an adoring crowd and boast of brutally beating a Black woman with impunity. How was this possible? And how could a smart scholar leading a major university still buy it another hundred years later?

The answer to these questions can be found, in part, in another speech given at the dedication of *Silent Sam*. This speech has received much less attention than Carr's, but it is more disturbing. Mrs. Marshall Williams, president of the North Carolina UDC, stood before the assembled and rejoiced: "Representing 4,000 Daughters of the Confederacy in the State, I voice their sentiment, when I say today is a proud and happy occasion."[39] She continues, speaking to their vast ambition, "The United Daughters of the Confederacy have erected 700 monuments to the Southern Cause. In all the history of the civilized world, there were never before so many monuments to a single cause."[40] This is both stunning and quite likely true. And then she turns poetic, offering a grand rumination on the operations of nations:

> Of all of the instincts in the human heart there is none more difficult of analysis than love of country, altogether inscrutable, altogether beyond the power of description. Vague it may be, vague the pale grey smoke of an Indian's Summer's evening along the hill-sides, mysterious as the glint of the moon rays through, barren wind-swayed branches, subtle as the sound of moving water, but he must be blind or deaf indeed who would deny it the mighty strength of passion woven from fibers of the first heart that ever throbbed in the misty dawn of time. This passionate love the United Daughters of the Confederacy have for the South, a love beyond analysis.[41]

She concludes, "May this shaft prove an inspiration to the students here as they come and go, and may they remember [the] courage and fidelity [of] those 'Boy Soldiers.'…The world unites in giving meed of praise to our soldiers, equal of the hardened legion of Caesar and the enthusiastic followers of Napoleon."[42] It might be easy to lose the thread in her lofty descriptions, but she is both offering an astute analysis of the operations of the nation and denying that the UDC had figured out as much as it had about how nations work. In fact, for thirty consequential years at the turn of the century, love of country was a powerful tool that the UDC harnessed, rather than something "beyond analysis."

And this is why the key to Carr's speech is not just the pleasure he was proud to share in horse-whipping a Black woman but also the reason he whipped her in public with such relish. You may recall that he told the gathered crowd that he had whipped the women in full sight of an entire garrison of federal soldiers because "she had publicly insulted and maligned a Southern lady."[43] So while no mention of slavery is made in the speeches given by Carr or Williams, or even in Folt's statement, the possibility of a Black woman publicly insulting a white woman, a "Southern lady," was an offense in Carr's telling that was universally assumed to be worthy of a violent response. He shares his pleasure in the violence but is also eager to report that despite his concerns, the entire garrison of soldiers did nothing. He makes the powerful point that whatever their differences, he and those soldiers and *Silent Sam* did in fact share something. They shared a world view in which the only reasonable response to a Black woman insulting a white woman was brutal public violence met with impunity. As he said, "All is well that ends well."

This may seem like a lot to claim based on a few speeches given to a crowd of a hundred people a long time ago in a small town. But the point is to try to understand something complicated: how big ideas that are untrue and mitigated against by daily lived experience come to be widely, nearly universally shared. The Jim Crow legal structures that were taking form across the United States in this period are clear evidence of one element of the process of maintaining structures of inequity, but those laws had to be driven by, justified by, more broadly shared ideas. These memorials, the fact that they mattered so much when they were built and have continued to matter so much since, are another site for understanding these processes. And for all of Mrs. Marshall Williams's denials of the ability of the

UDC to understand national passions, the ladies seem to have understood and manipulated them with remarkable clarity and precision.

Chancellor Folt's response to the *Silent Sam* controversy is powerful evidence of the UDC's success. And it is hard to know the extent to which Folt's statement about distinguishing between "those who commemorate their fallen and people who want a restoration of white rule" was something that she truly believed or something that seemed like a politically manageable line to walk in a tricky situation. But it is important to note that it doesn't matter if she believed it or if it was the politically possible thing to say. Either way, it is evidence of the long, striking, deeply embedded success of the UDC. It seems hard to imagine more explicit evidence, in the realm of rhetoric, that the UDC and the Lost Cause won. The distinction between the memory of innocent boys and a culture structured around racial violence has been so successfully collapsed that, despite its evident interconnection—despite the very direct language coming from people like Carr and Williams—even the *most highly educated people charged with thinking deeply about this question are unwilling or unable to see it.* (All's well that ends well.)

As Karen Cox, the foremost scholar on the UDC, states in no uncertain terms, "The whole point of Confederate monuments is to celebrate white supremacy."[44] This is the title of her 2017 op-ed in the *Washington Post*. It is startling, and the fact that it is startling is still further support for Cox's statement.

In 2022 781 of the UDC monuments still stand alongside more than 1,000 other public commemorations of the Confederacy.[45] (Union memorials to Abraham Lincoln dotted the landscape at a pretty steady rate from the end of the war into the beginning of the twentieth century. They celebrate Lincoln without the drama of naturalizing a fictional Lost Cause, but they were also not—it is worth noting—celebrations of emancipation that might have pushed back against the ideas the UDC was inscribing into the landscape.)

In 1913, Mrs. Marshall Williams bragged about seven hundred *Silent Sam*s across the South, but the UDC were just hitting their stride. The UDC memorials and other commemorations are mostly in the South but are also in forty of the fifty states. They include "109 public schools named for Robert E. Lee, Jefferson Davis or other Confederate icons; 80 counties and cities named for Confederates; 9 official Confederate holidays in six states; and 10 U.S. military bases named for Confederates."[46] This list does not include the hundreds of street names and Confederate flags flown in civic spaces (more on this in Chapter Five). Each of these elements of the campaign to win the Lost Cause, to maintain white supremacy, is slightly different, shaped by different sites and contexts. But they share a great deal, and they have been effectively working together for more than a hundred years.

It is stunning to think that there are nearly eight hundred memorials like *Silent Sam*; and while we can't examine them all, it would be invaluable for each of the 781 communities where they are displayed to do a "reading" like this of their local memorial. Asking just the most basic question—What was said at its dedication?—would quickly start to strip away the nearly intractable "heritage," "fallen sons," and "innocent boys" defenses to reveal the more pressing problems these memorials were intended to address. And, as with *Silent Sam*, tracking public statements from the dedication is important, but tracking public statements made since and the linguistic dexterity they have often required is just as important. (Think Carol Folt.) *Silent Sam* is a useful example of the things the memorials share. And if you are still unconvinced that the Lost Cause won, the question of what would become of *Silent Sam* after he was removed might be instructive. In 2019, the University settled a lawsuit filed by the Sons of Confederate Veterans (SCV) by donating the sculpture to the organization and giving the SCV $2.5 million for the care and preservation of the memorial. All's well that ends well?

Robert E. Lee memorials are the second most common Confederate memorial form of this period. Like the *Silent Sam*s, the Lee statues are not identical but share many common elements. The Robert E. Lee Monument in Richmond, Virginia, is a useful example. It was built on a larger scale than most, but it reflected the impulses that drove the building of Lee memorials across the South and beyond. It stood, until September 8, 2021, at the apex of Monument Avenue—a central point of the city through which east-west traffic flows—which was, until 2020, lined with Confederate memorials to J.E.B. Stewart, Stonewall Jackson, Jefferson Davis, and Matthew Fontaine Maury. The Lee memorial was at the center. It was built in 1890 and featured a bronze figure of Lee on a horse on a sixty-foot plinth. Together on top of the plinth, Lee and the horse stood fourteen feet tall. Sculpted by French artist Marius Mercie, it was the project of the Lee Monument Association led by Confederate veterans and the Ladies Lee Monument Association. Lee sat so fully upright that he almost appeared to be standing in his saddle. He held the reins of the horse, whose head was bowed in obedience. Lee looked thoughtfully into the near distance, a saber at his side. He was recognizably Lee, if you got close enough to see the details, but he was also a relatively generic leader on a horse.

At the dedication of the memorial, veteran, Southern Historical Society director, and donor to the memorial effort Archer Anderson led with a telling promise that Lee was a hero for all the nation, "Not Virginians only, not only those who dwell in the fair land stretching from the Potomac to the Rio Grande, but all who bear the American name may proudly consent that posterity shall judge them by the structure, which we are here to dedicate and crown with a heroic figure."[47] Arguing "that the character and fame of Robert Edward Lee are treasured as a 'possession for all time,'" Anderson claims a big victory for the Lost Cause, telling the crowd,

> That at the end of the first quarter of a century after the close of a stupendous civil war, in which more than a million men struggled for the mastery during four years of fierce and bloody conflict, we should see the Southern States in complete possession of their local self-government, the Federal Constitution unchanged save as respects the great issues submitted to the arbitrament of war, and the defeated party—whilst in full and patriotic sympathy with all the present grandeur and imperial promise of a reunited country—still not held to renounce any glorious memory, but free to heap honors upon their trusted leaders, living or dead—all this reveals a character in which the American people may well be content to be handed down to history.[48]

What Anderson wants to celebrate is partly the triumph of the ideology Lee fought for; but mostly he celebrates—in 1890—the triumph of the Lost Cause. He marches through a long and insistently adoring recounting of Lee's life and accomplishments, never explicitly speaking to the cause of the war, but only referring repeatedly to a call to duty that had to be answered. This is interesting because it would be hard, listening to the litany of praise, to discern that Lee lost. That he was a failed military leader is nowhere in Anderson's language, and certainly it is not reflected in the scale of the monument. But in the structure of the speech, once Anderson has claimed victory for the Lost Cause, "the defeated party...still not held to renounce any glorious memory," the rest is less important. It is hard to imagine a casual visitor to the memorial coming away with the impression that Lee lost. (But it is important to remember that he did.)

The scale of the victory Anderson claims is huge, matched by the scale of the monument itself. It is also reflected in the staying power of the Lee memorial 131 years later. In the summer of 2020, following the murder of George Floyd, protests erupted all over the country, and memorials started coming down in significant numbers—some were toppled by protesters, and some were removed by local governments. Virginia Governor Ralph Northam announced that the monuments of Monument Avenue would all come down—J.E.B. Stewart, Stonewall Jackson, Jefferson Davis, Matthew Fontaine Maury, and Lee himself. In short order, Stewart, Jackson, Davis, and Maury were removed. The Lee Memorial proved more difficult. It was massive and impossible to topple. And as it stood waiting for authorities to remove it, it was transformed. Artists and activists "transformed the base of the sculpture instead, covering the marble and granite with the names of victims of police violence, protest chants, calls for compassion, revolutionary symbols and anti-police slogans in dozens of colors." This transformation was so dramatic that the *New York Times* named it one of "The 25 Most Influential Works of American Protest Art Since World War II."[49] Images of people murdered by police and civil rights activists were projected onto the base; Breonna Taylor smiling back from the base of the memorial was undeniably powerful.

But even as this was happening, the best and longest advocates for the Lost Cause were not giving up, and they were not yet losing. As the other memorials on Monument Avenue were toppled and removed by municipal officials, a series of lawsuits saved the Lee Monument for another year. Supporters sued Governor Northam, arguing that he was breaking a commitment to "faithfully guard...and affectionately protect" the monument and to keep it "perpetually sacred."[50] In October 2020, a judge ruled that the state could, in fact, remove Lee because, in the words of Virginia Attorney General Mark Herring, "The Lee statue does not represent who we have become as Virginians and it sends the wrong message to the rest of the world that we continue to venerate an individual who fought to maintain the enslavement of human beings."[51]

Lee is gone, but the legal battles over toppled memorials are just beginning. The question has become, how racist can our cultural infrastructure be now? Again, it is telling that this is a question we are asking more than 150 years after the war.

Christopher Columbus memorials, which were also pulled down in large numbers in the summer of 2020, entered the memorial landscape at the same time as Robert E. Lee and *Silent Sam*. Starting around 1890, Italian Americans turned to him and fellow explorer Giuseppe da Verrazzano to stake their own claims to legitimacy. (This mostly meant claims to whiteness.) Seizing the opportunity presented by the 400th anniversary of Columbus's arrival in the Americas, they formed local organizations to promote ethnic pride and claim full American cultural citizenship by building memorials to, among other things, make the argument that the *first* founding fathers were Italians. Unlike the UDC or the DAR, they were not trying to *maintain* a racial order; they were trying to *modify* a white racial order to make it include them. In New York, especially, they dedicated time "to raising funds and lobbying for the construction of various monuments to the glory of Italian heroes, among whom were Giuseppe Garibaldi at Washington Square Park (1888) and on Staten Island (1896), Christopher Columbus at Columbus Circle (1892), Giuseppe Verdi between Broadway and 73rd Street (1906), Giovanni da Verrazzano in Battery Park (1909), and Dante Alighieri between Broadway and Columbus Avenue, near Lincoln Square (1921)."[52]

As historian Bénédicte Deschamps writes, "'Permeated with eugenic ideology,' the New York newspapers resented the 'dark faced Italians' who were 'swarming through the doors of Barge Office'" and Italian Americans sought to fight back against claims that they were overstepping their welcome by using "memorial building to get a greater exposure as an ethnic group and transcend the boundaries of the skimpy Little Italies."[53]

The impact that Columbus and da Verrazzano had on indigenous people of the Americas was very unlikely to have occupied these first- and second-generation immigrants struggling to shed the sins of being immigrants and "swarthy" and Catholic. They were seeking access to whiteness, not thinking about indigenous people. Banker Carlo Barotti was quoted in the *New York Times* boasting of the quality of the artwork, which would include "an Italian genius hovering" above "a bronze group representing America looking upward to the great navigator."[54] This is relatively unsubtle: the figure of the Italian standing tall forty feet above the street and being admired by figures of Americans frozen in bronze. Barotti takes pains to tell the paper that the memorial is being paid for by successful Italian American businessmen who could easily afford more than double what they are paying for this grand memorial.[55] (Again, the fate of indigenous people does not seem to be part of his thinking.) Another *New York Times* story published a few years later describes the Columbus memorial as "offered by the Italians resident in the United States as a testimonial of their love for the institutions of this Republic and a tribute to their great countryman."[56] It also mentions that Spanish Americans have tried, with less success, to build their own memorial to Columbus in the city, to claim him as their own.[57] In both of these cases, Italian Americans and Spanish Americans are using the power of cultural infrastructure to claim a place in the culture or, more specifically, the racial order, without thinking about the complicated, deadly impacts of the "genius" of these explorers.

If we return to both the basic principles for understanding all of these memorials and the questions to ask of all memorials, listed at the beginning of this chapter, with the Confederate and Columbus memorials in mind and with *Silent Sam*, the Robert E. Lee Monument in Richmond, and Columbus in New York as templates, we can start to see how valuable these principles and questions are.

The basic principles of memorials seem to reflect the memorial building boom of the 1890s–1920s. First, *they are powerful*: *Silent Sam* and Lee in Richmond both make this impossible to deny. Second, *they are doing their best work when they seem to fit seamlessly into the landscape; when they stop being noticeable, their job is done*: think of Carol Folt trying to argue that *Silent Sam* still has a place on her campus because he is simply a commemoration of "the fallen," or of the millions who have passed through Columbus Circle without thinking about the cost of Columbus's legacy. Third, *they are more about the time in which they are made than the time they memorialize*: remember Archer Anderson celebrating Lee as a hero for the entire nation and the excitement about a "full and patriotic sympathy with all the present grandeur and imperial promise of a reunited country." Fourth, *they are made by people who feel strongly that they have something very important to say*: Carr, Williams, and Anderson are all impassioned advocates for a forward-looking cause; they are not simply sharing grief. Fifth, *they are not neutral. Ever*: again, think of how deeply off Carol Folt's logic sounds in 2017 or of Mrs. Williams telling the crowd, "May this shaft prove an inspiration to the students here as they come and go, and may they remember... [the] courage and fidelity [of] those 'Boy Soldiers.'" Sixth, *they don't innocently remember a discrete event; they invent a particular past that they worry will not be recognized without a memorial*: Lee, even as he towered over the ceremonial space of Richmond, did not appear in any possible way to be the leader of a military failure who was responsible for the deaths of six hundred thousand young American men, and Columbus doesn't read as "ethnic other" but central to the culture. Seventh, *they are often inspired by anxiety, not the confidence the bronze and limestone might seem to project; they come from an unsettled moment*: the intense racial turbulence of this period—especially as it fought over Jim Crow laws and the federal support they found—is everywhere and hard to miss in the impassioned statement of many of these folks. And, eighth, *memorials use a few basic and familiar conventions to make their points*: Columbus towers above the city; and Lee on a horse and the single anonymous figure on the plinth with a rifle at his side use a very limited but scorchingly effective vocabulary with which to win the Lost Cause.

These principles, as they played out in the 1890s–1920s, make answering the key questions short work:

1. When was it built? We know that if it was built between roughly 1890 and 1920, it was part of a major memorial building boom that was largely focused on the Lost Cause.
2. By whom was it built? If it was built in this period, we know that it was likely built by a hereditary patriotic organization, probably a women's hereditary patriotic organization—the UDC or possibly the DAR—and that it required permission from the local government or state government, depending on where it was placed.
3. What was unsettled about the time in which it was made? We know that the legitimacy of a social order that put the enslavement of Black people at its center was at the heart of the Civil War and that finding a polite, indirect, but powerful way to maintain white supremacy was the driving force behind building these memorials. (We also know that there was an unspoken tension in these processes around the social position of women and their access to social power; these effective social tools were made by women

and shaped by their claim to moral authority and intimate roles as bearers of heritage at a time when their access to elected office and economic power was limited.)

4. What point did the builders want to make, and what past did they invent to make it? They wanted to maintain white supremacy for future generations, plain and simple. Grieving Civil War widows, innocent fallen boys, a world in which the public horse-whipping of a Black woman for insulting a "Southern lady" was a triumph of superior morality and divine order.

5. How, in what forms, did they try to make their point? The most common was the single soldier on the plinth or a victorious-looking Lee on a horse.

6. And, finally, what happened to the memorial in the summer of 2020? With *Silent Sam*, the jury is still out. Despite the fact that more than two hundred memorials came down after the murder of George Floyd in the summer of 2020, when *Silent Sam* was removed, the Sons of Confederate Veterans got both *Silent Sam* and $2.5 million.[58] And this was not the end of the story. First, in February 2020, a judge overruled the settlement with the SCV, revealing that the university had actually settled before the SCV had filed its suit, and raising more questions about the university's position. A lawyer for the UNC issued a statement saying, "The Board of Governors knew from the very beginning that this was a difficult but needed solution to meet all their goals to protect public safety of the University community, restore normality to campus, and be compliant with the Monuments Law."[59] The Monuments Law he refers to was passed in 2015 and requires that monuments "may not be removed, relocated, or altered in any way without the approval of the North Carolina Historical Commission" and an "object of remembrance located on public property may not be permanently removed and may only be relocated."[60] This little law, passed without much fanfare and with no mention of the Confederacy, slavery, the Lost Cause, or white supremacy, continues, quietly, to protect all of the above. And, as a result, the fate of *Silent Sam* is still, in 2022 up for grabs. So far, for the members of the UDC and their descendants, "All's well that ends well."

2

THE LOST CAUSE KEEPS WINNING

1920–1980: LIVING MEMORIALS AND DYING CITIES

The first thing to know about memorials in this period is that they went out of style. It is hard to know if this was *because* this period saw two world wars that produced a staggering *eighty million deaths worldwide* or *despite* eighty million deaths worldwide. In either case, during a sixty-year period in the middle of the twentieth century in the United States, the frenzy of memorial building that had preceded it receded, and there was generally much less interest in putting figures into civic spaces. That does not mean, however, that this is an unimportant period in the story of memorials as blunt instruments of social power or in the history of racist cultural infrastructure in the United States more broadly. This period is very important.

Americans continued to build traditional memorials in modest numbers—modest especially given that more than six hundred thousand American service men and women were killed in this period. And new kinds emerged. The Confederate memorials in the first boom often performed the sleight of hand of being very much about maintaining white supremacy without directly engaging with either slavery or race. They also could hardly have been more literal—bronze men on stone columns and plinths. Memorials built after 1920 were mostly for soldiers killed in

World War I, World War II, and, to a lesser extent, the Korean War. But they were much less literal.

In this period, most memorials were living memorials. Those who sought to commemorate built physical infrastructure and called it a memorial. This has been called a "living memorial movement." At the start of this period, as architectural historian Andrew Shanken describes it, "On one side stood those who advocated traditional forms of memorials such as statues, obelisks, triumphal arches, and other commemorative structures, those forms of memorials whose sole purpose is to serve as a memorial. On the other side of the debate stood those who supported 'living memorials,' useful projects such as community centers, libraries, forests, and even highways that were marked in some fashion, usually with plaques, as memorials."[1] The advocates for living memorials won in a landslide.

But while memorials became more abstract, and their relationship to thinking about race became less explicit, it is crucial to understand that this did not diminish the work they are doing and have done as cultural infrastructure shaping how we think about and experience race in the United States. No matter how you slice it, there is one pressing and undeniable takeaway: memorials became literal infrastructure, and that infrastructure was not only distributed inequitably but also distributed in ways that hardened racial lines indelibly and continues to be viscerally painful. This is a lot to claim for a highway with a plaque reading "Veterans Memorial Highway," but it is an important claim to make.

The first phase of memorial building in this period started in 1920, just two years after the end of the First World War. World War I memorials fall into two pretty distinct categories that align with the debate Shanken describes above. Local civic organizations, not especially women's organizations in this period, built either "doughboys" on courthouse lawns or living memorials—parks, libraries, auditoriums, bell towers, university buildings, swimming pools, basketball courts, and roadways.

A doughboy on a courthouse lawn was the most typical form of the traditional World War I memorial. The doughboy, a common nickname for an American enlisted man, came in a couple of mass-produced models, the most popular of which was *The Spirit of the American Doughboy*. This figure was a pressed copper sculpture designed by E.M. Viquesney. It was a carefully detailed figure of a man in uniform holding a hand grenade

FIGURE 6 *The Spirit of the American Doughboy*

in his raised right hand and a rifle in his left. He stared into the distance, his face both blank and pure. The Smithsonian Art Inventories Catalogue lists 163 Viquesney doughboys distributed across nearly every state.[2] So, clearly they were popular. And they cost only "$1,000 from the Sencer factory, plus the base."[3] They were a fast response to the deaths of 117,000 American men in one eighteen-month period. (See Figure 6.)

But in the eyes of many, they were relics from another time. They met with two forms of resistance. First, elites were worried about a landscape spotted with poor-quality art. Second, they seemed to be doing static memory work at a time when Americans wanted to move forward. As historian Jennifer Wingate relates, the chairman of the National Commission of Fine Arts, Charles Moore, worried in 1922 that "We of today laugh at the grotesque figures of the soldiers of the Civil War, with their strange uniforms, whether Union or Confederate. Will not the doughboy of the World War, with his clumsy helmet, his sagging belt and the other burdens of equipment, seem even more grotesque to the coming generations? And yet we are setting up doughboys all over the land."[4] According to Wingate, the Commission and other elites urged "local memorial committees to choose simple commemorative forms like decorative flagpoles instead of figurative sculpture produced by the nation's expanding commercial monument industry." From their perspective, no art was better than poor art. But they seemed to be missing what was most important to Viquesney. He explicitly advertised his doughboy as a response to post-war radicalism and labor organizing. Wingate tells us, "To counter the threat posed by groups like the Wobblies, the sculptor's advertisements urged communities to dedicate *The Spirit of the American Doughboy* as a sign of security and respect for 'democracy's greatest son—the American doughboy." Viquesney conflated nationalism with authenticity by selling a "100% perfect representation of an American soldier, a sales pitch that would have resonated with the interwar rhetoric of '100% Americanism.'"[5] So, while even the innocent-looking doughboy was quite explicitly designed to do public cultural work, these politics weren't what his detractors objected to—they worried about bad art but also about getting stuck in an old social model. They wanted to preserve social relations by enabling the living of social ideals rather than quietly commanding them in stone.

The problem with the doughboy was, for many, more about form in a moment in which people very much wanted to look forward. As Shanken argues, "Choosing a form of memorial was tantamount to choosing a form of society. Critics condemned traditional memorials as 'tawdry "monumental" monstrosities.' Building a victory column or a triumphal arch was anathema at a moment when many Americans experienced a compelling drive to move on and to forget war and the society that had fought two of them in quick succession."[6] He breaks down the argument: "To its sponsors, living memorials presented a way out of this dilemma, a means of folding the sacrifices of war into the pattern of democratic community life, gently kneading the past into the present, in the process altering the relation between public space and memory."[7] All of this is to say that World War I deaths stirred a serious debate about memorials in which, despite the 163 doughboys on plinth sold by the Sencer factory, the idea for "living memorials" emerged and triumphed.

Memorial halls, auditoriums, gymnasiums, and parks are evidence of the success of the push for living memorials. The extent of their triumph is such that most Americans are blissfully unaware of how much of the infrastructure of their daily lives is explicitly cultural infrastructure. Living memorials built after World War I include the Los Angeles Memorial Coliseum, the War Memorial Gymnasium at the University of Idaho, Memorial Auditorium in Kansas City, the Elks National Headquarters in Chicago, the American Legion Headquarters in Indianapolis, the War Memorial Auditorium in Nashville, the Civic Auditorium in Dallas, and many, many more. In New York City alone, more than *one hundred parks* have some World War I memorial element.[8]

Perhaps the most ambitious living memorial project after World War I was the Victory Highway. Planned by the Victory Highway Association, the highway was a trans-continental memorial. In the words of *Concrete Highway Magazine* in 1924, "Linking two oceans three thousand miles apart with a concrete chain, the Victory Highway will constitute one of the greatest memorials in history."[9] The plan involved not only the completion of the three-thousand-mile road but also Victory Highway Eagle Monuments along the way. By 1928, the highway was mostly completed; but as the federal government tried to regularize the newly emerging highway system, much of the Victory Highway was renamed I-40, and only six Eagle Monuments were completed.

Living memorials continued to be built across the 1930s, mostly by the Works Progress Administration of the New Deal. The Depression slowed the pace of all new building, and then the start of World War II turned attention away from remembering war and back to fighting. But when that war ended, Americans had four hundred thousand new deaths to mourn and very little interest left in figural sculptures in parks. Despite the huge number of deaths and the nearly universal support for the war, interest in memorials after World War II was modest at best. Maybe the most vivid evidence of this is in New York City. While there had been intense interest in memorializing the first war, after World War II, City Park Commissioner Robert Moses "expressed the hope that rather than the disparate group of World War I monuments scattered throughout the parks system, a plan be implemented to erect one consolidated memorial for each borough."[10] But even this was too ambitious. Eventually, one memorial was built: the Brooklyn War Memorial was dedicated in 1951 and "serves as a community facility and houses veterans organizations, parks operational personnel (including the monuments field office and shop), and an auditorium with honor rolls."[11] (That is a one-hundred-to-one ratio of interest in World War I memorials to those for World War II; in most communities, World War II was added to existing memorials in one way or another.) Living memorials, however, continued to be built apace after World War II.

There are two important points to make about living memorials. First, this infrastructure has mattered to people. Think of all the music heard, games played, peace enjoyed, lectures attended, afternoons whiled away, and childhoods played out in these places. Very few of the people enjoying these facilities are likely to have given much thought to the connection between their beloved pool or concert hall and dead American nineteen-year-olds in France, but the living memorials have enabled millions to enjoy the best of the ideals for which the doughboys and the GIs of World War II fought and died. (My children happily spent their childhoods in "Vets" sweatshirts because they swam for the Veterans Memorial Park swim team.) Second, despite the fact that all 163 of the doughboy memorials were white and that there doesn't seem to be explicit language about race in these memorials or spoken at their dedications, these living memorials are part of the cultural infrastructure that has shaped thinking about race and helped to maintain racial inequities in the United States.

This claim may seem like a stretch, but it is not. There are two specific ways in which living memorials have helped to maintain structures of inequity. The first is that although this beautiful new infrastructure was intended to enable Americans to enjoy the freedoms for which US soldiers had died—lazy afternoons at swimming pools, Saturdays in grassy parks, concert halls full of moving music—they also functioned to sharpen the lived experience of racial division. Americans shared this new infrastructure, but they shared it inequitably along racial lines—everywhere, not just in the South. In the 1920s and the 1960s across the United States, Black Americans had limited access to these beautiful new gifts to the nation, and this mattered.

Racialized access to living memorials was a basic fact of American life for the first three or four decades after they were built. As historian Victoria Wolcott writes, "Blacks wanted freedom and mobility without being 'beaten over the head.' They sought to live their lives fully as citizens and consumers without the constraints of segregation....They wished to protect their children from the reality of racism."[12] But they had the painful experience of explaining to their children that these beautiful pools and concert halls in particular, but often parks, too, were not for them. Famously, Dr. Martin Luther King Jr. wrote about this experience in his letter from Birmingham Jail, telling his readers that "When you suddenly find your tongue twisted and your speech stammering as you seek to explain to your six-year-old daughter why she can't go to the public amusement park that has just been advertised on television, and see tears welling up in her eyes when she is told that Funtown is closed to colored children...then you will understand why we find it difficult to wait."[13] The same would certainly be true for the shiny new memorial swimming pools, famously segregated across the United States, and bandstands built to commemorate the great wars. (If this seems to be making too much of post-war swimming pools, remember that Strom Thurmond famously said, in a stump speech for his 1948 presidential campaign, "I wanna tell you, ladies and gentlemen, that there's not enough troops in the army to force the Southern people to break down segregation and admit the Negro race into our theaters, into our swimming pools, into our homes, and into our churches.")

Building physical infrastructure that is accessible inequitably across racial lines is different from building a memorial to celebrate your ability to horse-whip a Black woman in public with impunity. Clearly. But that doesn't mean that building physical infrastructure to celebrate cultural values, which is accessible inequitably across racial lines, is not part of a system that has maintained basic untruths about racial logics everywhere in the United States.

Memorial highways that also served as cultural graveyards are the second way in which living memorials have helped to maintain structures of inequity. Again, this may seem like a leap, but it is very important to understand. After the Second World War, there was a highway building effort that remains unmatched by any physical infrastructure project in US history. It was certainly a logical development. American leadership in Europe during the war noted the value of big roads to move people and machinery in the context of a war, and Americans were experiencing a surge of affluence and moving out of cities into suburbs in record numbers. Cities had mostly been built before cars were invented, so big highways that could get commuters out to the suburbs to live and back into cities to work had to be retrofitted into existing cityscapes. This was a hugely significant, complicated, and impactful process, the effects of which have been woefully underestimated. But the short version of the long story is that the federal government subsidized the building of these highways, which enabled homeownership in new suburban developments, at a scale Americans had not experienced before. (All of this was also supported by the GI Bill and new federal home loan policies.) It was a beautifully effective way to build a healthy and newly affluent middle class.

Highways were key to facilitating the process. Why not make these highways memorial highways? Why not celebrate service and sacrifice with infrastructure to enable the American dream? It was an elegant system with a brutal, violent, fatal flaw. The problem was racial, and it was compound. First, to fit the highways into cities, parts of existing cities had to be torn down. In most cities, the neighborhoods that were torn down were not just African American neighborhoods but African American business districts.[14] This had a devastating impact—and is how these living memorial highways became cultural graveyards. Second, the new lending policies enabled white people to get nearly zero-interest loans to buy houses in the suburbs but precluded African Americans from buying in the suburbs *and* from buying or improving properties inside cities. The memorial highways were often constructed on the cultural graveyards of African American neighborhoods that were bulldozed to create space for the highways coming into cities; and the memorial pools were often built in suburbs to which African Americans were denied access by the Federal Housing Authority's redlining practices, which sharply restricted African Americans' access to mortgage loans, and by restrictive covenants. So, in the post-war United States, the highways were part of a web of infrastructure that simultaneously gave white Americans a big financial leg up and barred African Americans from access to this economic expansion by trapping them in cities experiencing radical disinvestment. Driving by roadside markers designating these highways as war memorial highways or memorials to heroic leaders or units who led the United States to help free Europe and Asia from racial tyranny must have had a bitter resonance for African Americans. And we can't fully understand how structures of inequity are maintained without understanding this part of the story. This is not to say that Carr-like speeches about barring little Black girls from memorial swimming pools were made at the dedications of these memorials, it is just to say that this is how these new memorials worked in the world.

By the time the Highway Act of 1956 was passed, the United States had already fought to a draw a post–World War II war in Korea, and public appetite for war memorials seems to have been seriously curtailed. The United States also already had soldiers on the ground in Vietnam, and public enthusiasm for both war and American GIs was about to make a dramatic shift that would end up profoundly changing memorials and monuments in the country for the foreseeable future.

Modest bicentennial memorials are the final element of the story of memorials in the United States between 1920 and 1980. The bicentennial fell months after the final United States withdrawal from the deeply unpopular Vietnam War, two years after Richard Nixon resigned in the face of the Watergate scandal, and as new levels of both disinvestment and segregation were roiling American cities. So while the celebration included some pomp and circumstance and some very interesting demonstrations of ethnic pride, the most notable thing about the bicentennial was probably its modesty.

The Memorial to the 56 Signers of the Declaration of Independence in Washington D.C. is a useful example of this humility. Approved by Congress in 1978, the memorial occupies some very valuable real estate on the National Mall, near the Daughters of the American Revolution headquarters. The memorial is a semi-circle of simple, unadorned stone just above knee height, carved with the names of the signers. It is exactly as exciting as it sounds.

So, the basic principles of memorials also seem to reflect, in some new ways, the memorials built between 1920 and 1980. First, *they are powerful*: the living memorials remade the American landscape and articulated in clear terms to whom it belonged. Second, *they are doing their best work when they seem to fit seamlessly into the landscape; when they stop being noticeable, their job is done*: the fact that they require so much introduction and explanation speaks to the extent to which they have disappeared into the landscape even as they continue to shape the culture. Third, *they are more about the time in which they are made than the time they memorialize*: the drive for the physical infrastructure of leisure seems a long way from either the challenge of getting Irish American teenagers and young German Americans to fight and die to save the British or the desire to avenge the attack on Pearl Harbor. Fourth, *they are made by people who feel strongly that they have something very important to say*: the builders of the living memorials did have something powerful to say—they wanted to look forward to define who we are and why the war was worth the loss of five hundred thousand soldiers, and the answer was a particular kind of future, a future of healthy white families in beautiful, shared public space. Fifth, *they are not neutral. Ever*: the seeming neutrality of the living memorial is belied by the way it was used and by whom. Sixth, *they don't innocently remember a discrete event; they invent a particular past that they worry will not be recognized without a memorial*: they want to respond to the scale of the losses with promises about a future without such losses. Seventh, *they are often inspired by anxiety, not the confidence the bronze and limestone might seem to project; they come from an unsettled moment*: the push to invest in physical infrastructure for recreation reflects a desire for a calmer, more peaceful future, if not an equitable one. And, eighth, *memorials use a few basic and familiar conventions to make their points*: here, new conventions are introduced—conventions that are essentially invisible but still have a significant impact.

These principles, as they played out between 1920 and 1980, make answering the key questions to ask possible, but not necessarily easy.

1. When was it built? We know that if it was built between roughly 1920 and 1980, it was likely part of a movement to build living memorials to respond to the scale of the mid-century losses.

2. By whom was it built? If it was built in this period, we know that it was likely built by local municipalities rather than hereditary patriotic organizations.

3. What was unsettled about the time in which it was made? This is the time of the long civil rights movement, the Great Depression, World War II, the Korean War, the Vietnam War, and the Black power movement. It was a long period of social turbulence, much of which turned on simultaneous efforts to undo and to maintain racist cultural logics.

4. What point did the builders want to make, and what past did they invent to make it? It is complicated in this period to state that they wanted to maintain white supremacy for future generations, plain and simple. It is more accurate to say that they wanted to lay the foundations for a future society that they, perhaps unthinkingly, imagined as essentially white.

5. How, in what forms, did they try to make their point? Swimming pools, parks, concert halls, and highways—resources for public use that were not equitably available to all.

6. And, finally, what happened to the memorial in the summer of 2020? The living memorials have gone largely unnoticed.

1980–2010: THE SECOND MEMORIAL BOOM IN THREE ACTS

The first and most important thing to know about the second American memorial boom that started in 1980 and stretched into the 2010s is that it was sparked by the Vietnam Veterans Memorial, which was dedicated in 1982. The Vietnam Veterans Memorial profoundly changed American memorial culture. It is easily the most significant memorial in the United States since the *Silent Sam*s and Robert E. Lees started to dot the landscape in the 1890s. Across the four decades that followed its dedication, it changed the culture of American memorials in three linked but quite distinct ways. First, it made memorials matter again in a way that raised the stakes for all memorials, and especially for war memorials. It led, in fact, to a boom in the building of war memorials in Washington D.C. that transformed the beloved National Mall. Second, it made memorials matter again in a way that inspired the building of a significant wave of civil rights memorials, not just across the South but across the whole country. And, third, it made memorials matter again in a way that changed how Americans interact with memorials and how they, more broadly, grieve together in public.[15] This may sound like a lot to claim for one memorial, but it is not accurate.

The Vietnam Veterans Memorial is a startling success in every conceivable sense and has had an impact well beyond the wildest dreams of its creators. The memorial was conceived by a group of veterans in 1979. They were led by Jan Scruggs and called themselves the Vietnam Veterans Memorial Fund. They were driven by the idea that Vietnam veterans deserved a memorial that distinguished between the young men who fought and died in the war and the government that sent them to fight and die. The Fund wanted a memorial on the National Mall because it would dignify their service and recognize its value, but they did not want a memorial that was funded by the government that had sent them to fight in a war about which many of them felt deeply ambivalent. Jan Scruggs was at the time studying Carl Jung, and he was interested in the collective unconscious and how a memorial might heal a nation that was wrenched apart by the pain wrought and the disagreements stirred by the war in Vietnam. It is a sign of the extent to which war memorials (or any kind of memorials) had gone out of fashion that so little attention was paid to the efforts of Scruggs and his compatriots, who were by no means Washington power brokers in 1979, that they were able to get a memorial *built* on the National Mall and *dedicated* within three years of their first press conference about the possibility. For memorials, this is moving at lightning speed. But it had been some time since a memorial of any consequence had been built on the Mall in Washington, and it's safe to say that the process didn't get much attention because memorials were not much on people's minds. (There was no backlog of memorials waiting for space, and they did not meet serious resistance at this stage.)

The memorial started to receive significant attention, however, when the selection committee put together by the Vietnam Veterans Memorial Fund reviewed designs submitted in an open competition and selected the design of a young woman who was an undergraduate studying architecture at Yale University. Maya Lin was not only very young, she was also Chinese American, and she designed a memorial that was explicitly ambivalent about the war itself.

The Vietnam Veterans Memorial is composed of two massive granite slabs in the shape of a wide V that cuts into the earth of the National Mall between the Jefferson Memorial and the Washington Monument. In our most sacred national symbolic space, Lin and Scruggs created a memorial that was unlike the neoclassical designs all around it. Lin's memorial is inscribed with the name of every man (and the eight women) who were killed in the Vietnam War or who were MIA or POWs who never returned: a total of 58,320 names. The names are listed on the memorial in the order in which they died rather than in alphabetical order. This builds a narrative in which the names on the memorial together are the names of people who died together. It is not a sea of Smiths or Hernandezes. It begins with the first death, of Michael Brutus in 1959, and ends with the death of Richard Vandegeer in 1975. The names are carved into reflective black granite so that as you stand looking at the memorial, you see the names and your own reflection; and depending on where you are standing, you might see either the Lincoln Memorial or the Washington Monument reflected as well.

This design was immediately highly controversial. It was called "the black gash of shame." It was seen as an outrage because it was not neoclassical, not figurative, not heroic, not manly, and not a celebration of either the war or the work done by the soldiers who fought in it. It may seem strange to us now, but in 1980 both the Vietnam War and the idea of a war memorial were seriously repugnant to many Americans; such an explicit statement of patriotism, however complicated it was, was simply off the collective radar. But suddenly, debates across the United States about how this new form was remembering a deeply divisive war sparked real interest in memorials and the work they do. When the memorial was dedicated in 1982, many of the early detractors changed their minds; and for the last forty years, crowds of people—more than three million every year—have shown up at "the Wall," as people have come to affectionately call the memorial, to quietly grieve, to pay their respects, and to be part of an American collective experience. The memorial has been undeniably popular, and it has had a remarkable impact.

Racial thinking at the Vietnam Veterans Memorial isn't immediately obvious. The memorial is mostly names carved in granite. It isn't until you look at a late addition to the design that you begin to see how racial thinking is actually very much alive at the site. Reagan officials who were unhappy with the mournful quality of Lin's design insisted that a heroic and masculine figural element be added. This resulted in the addition of the *Three Soldiers* to the memorial site; a straightforward piece of figural sculpture of three soldiers standing together. They are slightly larger than life size. They are not on a plinth—they stand on the ground together—but a quick reading of who they are and the dynamic between them reveals something important about how the Reagan-era officials imagined the US military and what they wanted to communicate about that imagery. It's not particularly complicated. The central figure is clearly white, and he is a half-step ahead of the other figures. He is holding up his arms as if to protect them. One of the figures at his side is African American, and the other Latino. So the shorthand you get when looking at the memorial is that the white figure is the lead, and he is protecting the other, somehow slightly lesser, soldiers. Again, this may seem like a lot to read into the three figures, but any ambiguity about the importance of this racial dynamic was clarified in pretty dramatic terms as conversations developed around other memorials that were built as correctives to the Vietnam Memorial.

Race, and the race of the soldiers, and the relationship between white soldiers and soldiers who are not white, became important and were fought over with serious intensity as the memorial landscape of the National Mall was reshaped in response to the Vietnam Memorial. In other words, the Reagan Department of the Interior celebrated figures who were not just heroic, were not just masculine, but also portrayed a narrative about race; the officials were never explicit about it, but once you identify it in the *Three Soldiers*, it is impossible to unsee. (It is also a dynamic in sculpture that we are going to encounter again in this book: the flanking of a white figure by non-white figures who serve, in the end, to emphasize his whiteness.)

Other war memorials on the National Mall built in direct response to the Vietnam Veterans Memorial are the first and most obvious evidence of the impact of this memorial. Between the dedication of the Wall in 1982 and the dedication of the national World War II Memorial in 2004, thinking about war memorials changed dramatically. In 1982, there were no national war memorials on the National Mall, and there had been *none* since its inception. The Korean War Veterans Memorial, dedicated in 1995, was the first memorial response to the Wall, and it could hardly be more explicitly a corrective. This is clear in nearly everything that the advocates for the Korean War memorial said during the process of designing and building it and is reflected in the completed memorial, which mimics the Wall on a smaller scale and without the names, and adds nineteen larger-than-life poncho-clad, helmet-wearing soldiers marching across the Mall toward a giant American flag. The World War II Memorial, dedicated in 2004, is if nothing else a triumph of a return to the neoclassical celebratory memorial architecture of an earlier era. It is an unambiguous celebration of a war that ended with more than sixty million dead. In both cases, as well as in the cases of many other memorials that were advocated for in this period, the builders were startlingly direct about the fact that they were building memorials in response to the Vietnam Veterans Memorial. Most frequently, what they meant—and what they were quite clear about—was that the ambivalence about dying in an American war expressed in the Vietnam Veterans Memorial was simply untenable as a lesson for the millions of middle schoolers and tourists who come to the National Mall to learn about their country and what it means to be part of it.

The Vietnam War ended with an end to conscription in the United States. There had been an active draft, on and off, in the United States from 1917 through 1974, but when the draft proved too unpopular to continue, military and political elites in Washington were anxious about recruiting an all-volunteer force. A big, immensely popular memorial that told kids tumbling out of school buses that dying in an American war was tragic rather than heroic directly mitigated against the needs of the contemporary military and was a problem that required fixing with the building of new, explicitly celebratory memorials that were much less interested in the past and the circumstances of the wars they remembered than in the future of bodies available for the United States military. So, the building of the Vietnam Veterans Memorial led to the building of new memorials in D.C. It also led to the building of more than one hundred local memorials for Vietnam veterans. Some of these are versions of the Wall, and many are variations on the theme of black granite and lists of names. And while all of this may seem to be wandering somewhat far afield from the story of cultural infrastructure that maintains structures of inequity, that is not—sadly—the case. In fact, the story of these memorials is focused on race to a surprising extent.

The Korean War Veterans Memorial could not have been more explicitly a response to the Vietnam Veterans Memorial. Those who advocated for it, and those who approved the design through a very complicated and involved process, were absolutely emphatic that they were building a corrective to the mournful, ambiguous, anti-heroic qualities of the Wall.[16] In part because it doesn't seem to have occurred to most advocates for memorials, despite the service of 350,000 African Americans in the First World War, that a doughboy on a plinth in a city might be figured as anything but white, and because the Second World War was so consistently remembered with living memorials, the problem of how to represent, in figural statues, a military that was increasingly diverse had not been raised or addressed across the history of the United States. There are, of course, a few memorials specifically for Black soldiers who served in the Civil War, but between the mass-produced doughboy and the living memorials, a real and important quandary went unaddressed for more than a hundred years. The builders of the Korean War Veterans Memorial wanted a heroic, inspiring memorial that honored and celebrated the service of individual soldiers. Its initial design included thirty-nine nine-foot-tall soldiers, and all of them were white—this despite the fact that the Korean War was the first war waged by a desegregated military in the United States. When the problem of using thirty-nine white figures to represent a desegregated, multi-racial military force was raised, it created significant problems for the memorial's advocates and designers. The extent of the problem was expressed by the sculptor, Frank Gaylord, who claimed that if he hadn't put helmets on the figures to cover their hair and therefore enable the blurring of their racial identities, the memorial would never have been built. The *representational* problem of the tradition of "the white soldier who gets remembered," despite the diversity of those who actually served in all wars waged by the United States, was raised for the first time in the 1980s when interest in memorials was renewed.

Two other memorials that were advocated for in this period offer some insight into this representational problem. The Black Revolutionary Patriots Memorial was an attempt to make a vivid and lasting argument on the National Mall about the important contributions that African Americans made to the founding of the United States through their service in the Revolutionary War. This memorial concept got congressional approval and a plum site on the National Mall, adjacent to the newly built Memorial to the 56 Signers of the Declaration of Independence, but decades after these initial successes it remains unbuilt principally because of the intensity of the arguments about how to put Black armed men in this sacred symbolic national space. For the memorial's advocates, displaying figures of Black armed soldiers who helped forge the nation was the whole point of building the memorial. Those who were pushing back against these figures, despite the delicate dances with language this required of them, simply seemed unable to find a way to imagine Black armed soldiers that they considered appropriate for the Mall. The compromise they offered was a group of Lilliputian figures, little armed soldiers who could be no more than knee high. This was frankly ridiculous and made the memorial very hard to sell to potential donors. It eventually killed the memorial. Some similar racial dynamics were at play in the story of the building of the Japanese American Memorial to Patriotism During World War II. In the case of that memorial, which was eventually built adjacent to the Capitol at the very far reaches of the eastern end of the National Mall, it was determined after intense debate that a memorial to the patriotism of Japanese Americans inside internment camps was acceptable, while a memorial that figured Japanese American soldiers, no matter how highly decorated they may have been, was unacceptable.

Perhaps what's most interesting about these examples, and about the struggle to figure out how to represent and commemorate a multi-ethnic American military, is the way in which the unspoken was set against the obvious. In other words, these examples have value because the Mall is an important place but also because they reveal implicit expectations in the work that commemoration does. It is fascinating that in the 1980s and 1990s, American officials charged with making these kinds of decisions were deeply uncomfortable with creating a public representation of the US military that wasn't all white. It speaks to the great success of previous generations' memorial efforts to use commemoration to make an implicit, powerful, insistent, emphatic argument about the nation as white, first and foremost. If the officials in Washington who took up these questions had been easily able to pivot, if it had not been controversial to represent the Korean War–era military as Black and white and Asian

American and Latino, that might have revealed limitations in the influence of earlier commemorative speech. But the struggles of the 1980s and 1990s do something quite distinct: they reveal the ongoing influence of memorials and commemorative culture as tools for making an argument about white supremacy and a white nation. It wasn't just important for Washington officials in this period to make a memorial landscape, for all those middle schoolers, that told them that dying in an American war was a good thing. It was also important for them to define heroism and service in white terms. (If this seems overwrought, think thirty-nine white figures to represent a desegregated military.)

The new memorial fever spread beyond Washington in a couple of different ways. Most of the new, non-military memorials were civil rights memorials but there were others. (The Ronald Reagan Legacy Projects is another good example of a successful memorial project set off in this second memorial boom.)

The civil rights memorials built across the United States in this period were explicitly inspired by the unexpected success of the Vietnam Veterans Memorial. As historian Dell Upton tells us, "The late-twentieth-century surge in monument building was also the product of an accident of history: the great, unexpected popular and critical success of Maya Lin's Vietnam Veterans Memorial. All subsequent monuments—especially, but not only, war memorials—stand in its shadow."[17] The Wall made memorials matter again. Upton continues, "Social changes ranging from the renewed vigor of religious fundamentalism to the reordering of gender and racial norms generated 'culture wars' over 'values'" that created a degree of social instability, and "Americans of all political persuasions were troubled by these changes and attempted to fix the national narrative in a manner congenial to their own views. Monuments became an important, if expensive, medium for doing so."[18] *Forty* important civil rights memorials were built between 1989 and 2010. Forty. (Those are not UDC numbers, but they are significant.)

The Civil Rights Memorial in Montgomery, Alabama, was designed, not coincidentally, by Maya Lin, and dedicated in 1989. Built by the Southern Poverty Law Center, the memorial was the first in a wave of memorials created to recognize the bravery and sacrifice of activists in the movement and to speak back to both white supremacy and the memorial conventions that have helped to maintain it.

As the memorial's website tells us, "Like the Vietnam Veterans Memorial, the Civil Rights Memorial invites visitors to touch the engraved names. As Lin envisioned, the Memorial plaza is 'a contemplative area—a place to remember the Civil Rights Movement, to honor those killed during the struggle, to appreciate how far the country has come in its quest for equality, and to consider how far it has to go.'"[19] The memorial consists of a curving black granite wall inscribed with these words, from Dr. Martin Luther King Jr.'s "I Have a Dream" speech: "Until Justice Rolls Down Like Mighty Waters and Righteousness Like a Mighty Stream." In front of the wall stands a black granite tabletop over which water flows and onto which are inscribed the names of forty-one Americans who were killed during the civil rights movement. Lin draws on both the design aesthetic and the symbolic vocabulary she used in the Vietnam Veterans Memorial. She makes the names of the dead the tangible, tactile center of the memorial and, in doing so, figures those killed in the civil rights movement as patriots like soldiers killed in an American war. Other civil rights memorials built in this period include the Lorraine Motel, the site of King's murder, which was turned into a memorial and National Civil Rights Museum in 1991; the Medgar Evers Memorial in Jackson, Mississippi, in 1992; the Albany Civil Rights Movement Memorial in 1992; the renovation and rededication of Kelly Ingram Park in Birmingham, Alabama—a living memorial to World War I sailor Ingram—as "A Place of Revolution & Reconciliation" to coincide with the opening of the Birmingham Civil Rights Institute in 1992; the Soda Fountain sculpture in Wichita, Kansas, in 1998; the Freedom Summer Memorial at Miami University, Oxford, Ohio, in 2000; Bridge to Freedom Memorial Park on Broad Street in Selma, Alabama, in 2001; and many more. (This last park, at the foot of the Edmund Pettus Bridge, is about a mile from the home of the Jefferson Davis memorial chair we started with.)

These memorials are a mix of forms. Many include black granite and lists of names of people killed in the movement. Some are more traditional figures of individual heroes. And some are revisions of living memorials of an earlier era or new kinds of living memorials—trails and parks with a wide range of commemorative sculpture. Many are also associated with new museums. (There was a museum building boom in this period, too, which we will turn to in the next chapters.) They all deserve close readings and careful analysis, but for our purposes here, it is important to understand that the builders of these monuments were seeking not only to reclaim public memorial space, space they often shared with Confederate memorials—think Arthur Ashe staring down Robert E. Lee on Monument Avenue in Richmond, Virginia—but also to undo the work that those Confederate memorials had been doing for so long. The fact that they continue to go up as the Confederate memorials are coming down is telling about the status of white supremacy in the United States. It is still very much a force to be reckoned with, and increasingly, communities are fighting back with the same tools that have helped to make it so successful.

Maybe the most vivid example of how high-stakes these memorials were—and continue to be—is the Emmitt Till memorial plaque that went up in 2008 at Graball Landing, near Glendora, Mississippi, where Till's body was found. The sign states that the site may have been the place where Till's brutalized body was pulled from the Tallahatchie River. It has been so frequently stolen or riddled with bullet holes that it was replaced in 2019 with a sign made of bulletproof materials.[20]

Participatory memorial practices are the third significant legacy of the Vietnam Veterans Memorial. Even before the memorial was completed, people had, in a way that was absolutely unexpected and uninvited, carried their personal, sometimes sacred, objects to the memorial and left them at its base. To most people in the United States, the practice of bringing things—teddy bears, flags, candles, combat boots, cans of beer—to a memorial or a site of a tragedy is familiar and ubiquitous as a collective practice of mourning. It is important to know that before the Vietnam Veterans Memorial, this practice was neither common nor ubiquitous. It simply didn't exist. People simply did not bring things to public memorials or sites of accidents or tragedy. The practice emerged at the Vietnam Veterans Memorial, and in the forty years since the dedication of the memorial, it has been contagious and a constant presence in the culture. More than a hundred thousand objects have been left at the base of the Vietnam Veterans Memorial. Most people in the United States also know that people carried objects to Ground Zero in New York City, the site of the Columbine shooting in Colorado, and the sites of pretty much every shared collective tragedy we have experienced in the United States since 1982. (The things brought to the site of the murder of George Floyd are a spectacular example of this practice.) Why did this practice emerge, seemingly out of nowhere, at the Vietnam Veterans Memorial?

The short answer to this complicated question is that it emerged in response to the new, increasingly multi-ethnic makeup of the US military, especially during the Vietnam War era. Working-class Mexican American Catholics, Irish American Catholics, Italian American Catholics, Puerto Ricans, African Americans, and American Indians all have traditions of grave decorations that involve leaving objects on graves. These populations were over-represented in the force that fought the Vietnam War and are over-represented, in relation to their numbers in the population, on the Vietnam Veterans Memorial. Their people brought these traditions to Washington D.C., where they became a shared national practice.

This is important to understand because the next big thing in memorials—their toppling—involves a lot of individual activism and community involvement. There is something about the leaving of things that opened up participation in commemorative culture, and the life of a memorial—what it says, what it does, and for whom—has been changed by these participatory practices. This is not to say that there is a direct line between bringing a can of Budweiser for your buddy you had promised a beer and leaving it at the Vietnam Veterans Memorial and throwing your own blood on the figure of a Confederate soldier who stands beloved and celebrated 150 years after the Civil War despite his willingness to die in defense of the enslavement of other humans. This is not a direct-line argument. But the extent and scale at which Americans in all kinds of contexts have stepped up and participated in memorial culture has opened a door, and part of what we are seeing in the toppling of monuments and a push to build new kinds of monuments is a legacy of this participatory tradition that emerged at the Vietnam Veterans Memorial.

So, the basic principles of memorials also seem to reflect, in some new ways, the memorials built between 1980 and 2010. First, *they are powerful*: the building of significant new memorials in our most sacred space, the National Mall, and across the South, again, is evidence that memorials matter again. People across the political spectrum are seeking to reimagine the American landscape and use memorials to articulate and rearticulate in clear terms to whom it belongs. Second, *they are doing their best work when they seem to fit seamlessly into the landscape; when they stop being noticeable, their job is done*: the story in this period is about a battle to reinscribe that landscape so that new logics will fit seamlessly into it. Third, *they are more about the time they are made than the time they memorialize*: the builders of the Vietnam Veterans Memorial and the Korean War Veterans Memorial were quite explicit that they were less interested in what had happened in the past than in the terms in which they wanted to remember it for the future, and the civil rights memorials reflect a new phase of the movement. The people they commemorate were fighting legal battles about access in more specific terms, while the folks rethinking memorials now are waging a broader, looser cultural battle about the endurance of white supremacy even in the context of transformed legal structures. Fourth, *they are made by people who feel strongly that they have something very important to say*: there are no wallflowers to be found anywhere in this part of the story. Fifth, *they are not neutral. Ever*: the Vietnam Veterans Memorial didn't make an explicit statement about the war because it didn't need to—Lin's rejection of the neoclassical was broadly understood to make a bold anti-war statement. Sixth, *they don't innocently remember a discrete event; they invent a particular past that they worry will not be recognized without a memorial*: think thirty-nine white men to remember forces who fought the Korean War or Ashe and Lee in Virginia. Seventh, *they are often inspired by anxiety, not the confidence the bronze and limestone might seem to project; they come from an unsettled moment*: anxiety about the military, anxiety about how we define who we are in the United States, and anxiety about the legacies of white supremacy seem to ricochet through these memorials like dangerous free radicals. And, eighth, *these memorials use a few basic and familiar conventions to make their points*: this period sees a blend of new conventions and old; the figure of the soldier or the civil rights hero is still very important, and the new convention of black granite inscribed with names is nearly ubiquitous.

These principles, as they played out between 1980 and 2010, make answering the key questions possible, but not necessarily easy.

1. When was it built? We know that if it was built between, roughly, 1980 and 2010, it was part of a second memorial boom that was responding to the challenges to definitions of inclusion and tenacious legacies of white supremacy.
2. By whom was it built? If it was built in this period, we know it was likely built by federal agencies in Washington or local municipalities and civil rights organizations rather than hereditary patriotic organizations.

3. What was unsettled about the time in which it was made? As Dell Upton put it, "In the years following the Vietnam War, waves of new immigrants entered the United States, encouraged by the abolition of country-of-origin restrictions in the 1965 immigration act. The collapse of the traditional industrial order, the outsourcing of manufacturing to Asia and Latin America, periodic energy crises, and economic deregulation leading to repeated episodes of financial chicanery destabilized the economy. The debacle in Vietnam and the intensification of militarism and xenophobic nationalism in reaction to it raised questions about the United States' role in the world."[21]

4. What point did the builders want to make, and what past did they invent to make it? In this period, two big ideas were expressed—in tension. In D.C., the point was that the US military was still something like the military called up by the Confederate memorials: it was white and heroic. *And* in cities across the South, especially, the point was that heroes of the civil rights movement deserve a place in public space every bit as much as the *Silent Sam*s. One impulse invents a heroic white past, and the other invents one in which civil rights activists are recognized as heroes.

5. How, in what forms, did they try to make their point? Figural statues and lists of names carved in black granite.

6. And, finally, what happened to these memorials in the summer of 2020? They were untouched. Although Black Lives Matters protesters were falsely accused, on Facebook, of defacing the Vietnam Veterans Memorial, memorials from this period withstood the summer of 2020.[22]

2010–PRESENT: TUMBLING DOWN AND RISING UP

Historians will likely look back on this period as the second most significant in the history of memorials and monuments in the United States. Starting most dramatically in 2015, after the murder of nine African Americans in a Bible study class at the Emanuel African Methodist Episcopal Church in South Carolina by a pro-Confederate white supremacist, a movement to remove Confederate memorials has been underway.

Between 2015 and 2019, fifty-eight Confederate memorials were removed. As historians Ethan Kytle and Blain Roberts put it, "Why, in the year 2015, should communal spaces in the South continue to be sullied by tributes to those who defended slavery? How can Americans ignore the pain that black citizens, especially, must feel when they walk by the Calhoun monument, or any similar statues, on their way to work, school, or Bible study?"[23]

The murder of George Floyd in 2020 dramatically turned up the intensity of the movement: 168 Confederate memorials came down in the summer of 2020.[24] According to the Southern Poverty Law Center, "2020 was a transformative year for the Confederate symbols movement. Over the course of seven months, more symbols of hate were removed from public property than in the preceding four years combined."[25] Yet, as the center's Lecia Brooks describes it, "These dehumanizing symbols of pain and oppression continue to serve as backdrops to important government buildings, halls of justice, public parks, and U.S. military properties, including 10 bases named after Confederate leaders across the South."[26]

Silent Sam splashed with human blood and groups of protesters collectively pulling down graffiti-covered Lee memorials may seem like a far cry from the modest gesture by Essie Mae Washington-Williams to get her name carved into her father's monument. But they are part of a long conversation that is important to understanding how this cultural infrastructure—these blunt instruments—in the United States has worked to maintain basic lies about race. They are also just one volley in a very long game. The legal battles to protect Confederate monuments have just begun. Alabama, Georgia, Mississippi, North Carolina, South Carolina, Tennessee, and Virginia have all enacted laws to prohibit their removal. None of this is over.

SECTION II

MUSEUMS

TWO MINUTES SPENT ON the sidewalk across Central Park West from the American Museum of Natural History, paying attention to the big gestures the exterior of the building makes, was, until very recently, just about as good a study in cultural infrastructure in the United States as you were likely to find anywhere. Without knowing any details about the place, you could discern a great deal. Even if you were not trying, a few major points were hard to avoid. (See Figure 7.)

First, the location is telling—this is seriously rarified real estate. Any large building here really matters. That is immediate and emphatic. Second, the architecture conveys a lot without requiring any analysis. (Think "Making Federal Buildings Beautiful Again.") An oversized, carefully articulated, neo-classical facade with a temple front and a grand staircase conveys not just that this place matters but that it is a place of authority. Whether it seems to be a place of benign authority or something else probably varies based on who is looking, but the big hit is "authority." This is underscored by the inscription across the facade: TRUTH, KNOWLEDGE, VISION. Moving from the building to the statue that stood, for more than eighty years, in front of the beautifully wrought metalwork on the massive front door, any observer gets a quick sense of the kind of authority being expressed. The figure of a man, Theodore Roosevelt, sat astride a noble beast and was flanked by two nearly naked men: a Black man and an Indian man. Roosevelt towered over them and conveyed something quite explicit about both what matters and what is "natural" in the natural

FIGURE 7 Teddy Roosevelt statue at the American Museum of Natural History

history to be revealed inside the building. The museum—before visitors even get in the door—threw all that authority behind a particular natural order in which the white man is at the apex of the "natural" hierarchy. It achieved what theorist Donna Haraway has described as the museum's purpose "of conservation, of preservation, of the production of permanence" in obvious terms.[1] It made clear just what the museum's TRUTH is all about. And at the same time, it demonstrated the claim made by scholar Sumaya Kassim: "Museums are not neutral in their preservation of history. In fact, arguably, they are sites of forgetfulness and fantasy."[2]

The problem with the figures of Roosevelt and the unnamed, barely dressed men seems straightforward, yet they have stood unaltered for more than eighty years. The removal of the figures was announced in the summer of 2020, after decades of complaints about the message the museum was conveying on the streets of a multiracial city. Museum president Ellen V. Futter wrote on the museum website, "The statue itself communicates a racial hierarchy that the Museum and members of the public have long found disturbing."[3] It was finally removed in January 2022.

Five million visitors, many of whom are kids on field trips or with their families, walked by that statue every year on their way into the museum (the eleventh most visited museum in the world).[4] Five million a year, year after year. That's a lot of children getting a very clear message; that is cultural infrastructure at work. And it begs the question: if it is so straightforward and so well understood, why did it take decades for the museum to make a change? Futter's answer is, essentially, the murder of George Floyd. This is worth pausing to reflect on for a minute. How could the facade of a natural history museum in Manhattan be connected to the death of an unarmed Black man in Minnesota? Futter explains, "Over the last few weeks, our museum community has been profoundly moved by the ever-widening movement for racial justice that has emerged after the killing of George Floyd. We have watched as the attention of the world and the country has increasingly turned to statues as powerful and hurtful symbols of systemic racism."[5] Interestingly, she is addressing the statue, not the content of her museum. She claims to have long been disturbed by what the exterior of her museum communicates, but this is a false distinction. If you go just a few steps into the museum, you encounter the William Andrew Mackay murals, which double down on the message about race conveyed by the statue—repeating the motif of Roosevelt flanked by "primitive" people of color—in beautiful, vivid color. This chapter will demonstrate that the figures outside reflect the "truths" that have been taught inside this museum and many, perhaps most museums in the United States. The movement for social justice in 2020 turned to memorials *and* museums because they continue to be sites not just for the expression of power but also for the active maintenance of structures of inequity.

As the facade of the American Museum of Natural History boldly states, museums use their institutional authority to define truth and knowledge and vision. This is consequential and linked to George Floyd because truth, knowledge, and vision have so often been defined and expressed in just the terms the Roosevelt statue so vividly embodied at the entrance to the museum.

The work of museums and historic sites, as cultural infrastructure, is accomplished in multiple ways. But there are four very basic elements of museums that have done this work pretty effectively—you don't need to dive into the details of particular exhibitions, although we will here, to understand how museums do big cultural work. The intentions of the people who founded and ran these institutions, the kinds of treasures they chose to collect, the exterior architecture, and the interior layout of the museums tell us pretty much everything we need to know about them as cultural infrastructure. It's not that the details of the exhibitions aren't important, because they are; it's simply that these are blunt instruments, and they have done their work in blunt ways. They were designed this way and often continue to operate this way, so we will look mostly at the big gestures. They were intended from the beginning to convey authority to the public. Their publics have always been broad; they have always been imagined for a general population that has included, importantly, non-English speakers and children—lots of children. So, while museums are not unsophisticated, they are also not subtle. As blunt gestures that intend to produce permanence and truth, they have been busy, and they are effective.

All of which is *not* to say that museums cannot be wonderful, magical places; they can be, and they are. Museums use the most fascinating products of the human imagination and the natural world to tell stories. They are temples to beauty and the mysteries of science, and they collect and protect treasurers of every possible kind. They can be fabulous, rich, soul-feeding places. It is just that we need to understand the nourishment they provide and the reverence they inspire *in the context of how* they have used their power.

In other words, again, thinking about museums as blunt instruments of social power requires holding two contradictory thoughts at the same time. It requires understanding that all infrastructure is cultural and that cultural infrastructures like museums are built with the explicit intent of shaping cultural life in particular ways that are not always explicit; *and* that in the United States, this basic fact about museums has been both marvelous and part of a larger project of maintaining dangerous, antiquated racial logics.

The point is not that museums can't escape their pasts or that some haven't; it is that museums can't leave behind the racial logics that have formed them without fully understanding and responding to their particular awful inheritance.

In other words, museums are not condemned by their histories—as we shall see—but they can't remake themselves without understanding these histories.

Museums are, in many ways, unlike memorials. They are institutions—complex, multifaceted institutions—rather than singular gestures. They are structured by the expectation of a certain amount of change: new exhibitions, new objects, new stories to tell. But it is important not to underestimate the extent to which they are similar to memorials.

Museums, like memorials, are big, blunt conveyors of cultural values. They emerged in Europe in the eighteenth century and became essential cultural institutions in Europe and the United States in the nineteenth century. They are almost always explicit sites for the expression of national power and ideas about the nation, in one form or another. But for all of this history and complexity, they still do fairly simple cultural work. They express authority while seeming benign and neutral, when they are neither benign nor neutral. And they repeat and repeat and repeat some very basic ideas about race and racial hierarchy in American culture. So while most good thinking about museums should be nuanced and attentive to small details of particular contexts and objects, there is also value in stressing the work they have done as blunt instruments.

Speaking at a recent symposium on race and museums, curator Terence Washington said that in order for museums to face their racial pasts, they "need to become unrecognizable to themselves."[6] This is a potent observation, and understanding it helps us understand how museums function as part of a system of racist cultural infrastructure and what the terms of the debate about museums are in 2021. Washington was making an Audre Lorde-style gesture—"the master's tools will never take down the master's house"—which is valuable here because it insists that we understand the relationship between museums and racial logics as structural, as built into the DNA of museums as institutions. So before we can get to making these institutions unrecognizable, we need to understand how this particular tool of "the master" has worked. Understanding the history of museums and how they work helps us to understand what it will take to change them.

MUSEUM BASICS

A few basic principles for understanding the cultural work that museums and historic sites have done, in big, broad terms, make understanding them as part of an effective web of racist cultural infrastructure relatively easy. First, *they are powerful.* Second, *they have been built and run by powerful people with big ideas to express.* Third, *architecture matters.* Fourth, *they are doing their best work when they seem to fit seamlessly into the landscape; when they stop being noticeable, their job is done.* Fifth, *they are not neutral. Ever.* And sixth, *museums have used a few basic and familiar conventions to make their points.*

Each of these principles deserves a little fleshing out.

So, first, they are powerful. This may not be immediately obvious, but it is crucial to understand. Dusty old collections of relics may not seem radiant with relevance, but museums are built to convey power—the power of the ideas of a particular group in a particular time and place—and power is always relevant. Museums claim shared public space with a largely unquestioned authority; they claim their ideas for all who share that public space—and for those who aspire to share it. The American Museum of Natural History, for instance, conveys serious authority about the order of things—about the very nature of the world—and for a long time offered a shorthand of what that looks like with Roosevelt and the nameless, shirtless men at his side for everyone on the streets of New York City as well as the five million visitors to the museum each year. And, this is, of course, just one example. Museums sit proudly in the center of civic space in virtually every big city in the United States. Schools everywhere make field trips to museums a priority. In 1786, Charles Willson Peale opened one of the first American museums in Philadelphia because it was the national capital. In 2022, the national capital is organized around the National Mall, a civic space lined with more than a dozen museums.

According to the head of the American Association of Museums, "If you add up the attendance for every major-league baseball, basketball, football and hockey game this year, the combined total will come to about 140 million people. That's a big number, but it's barely a fraction of the number of people who will visit American museums this year."[7] At the start of the twenty-first century, there were more than thirty-five thousand museums in the United States.[8] In 2019, more than 850 million people in the United States visited a museum, and museums contributed $50 billion to the US economy.[9] That is a lot of visitors and a lot of investment in the authority of these institutions.

Second, they have been built and run by powerful people with big ideas to express. Early on, American museums were sites for the expression of a unique American identity. As historian Karl Meyer has written, "Even before the American Revolution, the educated classes, made up of professional men, well-to-do merchants, and landowners, had begun to establish public galleries."[10] There was great excitement about these early museums and great investment in their potential as sites for telling the emerging American story. By 1876, there were already seventy-eight historical societies, most of which included a museum with collections of art, history, and natural history.[11] In the 1870s, there was a museum building boom in part because museums became sites for defining and teaching immigrant masses, who were often illiterate, what it meant to be American.[12] Industrialists joined forces and used museums as places to simultaneously display their wealth and make a nationalist argument. By the end of the nineteenth century, the founders of the large, significant museums were the robber barons: the industrialists who had made fortunes in steel and oil and railroads and banking and shipping and manufacturing. They founded museums on which their names were often inscribed, cementing (literally) their social power.

Third, architecture matters. It matters, of course, in the sense that beauty matters, but it also matters in the sense that architecture is an easily understood medium through which to express big ideas. Architecture is a tool that museums have long used to convey both their value to the culture and their authority. The language of the "Making Federal Buildings Beautiful Again" executive order, if we return to that, is evidence of an ongoing and serious investment in cultural infrastructure to do the work of maintaining a certain kind of social order very much like the work that the architecture of museums has long been doing.[13] It reads, "New Federal building designs should, like America's beloved landmark buildings, uplift and beautify public spaces, inspire the human spirit, ennoble the United States, command respect from the general public, and, as appropriate, respect the architectural heritage of a region."[14] Beauty, uplift, and the command of respect. That is a pretty good summary of the first century of museum architecture in the United States, or perhaps its entire history. And while museum architecture does become more complicated, does move beyond the neoclassical, it has yet to get anywhere near ceding authority.

Fourth, they are doing their best work when they seem to fit seamlessly into the landscape; when they stop being noticeable, their job is done. Or maybe it is more accurate to say that when they stop being noticeable, they are maintaining the power they express. In other words, they never stop working, but the less noticeable they are, the more effectively they have conveyed their message. If you walked by Roosevelt without recognizing the statue as conveying a specific, potent ideology, you were accepting that ideology as a natural part of the landscape. You were accepting, likely without thinking about it, a deeply fictionalized logic about the racial hierarchy as the natural order of things. (It is only when you reject the logic, push back against its appearance of being natural, that you question the extent to which the institution is benign and can begin to denaturalize those logics.)

Fifth, they are not neutral. Ever. Again, this may seem obvious, but it is an important point, and it extends well beyond the architecture of museums. Even the earliest European and American museums (cabinets of curiosities), which were largely the collections of wealthy collectors and seventeenth- and eighteenth-century explorers, had a particular point of view. They were made up of treasures looted and stolen and bought for nothing from people who were colonized and subjugated. They were full of amazing stuff, and the collectors were proud. And many of these things were fundamentally prizes extracted in often violent processes that made a claim for the prowess, potency, and superiority of the people who looted and stole and bought them for nothing. The possession of these objects, the curiosities in the cabinets, was presented as neutral, but the items had been procured by vast systems of power, which they could not help but implicitly express. They bore the authority of those who could travel the globe and bring home its treasures. This is simple, but it should not be overlooked. Having "their" treasures in "our" museums packs a powerful, if often not explicit, punch. It tells museum visitors something indelible about who we are.

Although often private and lacking the organization that would be the hallmark of later museums, these early collections shared an impulse to learn from, and express a kind of ownership over, treasures collected from colonization and exploration efforts. Amassing these treasures from far-flung places created a particular kind of knowledge with a particular point of view. As museums have evolved, they have come to emphasize the display of knowledge over the production of knowledge, but they began as places that toyed around with both. They were made by people who were, over a couple of centuries, "discovering" the world, delighting in the treasures they "found" along the way, and often making great fortunes in the process.

Perhaps an easy way to illustrate the problem of the seemingly neutral is with another oddity of American museums that is so familiar that it is hard to see just how odd it is. For 120 years, visitors, many of them school-children, have been visiting a grand neoclassical building in northwest Ohio to walk into a vast hall filled with precious artifacts from ancient Egypt. They are not there to see a film about the Egyptian treasures but to stand before the real things. It probably does not seem odd to them that the treasures—shards of pottery, whole sarcophagi, and other mas-terworks of antiquities from ancient Egypt—are in a mid-size town in Ohio. And they are unlikely to know that the reason the treasures ended up in Ohio is that Lake Erie sand has an unusually high silica content, which is good for making glass, and a Massachusetts industrialist moved his glass-making operation there in the 1880s and subsequently made a fortune, some of which he put toward buying precious artifacts from Egypt. William Libbey was by no means alone; he was among a throng in the late nineteenth century "who undertook widespread trenching of Egyptian sites primarily to enrich Western museum collections."[15] (A flood that Egyptian authorities worked unsuccessfully to stop until 1983. This is stunning in itself. Can you imagine Egyptians digging in Ohio, and Ohioans being unable to stop them?)

The unearthing of objects at these sites led to "the export and frag-mentation of assemblages across hundreds of the world's museums."[16] These treasurers were dug up and then spread out across museums in Europe and the United States, enabling them to own their piece of the ancient world as evidence of their influence or standing in a world order. The fact that this *does not* strike visitors as odd or nonsensical is evidence of both the success museums have had in naturalizing relations of power and the near invisibility of the process. Even kids who are barely paying attention leave the museum with a sense of the racialized power of their culture: "Of course their stuff should be in our museum." As critic Niel Harris has written, "Museums, then, were treated not as places where knowledge was disputed or contested, but as sanctuaries where it was se-cure."[17] This has enabled a lot to be both emphatically conveyed and un-said. Of course their stuff should be in our museum.

If museums were neutral, no one would ever bother to build one. Their magic is that they *seem* to be neutral—they seem to be benign expressions of shared foundational truths. But this is simply not true. One of the most interesting things about museums is the collective investment many have in the idea of their neutrality. Most art museums, for instance, have organized their galleries in a progressive narrative that moves in one way or another from antiquity to the achievements of modern art in the West, with side galleries that set the art of "Asia" or "Africa" not only outside of this narrative but also outside of culminating achievements of modern art. The fact that most museum-goers will understand, without thinking about it, that "modern" is a designation reserved for European and American work is telling, especially for institutions that have been so wedded to narratives of progress.

An arresting example of how the expectation of neutrality gives museums special power is an experimental exhibition created by artists Coco Fusco and Guillermo Gómez-Peña in 1992, in which they pretended to be—in museums across the United States—a pair of "undiscovered Amerindians"—who had been living untouched by the modern world.[18] Despite the pains the artists took to challenge this nonsensical idea in the exhibit itself, like wearing Nikes and working on laptops, they were amazed to find that most museum visitors believed the fake premise and took the suggestion that they were real live primitive people in a cage in a museum at face value. Some even complained to the museums about the living conditions of these "Indians." Fusco and Gómez-Peña were interested in playing around with what American museum visitors expect to see—but even they were surprised by the depth of the audience's acceptance of this crazy narrative as neutral because it was coming from a museum. (And because they are not surprised to find narratives about racial hierarchy in museums, particularly narratives about dark savages and white civilizers. Think Roosevelt at the American Museum of Natural History.)[19] As historian Carol Duncan writes, "We can also appreciate the ideological force of a cultural experience that claims for its truths the status of objective knowledge. To control a museum means precisely to control the representation of a community and its highest values and truths. It is also the power to define the relative standing of individuals within that community."[20]

Alongside the racial logics that seem so easy to identify in museums, there is other cultural work at play. Museums have been profoundly shaped by and have profoundly shaped ideas about nations. The two elements of cultural infrastructure have developed together. The modern museum was invented to do "national" cultural work and continues to be expected to do it. The Louvre Museum in Paris is the prime example of this. The short version of the story is that French revolutionaries wanted to make long-held royal art collections and the sites of their display *public* in 1793 as a demonstration of their commitment to liberty and equality. While it took some time for this gesture to reach most Parisians, the impulse was important and has shaped most museums since. Making the treasures of the elite accessible to the general population was a way to define the nation as democratic and egalitarian. Whether the treasure, art, or collected specimens of the world were once owned by the French monarchy or by a glass-making titan of industry in northwest Ohio, the impulse was the same. As Carol Duncan describes it, "The transformation of the old Royal Palace into the museum of the French Republic was high on the agenda of the French Revolutionary government. Already, public art museums were regarded as evidence of the political virtue, indicative of a government that provided the right thing for its people."[21] She goes on: "The West, then, has long known that public art museums are important, even necessary, fixtures of a well-furnished state."[22] Which is to say that museums have, from their inception, been intended to actively do cultural work.

And, finally, sixth, museums have used a few basic and familiar conventions to make their points. The most basic of these conventions involve things like height and scale and the scope of the collections. This could hardly be simpler, but a big museum makes a big statement. Beyond architecture, a few other very simple conventions make a real impact. First, the objects that are included tell a significant story in simple terms. Second, the organization of those objects conveys a great deal without ever needing to be explicit. A university art museum that opens with displays of treasured antiquities, moves to early Christian art through Renaissance paintings, and then continues to modern and contemporary European and American art never has to be explicit about whose stories matter and whose art matters to make a particular argument about it. In a sense, the simplicity of the process is linked to its invisibility. Finally, the ownership of "their" art in "our" museums is an insistent shorthand for how power works in the world. It is an important convention, and it is also almost invisible despite its potency.

All of these conventions are put to use in a short, pivotal scene in the movie *Black Panther*. The scene is preceded by an establishing shot of the exterior of the Museum of Great Britain, a fictionalized version of the British Museum. It opens with a Black man standing, flanked by watchful museum guards, in a clean, well-lit, oversized exhibit hall filled with objects from Africa in gleaming cases. The white museum director approaches him and informs him of the history of the objects; when he corrects her about a particular artifact, she responds, "I beg your pardon?" When he tells her that he is going to take the artifact, she tells him it isn't for sale, and he responds, "How do you think your ancestors got these? Do you think they paid a fair price? Or, did they take it like they took everything else?" He also comments about "all this security watching me ever since I walked in." The stealing, or taking back, of the treasured artifact sets the thief on a path to the discovery of a powerful Black world beyond the reach of colonialism and its brutal histories. In other words, a comic-based movie is able, in one minute and thirty seconds, to put the conventions of museums to work to start its plot churning—the conventions' relationship to race and power are so commonly understood that, with very little work, they stand in for a larger commentary on race for the audience of a Marvel movie.

Taken together, these principles make the work of understanding museums and historic sites relatively straightforward. They set up a clear set of questions to ask of any museum: (1) When was it built? (2) By whom was it built? (3) What does it look like? (4) How is it organized? (5) How has its point of view been sustained, and how has it been challenged?

Because the first question, "When was the museum built?" is so fundamental, a timeline that tracks the building of museums in the United States is a crucial tool. And while this timeline does not try to be absolute or definitive, it is possible to characterize the impulses that drove the building of museums and historic sites in a given period, and these characterizations can be a useful shorthand for understanding the work that a given museum was intended to do.

The two chapters in this section take up key periods in the life of American museums, as follows. They don't try to tell an encyclopedic history; rather, they offer a quick hit on a series of valuable examples. Chapter Three takes up the pre-1870 period and the period 1870–1940. The pre-1870 period is, of course, nearly the first whole century of American life, during which there was great enthusiasm for American museums and historic sites, many of which were founded by local historical and ladies' societies. 1870–1940 saw the first museum building boom in which most significant American museums were built. Chapter Four discusses the period 1965–2020 and the summer of 2020. 1965–2020 is a second robust period of museum building—a new golden age that saw new kinds of museums with new missions, a surge in the building of civil rights museums, and a tug of war at the Smithsonian over whose stories could be told. And in summer of 2020, the murder of George Floyd inspired what could become a significant reckoning for these institutions.

3

WHITE TEMPLES EMERGED

The pre-1870 period is marked mostly by three developments. The first is the formation of local historical and scientific societies, which often included a collection and some kind of gallery for its display. The second is the collecting and ordering of a mixed bag of curiosities—relics, art, and flora and fauna owned by individual wealthy enthusiasts who often made their "cabinets of curiosities" public in a limited way. The third is the emergence of ladies' associations dedicated to physical and ideological preservation. (Think UDC and DAR.)

A quick look at these developments and a brief walk through the early history of museums make clear that while some of the big claims this chapter makes about museums—that they are part of a system of racist cultural infrastructure, for example—may seem incendiary or very much of the moment of racial reckoning in 2022, evidence for these claims about race and power is quite simply everywhere in the DNA of American museums. They have always been profoundly shaped by thinking about race. Knowledge, social power, and a narrative about progress from savagery to civilization were embedded in all aspects of museums in this period.

Museum founder Charles Willson Peale painted a self-portrait titled *The Artist in His Museum* in 1822, and it provides an easy shorthand for this early period. In the painting, as he lifts a heavy curtain, his open palm makes a gesture of invitation to see what he has to reveal: an orderly collection of treasures. Although they are not all visible in the painting, the museum "contained displays of quadrupeds, birds, amphibians and insects, minerals and fossils, as well as wax figures of racial types, and examples of cultural artifacts from a variety of areas."[1] As museum scholar Ellen Saco describes it, "Peale was concerned with the grounding of social order, and his displays made explicit the relation between taxonomic natural science and political order through a static, synchronous presentation of knowledge."[2] This included the display of a *living enslaved* person and an emphasis on the flawed science of racial types. For Peale, the museum was not just a place to display the treasures he had collected but also a place to make an emphatic argument about the "natural" order of the social world. Making this argument was the reason to show the treasures—and the order was, in part, a racial order.

And Peale was not alone. In the last two hundred years, "Collecting objects and material of cultural, historical, and religious significance, preserving them, researching them, and presenting them to the public for education and enjoyment has been the traditional role of museums."[3] They are institutions that are designed to provide "people with a sense of place, purpose, and a place to celebrate achievements."[4] It is important to understand that these celebrations honor not only the objects themselves but also the fact of the ownership of the objects—and this has been a celebration of power relations.

The fact of the ownership of the objects is as salient as anything else about the museum. Critics thinking about this argue that "Colonial rule is not accomplished by sheer force alone. In order to justify continued oppression of subordinate groups, the dominant group needs to dominate physically and mentally. That is, they need to convince all groups that a racial hierarchy exists and that at the top of that hierarchy sits a group that is superior because they excel in intellectual thought, architecture, the sciences, art, and culture. The claim is that the road toward a greater civilization is rooted in Whiteness."[5] In other words, keeping "their" treasures in "our" institutions can't help but be an expression of power. This expression of power is not military or explicitly political but soft, cultural power. For institutions founded in periods in which slavery was the coin of the realm, in which structures of inequity were the explicit political and economic foundations of the culture, this kind of expression of power—white supremacy, which sounds like a radical claim now—would have been key to the "natural" order they were displaying. (A working enslaved person on display makes sense in this context.)

The very first European museums date back to the eighteenth century, when they were, for the most part, originally "cabinets of curiosities" like Peale's museum. They held wonders collected from newly explored colonial sites and carried home to Europe and Great Britain by individual men of wealth and sometimes of science. These original cabinets of curiosities were privately held collections of botanical, ethnographic, and sometimes artistic objects of merit, and, crucially, they evolved at the same moment when nations formed as social organizations.

Across the century, as nations emerged, these private cabinets of curiosities took on a civic aspect, and the modern museum was born. The collections were always a kind of expression of power, and when they became national or civic institutions, they became new kinds of expressions of power.

As cultural theorist Stuart Hall describes it,

> From its earliest history in western societies—in the heterogeneous assemblages of the 'cabinets of curiosity and wonder'—collections have adorned the position of people of power and influence—kings, princes, popes, landowners and merchants—whose wealth and status they amplified. They have always been related to the exercise of 'power' in another sense—the symbolic power to order knowledge, to rank, classify and arrange, and thus to give meaning to objects and things through the imposition of interpretative schémas, scholarship and the authority of connoisseurship.

In other words, it would be a mistake to underestimate the cultural work that ordering curiosities has done and is doing.[6] All of which is to say that in the history of museums, it is not possible to disaggregate collecting, owning, ordering, and racial thinking on a national scale. (Think *Black Panther*.)

The British Museum is perhaps the first and the best example of the modern museum. (Again, think *Black Panther*.) Founded in 1750, it is a fusion of the consolidation of wealth, the emergence of nationalism, colonial expansion, ideas about democracy, and the Enlightenment. The British Museum started with the collection of one man, Sir Hans Sloane. It is worth spending a little time on Sloane as an archetypal museum founder. Born into humble circumstances in Ireland in 1660, Sloane was a brilliant scientist, naturalist, and respected physician. He traveled as a young man to the Caribbean, where he met and married a widow with a title and significant investments in plantations in Jamaica. He collected all kinds of objects and studied the local flora and fauna. (He also famously invented hot chocolate while in Jamaica.) He returned to Britain and continued to invest—in companies that amassed fortunes based on enslavement—and to collect objects from around the world. His fortune and his collections grew apace. He eventually donated his collection, and his framework for understanding it, to create the British Museum. This modern museum was distinct from a cabinet of curiosities in important ways.

First, modern museums look important. They are almost always big, significant pieces of neoclassical architecture: a white temple with a grand staircase leading into vast high-ceilinged halls where objects of import are displayed. But, second, they are also all about organization, in contrast to the cabinets of curiosities, which were often seriously disorganized. The modern museum's organization reflected the development of scientific disciplines and Enlightenment ideas about order and progress. Early modern museums were heavily invested in differentiation and categorization. And it is important to note that this differentiation and categorization was not due to neutral science or following an inevitable, natural logic. (Think Peale.) These modes of organization in early museums almost always told narratives of progress, and these narratives were almost always about development from "savagery" to "civilization" in one form or another. As historian Steven Conn describes it, "Almost without exception...a trip through the galleries followed a trajectory from simple to complex, from savage to civilized, from ancient to modern."[7] The logic of the museum—creating a narrative of European and, later, American, triumph—requires some cherry-picking of times and places. (If one had to rely only on museum displays to understand where different parts of the world fall in terms of modernization, one would think that the Middle

East is ancient and remains so, and that Asia, too, is locked in the past, but that the story of art in Europe is one of both artistic and intellectual development.)

An emphasis on differentiation enabled this kind of unspoken logic to articulate big ideas without making them explicit. It also led to specializations of types of museums: art museums and natural history museums and ethnographic museums (although it is worth noting that natural history museums and the ethnographic museums were often organized together under one roof, blurring the lines between non-white humans and the natural world). So, in the end, the amassing of fortunes based on exploration of all forms is very deep in the history of museums. Wealth built by pillaging was organized and displayed to enable an argument about the superiority of the pillager over the pillaged. This may seem too blunt or like a crass overgeneralization, but, in fact, it is a fundamental fact of modern museums.

Certainly this is the history of museums in the United States and Europe, and it carries a logic with a long shadow. This logic continues to impact museums and how they work in the culture. It is this logic that gives them their power as blunt instruments of a racist cultural infrastructure. This is not to say that the founders of the Charleston Museum, for instance, had a plan in mind that specifically involved maintaining structures of inequity, but that is how it has worked. Understanding the history of museums and how they function helps us understand the work they're continuing to do today and what it will take to change them.

The Charleston Museum is the first American museum. Founded in 1773, it predated the Louvre as a public institution by twenty years and was explicitly inspired by the British Museum. It was "established by the Charleston Library Society on the eve of the American Revolution and its early history was characterized by association with distinguished South Carolinians and scientific figures including Charles Cotesworth Pinckney, Thomas Heyward, Jr., Reverend John Bachman, and John J. Audubon."[8] But while it was intended to be a tool for education and to bring credit to the city, it was a pretty modest operation until well after the Civil War. Peale's Philadelphia Museum was opened in 1786, the East India Marine Hall (now the Peabody Essex Museum) was founded in 1799, and a bloom of local historical societies with collections appeared in this period.

Peale's Philadelphia Museum usefully marks the transition from the cabinets of curiosities to the more formal civic museum. His cabinet of curiosities began in the 1780s as a gallery for his paintings and miscellaneous collections but evolved over time to emphasize natural history. Its 1794 building had a grand, oversized facade with neoclassical references, big white pillars, and somewhat more orderly exhibits. It was part funky personal collection, part entertainment for the masses, and part national repository of natural history. Peale was a renaissance man and an entrepreneur. He pitched a series of versions of what an "American national museum" might look like and was most successful when he landed on the idea that "museums should perform a vital educational function for a democratic society."[9] Serious interest in this idea was evidenced by the fact that his first board of advisors for the museum included Alexander Hamilton, James Madison, and Thomas Jefferson.

Jefferson, himself a man of science, was taken with Peale, and he "presented the minerals collected by the Lewis and Clark expedition to Peale's museum in Philadelphia." As museum historian Stephen Conn sees it, "By doing so Jefferson drew a correlation between the nation's project of taming and ordering the wilderness and the way Peale's Museum functioned to do the same."[10] This might be a bit of an overstatement on Conn's part, but it is a useful overstatement. Peale's collections were idiosyncratic, but they were not random. They included "a mammoth's tooth from the Ohio, and a woman's shoe from Canton; nests of the kind used to make soup of, and a Chinese fan six feet long, bits of asbestos, belts of wampum, stuffed birds and feathers from the Friendly Islands, scalps, tomahawks, and long lines of portraits of great men of the Revolutionary War."[11] His "use of wax figures in displaying the races of man, the staging of American Indian remains, the divisions and placement of his portrait collection, even the location of (his former slave on display working in the museum)…bespoke a particular awareness of the boundaries of Americanness."[12]

The museum failed in the 1830s, in part because the Smithsonian was emerging as "the" national museum, but Peale did much to establish the template for the thousands of American museums that would follow—the messy magpie nests that were the early cabinets of curiosities came to have a firm and consistent reliance on a racialized natural order in which it made sense to put a working slave and dead Indian people on display.

The East India Marine Hall was founded in 1799—not to collect and catalogue American flora and fauna or art but to bring together the collections and shared knowledge of seamen "who had sailed beyond either the Cape of Good Hope or Cape Horn."[13] The collections of the East India Marine Hall were varied—from "civilized areas, the shipmaster often brought back knickknacks, trade objects, and profitless tourist 'curiosities'" and from the Pacific islands and other "uncivilized regions they brought home weapons, household utensils, and other objects of primitive manufacture that are today of fundamental importance to the ethnologist and anthropologist."[14]

As a loving 1949 history of the museum tells it, "At first glance the founding of a museum hardly seems a likely activity for shipmasters, but the wealth of Salem came from the sea, and we are all acquainted with the human foible of wishing to be admired for irrelevant reasons."[15] It goes on, "For a brief golden age, the Salem shipmasters were thrice-happy.... By following the sea and doing what by experience they were best fitted for, they gained not only the approbation of the polite and cultured landsmen, but the blessing of the Almighty Himself."[16] So, these nautical adventurers were celebrated by their community and by God for opening "the way to the riches of the orient," for collecting the spoils of their adventures, and for demonstrating their mastery with the displays of the spoils. As odd as it may seem, American museums started, in part, with a group of sailors who had a specific and freighted world view—gleaned by sailing to Africa and beyond—to share.

These early museums were both local and national endeavors. A key theorist of nationalism, Benedict Anderson, has written a good deal about the importance of museums in creating national culture.[17] As critic Daniel Trilling notes about Anderson's formation, "National museums—museums that are supposed to speak for or to a country—play a somewhat odd role in this arrangement."[18] He continues, "Their frame of reference might stretch back thousands of years, or across continents. Yet they are generally consigned to a single building, in a fixed location. This is often turned into a declaration of power—the national government places the national museum in the capital city of the nation."[19] In other words, museums became requirements for emerging nations—and they have been, since then, sites for defining and promoting ideas of and about the nation. And Americans have been enthusiastic participants in this cultural infrastructure.

The Mount Vernon Ladies' Association (MVLA), a relatively early American patriotic organization that emerged in this period, set another important template for a hybrid museum and historic house that would become a staple of the museum landscape in the United States. The MVLA was founded in 1853. As the story goes, Louisa Bird Cunningham was traveling on the Potomac River when she noticed the rundown state of George Washington's once glorious plantation. Her daughter, Ann Pamela Cunningham, took up the challenge—two decades before the founding of the United Daughters of the Revolution and the United Daughters of the Confederacy—and formed a national association. She called on her fellow ladies, writing, "Will you, can you, look on passively and behold the home and grave of the matchless patriot, who is so completely identified with your land, sold as a possession to speculators?" and she asked them to join her in protecting "the shrine of pure patriotism.[20]

"There is no doubt that this seemingly mild-mannered lady from South Carolina recognized," the MVLA website tells us, "the untapped power and determination of American women early on."[21] Certainly, "the MVLA established a model for a host of similar women's organizations at the end of the nineteenth century." In fact, "By 1910, there were one hundred American historic house museums, the vast majority privately owned. Many of these museums were staffed by women, and most celebrated a great patriot or great historical event in the United States."[22]

The mission of the MVLA was to raise funds to buy the plantation and restore it to its original glory. (The Washington family had fallen on hard times, surviving only on "wheat and potato production, woodcutting, selling enslaved people and outsourcing enslaved labor, collecting land rents, and (a) herring operation on the Potomac River."[23]) The ladies were "astonishingly successful" in preserving both the physical structure and the world view that the plantation embodied. A 1932 illustrated guide to the plantation published by the MVLA offers a quick sense of what this meant. Slaves and slavery are not present anywhere in the guide. (This was also true for presentations to visitors to the plantation.) The section of the book titled "Servants Quarters" describes "the quarters for a limited number of servants needed at the mansion."[24] It goes on, "Comfortable cabins that housed the rest of the Negroes were located at convenient distances about the plantation."[25] In other words, the ladies of Mount Vernon were dedicated to a kind of "historic preservation" that meticulously preserved the fictionalized in bold and blatant terms. The guide book lists all thirty-four varieties of trees on the map of the plantation in the book but does not include slave quarters—only a "Butler's House" and "Quarter Buildings."

This, of course, gives *preservation* a whole new meaning that is resonant for the historic sites and the museums in this early period. And, like the work of the ladies of the UDC and the DAR who would follow in their footsteps, the ideological preservation work of the ladies at Mount Vernon has been remarkably effective for a very long time. Although they dedicated a memorial stone to "faithful colored slaves" in 1929 and added a modest slave memorial in 1983, it was still easy for the casual visitor to notice "the almost total absence of slavery, enslaved people."[26] (I have a vivid memory of visiting Mount Vernon as an unsophisticed third grader and of thinking *What the heck? Where are the slaves?*)

In 2022, visitors can take a "slavery tour"; but as visitors have asked, "Why segregate attention to slavery entirely into a once-daily slave-life tour that many visitors will never take (and that, at the very least, should be renamed)? Such an arrangement makes dealing with or even acknowledging slavery and enslaved men and women optional, both at Mount Vernon and by extension in the history of the United States."[27] In 2022, most tours at Mount Vernon mention slavery in some way, but the unmistakable truth here is that these house museums were not formed to remember the experience of enslaved people; they were founded to celebrate the men who oversaw enslavement, and their creators have insistently resisted rethinking this initial impulse. This makes them blunt instruments indeed.

So, the basic principles for understanding the cultural work that museums and historic sites do, in broad terms, emerged pretty clearly in this first period. First, *they are powerful*: they took up then, and continue to take up, significant civic space. Second, *they have been built and run by powerful people with big ideas to express*: Hamilton, Jefferson, and Madison on a museum board convey this pretty well. Third, *architecture matters*: meticulously restoring Mount Vernon while ignoring the slave quarters is a good shorthand for this. Architecture matters, and it actively does all kinds of ideological work. Fourth, *they are doing their best work when they seem to fit seamlessly into the landscape; when they stop being noticeable, their job is done*: if visitors don't notice the lessons about the social order embedded in the lessons about natural science at a place like the Peabody Essex Museum, it is working. Fifth, *they are not neutral. Ever.* Again, meticulously restoring Mount Vernon while ignoring the slave quarters is a good shorthand for this. And sixth, *museums have used a few basic and familiar conventions to make their points*: for instance, they naturalize, in art and science and history, a progression from savagery to civilization by repeating it with quiet but weighty neoclassically framed authority.

These principles, as they played out before the 1870s, make answering the key questions about them pretty straightforward.

1. When was it built? If it was founded before 1870, we know that it was likely a hybrid of the old cabinet of curiosities and the emerging modern museum.
2. By whom was it built? In this period, it was likely the work of an ambitious local historical association, often of sailors, scientists, or ladies bent on a particular kind of preservation.
3. What does it look like? The architectural vocabulary of museums was just developing in this period, but most had some elements of what would become the archetypal museum (pillars, a faux Greek peak or two, an oversized facade).
4. How is it organized? Increasingly, across this period, tightly and with an emphasis on natural science and a natural order of things—a movement from savagery to civilization.
5. How has its point of view been sustained, and how has it been challenged? Please see the next section for answers to these big questions.

1870–1940: THE FIRST GOLDEN AGE OF AMERICAN MUSEUMS

This first golden age, from 1870 to 1940, is defined by the founding of the most significant American museums and the establishment of the Smithsonian Institution as an expansive system of national museums. These developments share an impulse to convey a natural scientific and social order, celebrate American achievements, and educate an expanding population. These are good and admirable impulses. The museums and historic sites founded in this period have been doing work of real value for 150 years, and this is the era of the "white temple."

Calling these museums "white temples" is accurate both in terms of their architecture and in terms of their content. And "white temples" feels like something of a cheap shot. It is worth reiterating here that these institutions are complicated, the impulses that drive them are complicated, and condemning them all as bastions of power dedicated to the maintenance of white supremacy would be a mistake. Doing this would miss the enormous good they have done—teaching, sharing beauty, inspiring all kinds of wonder. This would be a mistake. Neglecting the inequitable distribution of all of these good things would also be a mistake. So would ignoring the power of the cultural logics museums convey as neural knowledge.

In other words, *again*, thinking about museums as blunt instruments of social power requires holding two contradictory thoughts. As I have said, it requires understanding that all infrastructure is cultural, that cultural infrastructures like museums and historic sites are built with the explicit intent of shaping cultural life, *and* that in the United States, this has been both marvelous and dangerous—and it has mattered. As historian Michael Kammen has argued in his history of American patriotism, "One of the most important trends in American cultural life ever since the 1870s has involved the founding of museums."[28]

The Metropolitan Museum of Art in New York and the Museum of Fine Arts in Boston were both founded by groups of wealthy private citizens in 1870. They set off a long museum building boom. As historian Bonnie Pitman tells us, "The 1870s, following the years of the Civil War, were a time of industrial and commercial expansion. During this period the Metropolitan Museum of Art, the American Museum of Natural History, the Museum of Fine Arts in Boston, and the Philadelphia Museum of Art were founded. Each, established with a different purpose, perceived its collections differently" and was "dedicated to educating the public."[29]

Although the Met and the Museum of Fine Arts in Boston represent somewhat distinct origins—the Museum of Fine Arts started as a school, and the Met "was established to exhibit the objects d'art collected by its wealthy benefactors"—as institutions, they established a model that became ubiquitous.[30] They were underwritten by one or two industrialists to start, and then they developed boards made up of the most elite industrialists and, later, sometimes their wives. In New York, "After the election of J. P. Morgan to the Metropolitan's board in 1888, he filled vacancies on the board with millionaires like himself, including Henry Clay Frick, Henry Walters, and others of comparable wealth." This idea spread: "Other art museum boards followed this same model, including Chicago, Detroit, San Francisco, and Washington."[31] As an exhibit celebrating the 150th anniversary of the Met describes it, "In a flush of optimism following the Civil War, a group of businessmen, civic leaders, and artists determined to found an art museum in New York City."[32]

Before we give these robber barons too much credit for their civic generosity, it is worth noting that two laws granting tax relief to generous museum donors played a big part in the appeal of giving. (The Payne-Aldrich Tariff Act made importing art a wise investment, and the charitable deductions that became available in federal and state taxation of income and estates were another incentive.)[33] These inducements certainly sweetened the pot; you could get your name in limestone on a white temple in the heart of your city, be acclaimed as a philanthropist, and save big dollars all at the same time.

White temples is certainly a good shorthand for the architecture of the museums built in this era. Vast, neoclassical, out-scaled buildings with long halls, high ceilings, a temple facade, and grand staircases leading from bustling streets into quiet sanctuaries were the order of the day. (Think the Met, the Museum of Fine Arts in Boston, the Art Institute of Chicago, the Philadelphia Museum of Art, the San Francisco Museum of Art, the Detroit Institute of Arts…) The architecture of the museums was as important as the art.[34] It was intended to communicate the importance of an emerging cultural form—and it did so quite emphatically.

"From 1890 onwards," architectural historian Ingrid Steffensen-Bruce tells us, "the architectural language on which members of the American Museum establishment settled was one imbued with history and culture." She helpfully calls the style "monumental classical, executed with Beaux-Arts sophistication."[35] Of course, there are subtleties and distinctions among these buildings that might be pointed to, but the blunt hit of it—the idea that was meant to be communicated and the ubiquity of the form—is pretty hard to deny. Most people over ten years old in the United States could answer the question "What does a museum look like?" easily and accurately. (This is why exceptions to the rule are so notable—think David Adjaye's African-architecture-meets-neoclassical-architecture inspired design for the National Museum of African American Culture and History.)

The internal logics of museums in this period are also, of course, important to note. These late-Victorian museums were shrines to order. This is true of art museums and science and history museums. Drawing on the foundations laid by Peale and those of his generation, interior spaces were marked both by scale (lots of big rooms) and by the emphasis on narrative and order in which the objects of all kinds were displayed. Museums were filled with "endless glass cases" in which treasures were laid before visitors to demonstrate a rational, orderly, systematic narrative about the nature of the world we inhabit.[36] These museums, then, as one historian has put it, "created, reified, and institutionalized categories of knowledge as unassailable truths" that inescapably reflect the operations of power.[37] Scholars have argued about the extent to which this was to exert control over the public or to pull the public into a kind of "complicity with power by placing them on this side of a power which it represented as its own."[38] But for our purposes, this is less important than the idea that knowledge, social power, and a narrative about progress from savagery to civilization were linked to and embedded in all aspects of museums in this period.

The American Museum of Natural History in New York is a useful example of all of the above. It has what Donna Haraway has described as a "palatial fortress-like Seventy-Seventh Street façade," not to mention the figures of Roosevelt and his undressed, unnamed companions.[39] It has an interior logic that builds on these big, blunt initial hits. "Passing through the Museum's Roosevelt Memorial atrium into the African Hall," writes Haraway, "the ordinary citizen may enter a privileged space and time: the Age of Mammals in the heart of Africa, scene of the origin."[40] But it is important to remember that these were carefully, thoughtfully executed spaces—spaces made by people with a point of view to express—and that the museum was not only a site for the expression of those ideas but also a site for their development and legitimization. So, the example of the museum's role in supporting and legitimizing the eugenics movement is useful to note here.

In 1921, the museum hosted the Second International Congress of Eugenics. Madison Grant, who would become one of the most vocal proponents of both scientific racism (a strain of pseudoscience that sought to find empirical evidence for racism) and eugenics (the study of human traits to enable to "improvement" and "purification" of human populations) was on the board of the American Museum of Natural History and was eager to host the Congress of Eugenics. The basic position of the Congress was that there was a correlation between "certain negative and deviant social behaviors—including criminality, insanity, and feeblemindedness (a term that captured any number of mental disorders)—with particular ethnic and racial populations, and [it] claimed these behaviors to be inherited via the gene."[41] These were people for whom white supremacy was a given for which they were seeking scientific evidence and legitimacy. At the event, papers were presented, Madison's book *The Passing of the Great Race* was given its own exhibition, and other consequential exhibits were created to coincide with the meeting. One of note was "about the dangers of immigration." It was visited "by thousands of New York City schoolchildren" and would eventually "travel to Congress," where it was one of the "visual aids offered in support of the winning passage of the National Origins Act."[42]

One speaker at the meeting, Charles Davenport, opined, "Not only our physical but also our mental and temperamental characteristics have a hereditary basis." He continued, "The study of racial characters will lead men to a broader vision of the human race and the fact that its fate is controllable."[43] The Museum's annual report boasted, "Inasmuch as the World War left the finest racial stocks in many countries so depleted that there is a danger of their extinction, and inasmuch as our own race is threatened with submergence by the influx of other races, it was felt by all present and especially by our foreign guests that the American Museum of Natural History had rendered a signal service in providing for the reception and entertainment of the large number of distinguished men and women who attended the conference."[44] Davenport, who also claimed, "We are driven to the conclusion that there is a constitutional, hereditary, genetic basis for the difference between the two races [whites and blacks] in mental tests. We have to conclude that there are racial differences in mental capacity," captured their logic fairly well.[45]

Madison Grant was a busy figure in the early twentieth-century United States. He was not only a best-selling author and on the board of the American Museum of Natural History but also the director of the American Eugenics Society, vice president of the Immigration Restriction League, and a founder of the Bronx Zoo, one of many United States museums to exhibit humans alongside animals and artifacts. It is worth including, very briefly, two stories of humans who were put on display in this period, to convey a sense of the everyday quality of the racial logics that were so deeply ingrained in the golden era of American museums.

Ota Benga was put on display at the Bronx Zoo in 1906. He was captured and enslaved in his native Congo in 1904 and brought to the United States to be displayed at the St. Louis World's Fair, where he learned how to perform in his exhibition by watching Apache Chief Geronimo performing in his.[46] He was later taken to the American Museum of Natural History, where he lived before he was moved to the newly opened Bronx Zoo in 1906. The label for his exhibit, in the monkey cage, read "The African Pygmy, 'Ota Benga.' Age, 23 years. Height, 4 feet 11 inches. Weight, 103 pounds. Brought from the Kasai River, Congo Free State, South Central Africa, by Dr. Samuel P. Verner. Exhibited each afternoon during September."[47] The *New York Times* reported, "To increase the picturesqueness of the exhibition, moreover, an orang-outang named Dohong, which has been widely described as showing almost human intelligence, was put in the cage with the Bushman." And although the story in the *Times* is, in part, about the outrage of "colored ministers," it quotes the Zoo director defending his decision with the authority of Madison Grant. He told the reporter, "What is being done in the matter is with the acquiescence of the society. The Secretary, Mr. Madison Grant, was present when I made the arrangements...for the keep of the little African savage."[48]

A few years later, Ishi, the last surviving member of his California tribe, was "discovered" and put on display at both the Pan-Pacific International Exposition in San Francisco and the new museum of anthropology there. Benga took his own life just two days before Ishi died of tuberculosis, to which he was exposed while on display. (In 1999, Ishi's brain was "discovered" to still be in a museum collection—it was held "in a tank in Maryland by the Smithsonian."[49] It was eventually returned to California, to the Yana people, to be buried with the rest of his body.)

So, while it may seem like a big leap to say that Roosevelt on a statue in front of a museum, or the architecture of the white pillars, or rows and rows of artifacts of the daily lives of indigenous people locked in glass cases in Washington D.C. are explicitly part of a system of racist cultural infrastructure, it doesn't take too much digging into the history of these institutions and the thinking of the people who founded them to find that the worst accusations, and what might seem like the easiest swipes to take in 2022, play out over and over again in the histories of these institutions.

To paraphrase Maya Angelou, when they try to tell us who they are, we should believe them, and we should take them seriously. The point is not to go back and cherry-pick the worst of the impulses of American museums around the turn of the twentieth century. The point is to demonstrate that these were institutions built for the personal gratification of the wealthy and the education and the edification of the masses, in which the profoundly distorted display of a single human being was made logical by the thinking that organized the whole enterprise. In other words, it shouldn't come as a surprise that museum-goers were willing to believe that Coco Fusco and Guillermo Gómez-Peña were exotic "tribespeople" who were put in a museum for display in the 1990s; this made sense to people because of what they understood, implicitly, about the work that museums do.

The Smithsonian Institution's founding is the next significant development in the story of the golden age of museums in the United States. At the moment when these other great institutions were being formed, Congress was several decades into fussing over what to do with a gift that had come to the United States from an English man named John Smithson. Lots of ink has been spilled on this story, but the short version is that he donated a fortune for the "increase and diffusion of knowledge" in the United States and left little evidence as to exactly what he meant by that. So even though the gift came in the 1830s, and the Smithsonian had a secretary and began some modest collecting, the question of how the money would be spent and what the "increase and diffusion of knowledge" should look like was still a matter of debate in the 1870s.

One solution arose around the occasion of the US Centennial in 1876. As the Philadelphia Exposition was being planned, it was determined that some of the Smithsonian resources would go to collecting the materials of indigenous people in the American West. So the US government exhibits at the fair, part of the foundation for the now much broader Smithsonian Institution, involved the display of Indian tools and art in cases right next to taxidermy and other objects of scientific interest from the natural world. These exhibits look very much like the typical museum exhibits of this era—high-ceilinged halls filled with rows of glass cases that made little or no distinction between human artifacts and natural artifacts. They made artifacts produced by native people equivalent to found objects like fossils and moose antlers. They used these objects to tell an invented story of the "natural" order of the world.

Spencer Fullerton Baird, founding curator of the United States National Museum, as the Smithsonian was called then, wanted to include living Indigenous people in this exhibit but worried about "their mixture with whites or negroes" and that the "adaptation of their manners and culture" might render them "less interesting as objects of ethnological display."[50] Baird didn't decide against exhibiting Indigenous people because it was unethical. He decided against it because *actual* Indigenous people had been tainted by the modern world and were therefore not "authentic" enough for the story he wanted the exhibit to tell.

So, at its inception, the Smithsonian wanted to display artifacts that would tell a particular story about racial purity and racial hierarchy and was inconvenienced because some of the artifacts (real Indigenous people) did not support that narrative. Baird's solution was to dress mannequins up in a hodgepodge of "authentic garb" that included a "belt of human scalps."

In 1881, the first official United States National Museum was completed in Washington, and the Smithsonian, as we know it now, started to take shape. (Today it includes nineteen museums, twenty-one libraries, nine research centers, a handful of historic sites, and a zoo. It also includes 150 million objects.) And native objects—including Indigenous bodies—have been central to the Smithsonian across this time.

The display or study of native objects certainly does not always have to be an expression of racism or racist cultural logics. It is just that in the case of the Smithsonian, and American museums in this period more broadly, that was a big part of the story for a very long time. One anecdote demonstrates the long shadow cast by this founding framework for the Smithsonian. Recounting a visit to the natural history museum on the Mall in the late 1980s, a story in the *Native American Rights Fund Legal Review* reads,

[A] number of Northern Cheyenne chiefs visited Washington D.C. During the course of their visit they arranged to tour the Smithsonian Institution's Cheyenne collection at the National Museum of Natural History. "As we were walking out," a Northern Cheyenne woman who worked on Capitol Hill later recalled, "we saw [the] huge ceilings in the room, with row upon row of drawers. Someone remarked that there must be a lot of Indian stuff in those drawers. Quite casually, a curator with us said, 'Oh, this is where we keep the skeletal remains,' and he told us how many—18,500. Everyone was shocked."[51]

In 1986, there were 18,500 skeletal remains on the National Mall in Washington D.C., some of which had been collected as recently as the 1930s. (This would include the grandparents of living people in the 1980s.) The collections also included nine brains. That seems to qualify as shocking. And while "It may be hard to imagine that our government has had a firm policy which encouraged the acquisition and retention of Native American human remains…that is the case."[52] (A few years later a federal law—The Native American Grave Protection and Repatriation Act—would begin to require these remains to be returned. This was an important move toward racial equity in museums and the fact that we needed such a law is worth noting here. Also, it is worth saying that volumes could be filled with stories of the tenacity with which museums are still fighting this requirement.)

The Smithsonian's National Museum of Natural History was approved as part of a 1902 plan to reclaim the long-neglected National Mall, and it is as typical an example of museum architecture as you might hope to find. Gleaming white pillars and a grand staircase lead into oversized halls full of carefully organized objects that seek to achieve the diffusion of knowledge. The papers of one of its early leaders, George Brown Goode, reveal lots of interesting and sophisticated material on the relationship between art and the natural world. He comes across as an ambitious optimist rather than a rabid enforcer of a system of brutal racism. He argued, "The people's museum should be much more than a house full of specimens in glass cases. It should be a house full of ideas, arranged with the strictest attention to systems." And he claimed that "The museum of the future may be made one of the chief agencies of the higher civilization."[53]

But for Goode, in practice, this meant using objects collected from around the world to tell a story that was very much about racial order. In 1919, for instance, the African ethnography exhibit included a hierarchical display of seven miniature figures that represented African racialized types that were ranked, geographically, from north to south.[54] Diminutive wax figures in glass cases dressed in (likely stolen) artifacts were used to teach exoticized (and fictional) racial types. (Can you help but think *Black Panther?*)

The Smithsonian's National Gallery of Art was founded at the end of the golden age of museums, and art museums were not exempt from the logics that drove other kinds of museums in this period. The National

Gallery was typical: its exterior is a big, neoclassical expression of authority (and beauty); its founder, Andrew Mellon, was an industrialist whose enormous wealth enabled him to collect the works of old masters from cash-strapped Europeans after the First World War; and its collections made an argument about civilization that continues to shape it today.

And while there is a great deal to be said—whole fields of vital knowledge have been developed—about the collection and display of art, some basic elements of this story are surprisingly uncomplicated. A useful shorthand for blunt meaning-making in art museums is the tenacity of the organization of museums around halls devoted to European and American art as the pinnacle of human achievement, which have explicitly classified art produced by people from other parts of the world as "primitive" for more than a century.

This logic for art museums is so persistent that as recently as 2020, when the Met celebrated its 150th anniversary with a sweeping exhibition, the museum paid very little attention to its history of investment in the category of "Primitive Art." They "chose not to compose even a short separate paragraph expounding why 'Primitive Art' is now regarded as an inappropriate label, reflective of the reductive, racist biases of the first collectors of African, Oceanic, and Indigenous art from the Americas, which distorted generations of scholarship."[55] It doesn't get much blunter than organizing a museum around the distinction between "primitive" and "modern" art. The fact that this model lived for long in so many museums in the United States is evidence of how deeply reliant museums have been on racial logics. This was true in 1870, and if you take the time to read the wave of anti-racist statements issued by every kind of museum in 2020, you will see that they are still contending with these logics.

(Another easy shorthand for the expression of cultural power in art museums is the still-potent 1989 work by Guerrilla Girls that asked, "Do women have to be naked to get into the Met. Museum? Less than 5% of the artists in the Modern Art sections are women, but 85% of nudes are female." Again, it doesn't get much blunter than that.)

In other words, you don't need to know the details of these histories—that Sir Hans Sloane made his fortune from the labor of enslaved people and used it to display their cultures as fascinatingly primitive at the British Museum or that the Smithsonian started with an impulse to display real living Indigenous people but stopped short because real Indigenous people didn't conform to the narratives of racial hierarchy they wanted to convey—in order to get to a *Black Panther*-style hit of how power operates in museums. If Marvel movie folks can safely assume that African objects in white museums will make sense to viewers as a key to unlocking colonial power structures, then even though it usually goes unsaid, we can safely assume that we all understand how museums work as blunt instruments of racist cultural infrastructure. We just don't often make it explicit.

If this seems hyperbolic or overwrought, it is useful to recall that in the period of the first golden age of museums in the United States— when museums and historic sites were forged with and by not just racial but profoundly racist logics—these logics were, indeed, based on untruths. This seems ridiculous to state, but I am going to state it anyway. People living in the United States were constantly exposed to evidence that white supremacy was a lie. (Again, this may seem like an odd point to make, but it is important.) White people were not fundamentally superior to people who were not white in the 1870s, despite their distinct legal status. White supremacy was then, as it is now, a fiction that needed to be maintained by things like infrastructures that called non-white art "primitive" or architecture that worked to give this point authority and permanence. In 1906, when Ota Benga was put on display in the Bronx Zoo, New York was fairly exploding with evidence of the absurdity of this fiction. A Black middle class was booming in nearly every American city; a Black literary canon was exploding; there were seventy-eight Black colleges and universities in the United States; and African Americans were thirty years into a struggle to get respectful recognition at the World's Fairs in the United States by producing their own buildings and exhibits demonstrating Black achievements and an African American vision of the future.[56] (It is also true that at least sixty-two African Americans were lynched with impunity in the same year.)[57] Obviously this ridiculous list could go on and on. In other words, it is *not* the case that white supremacy made more sense in the past. It has always been a fiction that has needed powerful institutions to support it, and it has always been met with resistance. But the power of museums in the United States has also always been, right alongside the wondrous objects they include, the combination of the heavy weight of assumed neutral authority (think the facade of the Met) and the fictions within (think of the fake Indians at the Centennial).

Much of the 2020 conversation about museums was about "decolonizing" the museum—ridding it of these colonial roots. But how do you change these institutions so they are not comic-book-easy stand-ins for maintaining white supremacy? Many have argued that it is hopeless. "Decolonizing is deeper than just being represented," argues Sumaya Kassim.[58] She worries about "whether, in fact, they are so embedded in the history and power structures that decoloniality challenges, that they will only end up co-opting decoloniality."[59] And she calls on us to be suspicious:

> When projects and institutions proclaim a commitment to "diversity," "inclusion" or "decoloniality" we need to attend to these claims with a critical eye. Decoloniality is a complex set of ideas—it requires complex processes, space, money, and time, otherwise it runs the risk of becoming another buzzword, like "diversity." As interest in decolonial thought grows, we must beware of museums' and other institutions' propensity to collect and exhibit because there is a danger (some may argue an inevitability) that the museum will exhibit decoloniality in much the same way they display/ed black and brown bodies as part of Empire's "collection."[60]

But while it is nearly impossible to disaggregate the impulses that drove the building of museums in this era from the dominant racial logics of the period—and that makes it important to take them seriously as racist cultural infrastructure—work in museums in the next period does begin to successfully put the power of museums to new kinds of uses. As we will see, this has not been easy because museums seem benign, but they are not benign, and they have long been shaped by deeply untrue, even in their own moments, racial logics.

So, the basic principles for understanding the cultural work that museums and historic sites do, in broad terms, emerge pretty clearly in this golden age. First, *they are powerful*: museums got bigger and grander and more permanent and continued to take up significant civic space. Second, *they have been built and run by powerful people with big ideas to express*: Andrew Mellon, J.P. Morgan, Henry Clay Frick, and their fellow robber barons put their dollars into these institutions and, often, their names on the buildings. Third, *architecture matters*: the same architect, John Russell Pope, designed the National Gallery of Art in Washington and the American Museum of Natural History in New York. Both are archetypal museums—neoclassical, grand in scale, and weighty in authority. Fourth, *they are doing their best work when they seem to fit seamlessly into the landscape; when they stop being noticeable, their job is done*: if you don't notice the lessons about the social order embedded in the lessons about natural science in a place like the American Museum of Natural History, the lessons are working. Fifth, *they are not neutral. Ever*: meticulously restoring Mount Vernon while ignoring the slave quarters is still a good shorthand for this. And, sixth, *museums have used a few basic and familiar conventions to make their points*: for instance, they naturalize, in art and science and history, a progression from savagery to civilization by repeating it with quiet but weighty authority.

These principles, as they played out, make answering the key questions about them pretty straightforward.

1. When was it built? If it was founded between 1870 and 1940, we know that it was part of the first golden age of American museums.
2. By whom was it built? In this period, it was likely the work of ambitious, wealthy industrialists interested in public education, tax breaks, and, maybe, self-promotion.
3. What does it look like? The architectural vocabulary of museums in this period is firmly engraved in the public consciousness: neoclassical, out-sized, stone, pillared, and often domed.
4. How is it organized? Increasingly, across this period, tightly and with an emphasis in natural science and a natural order of things or a progressive narrative of development from savagery to civilization.
5. How has its point of view been sustained, and how has it been challenged? These are big questions with relatively easy answers. Their point of view has been sustained by repetition, longevity, and the power of the authority they express. (Think the figures that flanked Roosevelt in New York.) This perspective has been challenged by scholars, activists, and people working in museums for decades. And while it may seem strange to add his name to the pantheon of museum history—Peale, Goode, Frick, Mellon, J.P. Morgan—George Floyd has opened up new space for a bigger conversation about how to challenge this authority.

4

WHITE TEMPLES
RESHAPED?

1965–2020: KING TUT AND EMMETT TILL— THE OLD SCHOOL BLOCKBUSTER AND THE NEW PERMANENCE OF "NEGRO BUILDINGS"

The period from 1965 to 2020 marked a second golden age of the American museum, of a sort. It was a golden age in that a huge number of new museums were built, and existing museums expanded both their physical and cultural footprints. But if *golden age* implies *easy* growth, the label is less accurate; this period was expansive but fraught. It is tempting to describe this second golden age in the life of American museums as taking us from King Tut to Emmett Till—from Tut to Till. This framing is a little tricky, but it usefully captures the struggle of many to face the particular awful inheritance of museums in this period.

The 1975 blockbuster King Tutankhamun exhibit traveled to museums across the United States for five years. It represents, perhaps, a culmination of the logics that were developed and expressed in the first golden era of museums. The King Tut show launched new levels of interest in American museums in a couple of ways. First, it was a new kind of exhibit, a "blockbuster" traveling exhibit that draws huge crowds to museums and generates significant profits for them. Second, it was something of a victory lap for the first golden era. It is the story of an erroneous, illogical reclaiming of "our treasures" from "their land." It was a deeply racialized exhibition, like many in the earlier period. And even though plenty of people clearly articulated this problem, the exhibit was a huge success—people went in record numbers to see it.

The Emmett Till part of this framing is a reference to the inclusion at the National Museum of African American History and Culture, opened on the National Mall in 2016, of the coffin in which Emmett Till was buried. Emmett Till was 14 years old in 1955 when he was brutally murdered—tortured and shot and drowned—in Mississippi for allegedly being disrespectful to a white woman in a grocery store. (The memorial for him has recently been made bulletproof in Glendora, Mississippi, because it has been shot at so many times in the last few years.) Including such a vivid and fraught object as his coffin—a relic of the violence white supremacy has inspired, or maybe requires?—in a museum exhibit feels like a culmination of the work that began in the "Negro Buildings" at the world's fairs. A few years later the National Museum of American History collected and exhibited—in the front of the museum and in front of the star-spangled banner—one of these Till memorial markers that is riddled with thirty-one bullet holes. Certainly, both of these Till exhibits use race in museums in new ways. And they both build on the efforts and energies of the many African Americans who turned to the work of making their own history museums in the 1960s and 1970s. They founded scores of local and, later national, African American history museums.

As a shorthand, this framing for the period, Tut to Till, is useful because it addresses two simultaneous and competing dynamics: a new embrace of old museums by the public *and* the success of many efforts to reframe the work museums can do in the culture. It is not quite right, though, in that it suggests a kind of narrative of progress. As in, we used to be the people who loved going to see the treasures of King Tut—which were unearthed by British archaeologists and museologists and were used to make a claim about the superiority of white culture in a wildly untrue but broadly accepted sleight of hand—and now we are the people who are using our museums to disrupt narratives of white supremacy and rethink the possibilities of the institutions themselves. The problem with this narrative is that it implies a direct kind of progress, when the situation on the ground has involved much more of a complicated back and forth. Both of these museum narratives are very much alive in the present, and the ongoing struggle over who museums are for and what work they can do in the culture is important to understand.

The *Treasures of Tutankhamun* exhibition opened at the Metropolitan Museum of Art in New York in 1975. Over the next five years, it traveled to the Field Museum of Natural History in Chicago, the New Orleans Museum of Art, the Los Angeles County Museum of Art, the Seattle Art Museum, the Metropolitan Museum of Art in New York (again), and the M. H. de Young Memorial Museum in San Francisco. The exhibit broke museum attendance records in nearly all of these cities. It was an opulent display of the treasures unearthed in the tomb of King Tutankhamun; Tut ruled Egypt in ca. 1332–1323 BC, and his tomb was packed with at least five thousand priceless, showy objects, including a solid gold coffin weighing two hundred pounds. The exhibit was full of dazzling, wonder-inspiring objects

These objects and their travel in exhibitions across the United States and around the globe in the twentieth century mark a new phase in the history of museums—perhaps they marked the peak of the modern museum. The objects were pulled from the tomb and ended up in museums in a you-can't-make-this-stuff-up story of colonialism, race, and museums. In 1907, Lord Carnarvon, who lived in the castle in which the *Downton Abbey* television show was filmed, invested in an excavation in Egypt. Egypt was then a British colonial territory. Lord Carnarvon could do this because he had married Almina Victoria Maria Alexandra Wombwell, the illegitimate daughter of the Jewish millionaire banker Alfred de Rothschild. The money de Rothschild gave Lord Carnarvon on the occasion of the marriage bought his daughter respectability, paid the Carnarvon's family debt, and funded the digging up of ancient Egyptian treasures, which Lady Carnarvon would later, as Egypt was fighting for independence from Britain, sell to the Egyptians for a handsome sum. Got that? *Downton Abbey*, buying respectability for a Jewish woman of illegitimate birth, and British archeology create the circumstances in which Tut's treasures belong to Lady Carnarvon, and the Egyptians buy them to keep them in Egypt and then eventually let the treasures travel as the discoveries of enterprising, brilliant English men of science.

The framing of the blockbuster exhibit was, indeed, through the eyes of these British archeologists, and the objects were displayed as they were "discovered." In this way, the objects from the tomb were not displayed as examples of achievements in Egyptian or African or Middle Eastern civilization, but were presented as Western prizes and were consistently described as examples of achievements of "humankind." The importance of this story at that moment is underscored both by the direct intervention of President Nixon and Secretary of State Henry Kissinger in support of the exhibit and the significant financial contributions made by the Exxon Corporation.

As historian Melani McAlister has described it, the exhibit was "a site of struggle over both the nature of American world power and domestic politics of race."[1] She argues that, "At that particular historical moment the Tut exhibit became an extraordinary nexus where...the construction of American relations to the Middle East...and racial identity [in] the United States were combined, contested and revised."[2] Which is to say that these objects of Egyptian history ended up being used to make an argument about white European ownership that doesn't, removed from all of this context, make a lot of sense.

As McAlister describes it, "The 'official' Tut narrative—as produced by museum curators, Egyptologists, and the mainstream press—aestheticized the Tut treasures, constructing them as 'universal' art, something too ennobling and too precious (too 'human') to belong to any one people (Arabs) or any one nation (Egypt) " (So, at a time when nearly all the other objects from Africa and the Middle East in these museums were trapped in collections of the "primitive" or the "ancient," these objects were displayed as prized shared possessions—the "discovery" of which implied Western ownership.)

Even more specious were the strange discussions of Tut's race that surrounded the exhibit. Tut was figured as white, or maybe more accurately as not Black. The Met produced a booklet titled "Tutankhamun and the African Heritage" that conceded the Egyptian population did include some "Negroes and individuals with negroid traits" but said it had consisted "mostly of individuals essentially europoid or caucasoid."[3] In other words, Tut's treasures were produced by people who were "essentially" European. As if to stress this point, the official exhibition catalogue describes a black image of Tut with this clarification, "Clearly the [black] color [of the face] has no ethnic significance, but its precise meaning is not easy to explain."[4]

Of course, many pushed back against this narrative. As McAlister tells it, "It was sharply contested by African American journalists and scholars, who refused to see the Tut Treasures as 'universal art' and thus countered the logic that read the Tut exhibit through a narrative of resource rescue."[5] Claiming Tut as Black seemed like a radical act and was met with bewilderment and derision.

So, let me repeat that. In the 1970s, the Metropolitan Museum of Art published a booklet for visitors to an exhibition of the treasures of the tomb of King Tutankhamun in which the museum argued that Egyptians were more European than African. Does that make any sense? Does that make big claims about the white supremacist impulses of American museums seem a little less overwrought or of the moment of 2022? Of course, the actual racial makeup of a transcontinental country is complex. The veracity of the claim is almost beside the point—which is that the Metropolitan Museum of Art, then in a city that was nearly 25 percent Black, went to the trouble to commission, print, and distribute such a booklet. Why would the museum care? What are the stakes in Tut's race? What would be lost by acknowledging that these treasures were produced by people who might possibly have been something other than white? These questions are easy to answer. They are also painful to answer. What could it be other than a deep investment in whiteness in the exhibit?

(As the exhibit traveled the US, comedian Steve Martin had a hit song about the boy king in which he sang, "He's my favorite honky!" There is not point in making too much of this, but it suggests that the Met's message about Tut's race got some attention and seemed worth making fun of.)

In the end, most people probably waited in lines that snaked outside of museums' doors to see all the gold, but they were shown a lot more. Certainly, the Met's arguments stood in tension with efforts of African Americans to claim a dignified place for themselves in the museum.

The "Century of Negro Progress Exposition" opened in 1963, a decade before the great rush to see the Tut treasures. It celebrated one hundred years since emancipation. As had been the tradition in African American contributions to the world's fairs, Black businesses and civic associations and local community organizations worked together with some corporate sponsors to produce exhibits on Black history and culture. According to historian Mabel Wilson, "[The 'Century of Negro Progress Exposition'] organizers claimed 'the elements of justice, equality and liberty, within the chemistry of Democracy, acts as a catalyst upon its principal component—FREEDOM—and forces out of it those impurity such as prejudice, hate and fear.'"[6] This exhibition, the last big effort of its kind, came just a few years after the founding of an early African American history museum in Chicago and inspired the founding of many more.

The Ebony Museum of Negro History and Art, now the DuSable Museum of African American History, was founded in 1961 in the home of Margaret and Charles Burroughs on South Michigan Avenue. Well-to-do activists, the Burroughs had a vision for their museum that was about the future as much as it was about the past. According to Wilson, their early work included presentations titled "Africa and the Freedom Rides" and "New Opportunities and Responsibilities of the Afro-American Writer."[7] The Burroughs wanted to create cultural infrastructure that would tell a story that was outside of the logics of most museums, and they were not alone.

The African American Museum in Cleveland was the first African American museum that was *not* part of a historically Black college or university. (It was founded in 1953 by Icabod Flewellen after the Black history materials he had been collecting since he was a teen were burned, shortly after his return from service in World War II, in a fire set by white supremacists at his home.)[8] In 1963, the American Negro History Museum was founded in Boston.

In 1965, the International Afro-American Museum, now the Charles H. Wright Museum of African American History, was founded in Detroit. For Charles Wright, the time had come for a museum "devoted to the past and present fight for freedom of the American negro."[9] Inspired in part by an exhibit on Nazi resistance he had seen in Denmark, he wanted to build a museum to display the African American's "opinion of himself." Wright described this as "one of the most important tasks of our times."[10] And as the museum website tells it now, "Dr. Wright would later remark, '[it] ensur[es] that generations, especially young African Americans, are made aware of and take pride in the history of their forebears and their remarkable struggle for freedom.'"[11]

Over the next twenty-five years, more than 150 African American museums would be established in American cities. Historian Fath Ruffins writes, "These new museums were founded by community activists who had worked in the civil rights movement at some level and now wanted to use that expertise for a cultural agenda," and they were founded by people who were inspired by an idea of empowerment through cultural institutions.[12] Although many were drawing on their civil rights movement experience, founders at the early end of this movement tended to be educators and affluent business people. Further into the 1960s, a younger generation stepped up who saw museums "as cultural centers that supported a constructive pathway towards the development of ethnic and personal 'pride.'"[13]

It is important to observe that these museums were mostly built in cities, and generally in cities undergoing dramatic racial transformation. In the post–World War II era, with some dramatic acceleration in the late 1960s, US federal housing policy and the building of highways, which were often also war memorials, were turning majority-white cities into majority-Black cities. In Detroit, the transition from a white city to a Black city was particularly dramatic, and the damage done by transforming huge numbers of acres of city into acres of highway was particularly acute. Newly Black city governments had very limited resources but the will to support these new museums, and in the 1970s into the 1990s, they became important cultural institutions. They often started in houses, and over the course of a couple of decades grew to include substantial collections in substantial museum buildings.

In fact, the International Afro-American Museum was originally in Wright's home on West Grand Boulevard, and it was just barely spared the wrecking ball to make way for a "newly erected concrete spaghetti" of highways. As Wilson puts it, "In the 1950s, the black areas of the Westside bore the negative externalities of new canyons where the north-south Jeffries Freeway bisected the western spur of the Ford Freeway, one block north of Wright's home on West Grand Boulevard."[14]

While it survived highway removal clearance, the museum was never intended to remain in a house. Its advocates had always assumed that it would eventually be housed in a museum building. And while they were unable to get support from the state of Michigan, they eventually found an ally in the city's first African American mayor, Coleman Young. Young agreed to lease a plot of land to the museum in the heart of the city's cultural center and next to the Detroit Institute of Arts, an institution that had yet to demonstrate support of or interest in African American art.

According to Wilson, "A deft political tactician, Young pieced together $2.3 million from federal Housing and Urban Development block grants to pay for construction" of the new museum.[15]

The Charles H. Wright Museum of African American History was dedicated in 1987. It was a two-floor, twenty-eight-thousand-square-foot building with an exterior that looked nothing like the neoclassical Detroit Institute of Arts next to which it stood. The design of the Wright Museum was "a large gray trapezoid clad in cast concrete panels" with the playful addition of "a silhouette of African domed roofs—shaped from bent steel and painted red" to "enliven" the facade.[16] It was decidedly not neoclassical and used the tools of the postmodern architecture of the day to gesture toward the African roots of the people whose story would be told inside. It worked, successfully, to convey that it would not be business as usual in this museum.

Inside, the museum also offered a different kind of narrative that fundamentally challenged who was civilized and who was savage. (It began with the story of enslavement, which in that context is nearly impossible to see as anything but savagery, and thus rewrote the savagery-to-civilization narrative so familiar in museums.)

African Americans were not alone in their work to use cultural infrastructure to try to rewrite narratives of belonging and racial logics in the culture. Across this period, Latinos, Chinese Americans, Japanese Americans, and later Arab Americans stepped up to create museums intended to do new kinds of work as cultural infrastructure.

The Museum of Chinese in America was founded in New York City in 1980. It wanted to take up subject matter—the experience of Chinese Americans—that had not been represented in historical museums or art museums. It was a seriously ambitious effort from the start and was designed to rethink the museum in a fundamental way. Scholar and brilliant strategic thinker Jack Chen was among the museum's founders, and he had a vision for what he called a "dialogic museum." He was well aware of the racial freight carried by museums as institutions in the United States and wanted to develop a model that could mitigate against that history. His idea was a museum that was created in dialogue with a community as a new model that upended the old model of authority and white pillars and limestone and logics about progress from savagery to civilization. The museum was initially relatively modest, in a storefront in Chinatown in

New York City, and its early years involved small exhibitions and collective community outreach efforts to build an archive and collections. It was at the beginning of a wave of interest in the museum as a "forum" as opposed to the museum as a site to receive wisdom from all-knowing experts. It began developing a new model with which museum directors and curators would experiment for the next four decades. In 2009, it moved into a marquee new building designed by Maya Lin, the architect of the Vietnam Veterans Memorial, the Civil Rights Memorial in Birmingham, Alabama, and the Civil Rights Museum.

In this new space, which was designed to build on the dialogic spirit of Chen's initial ideal, the museum has continued to try to develop models that leave the racial freight of the museum behind. As the permanent exhibit reads, "We are a 'we' of glorious, expansive diversity. But at last, for all of us, the United States of America can be our home. Chinese Americans, excluded and marginalized, stereotyped and violated, at last have become part of 'We, the People.' Now we must right the wrongs and rewrite the history."[17]

This impulse to rewrite the history, to move from Tut to Till, played out vividly at the Smithsonian Institution, as well as in the founding of new museums like the Museum of Chinese in America and the Charles Wright Museum, in dramatic terms in this period. The Smithsonian was not immune to the changes afoot in this second golden age of museums, but large-scale institutional change was neither easy nor consistent nor progressive.

Without a doubt, the Smithsonian expanded dramatically in this second golden age for American museums. At the end of the first golden age, in 1940, there were four Smithsonian museum buildings: the Castle, the Arts and Industry Building, the National Zoo, and the National Museum of Natural History. Between 1964 and 2016, eleven new museum buildings were built and opened to the public. In 1964, the Museum of History and Technology, which would later be renamed the National Museum of American History, was opened. The Anacostia Community Museum was dedicated in 1967; it is a fascinating hybrid of a local African American Museum and a national museum within the Smithsonian Institution. Also in 1968, the Smithsonian dedicated the National Portrait Gallery and the Smithsonian American Art Museum. The Cooper Union Museum for the Arts of Decoration followed in 1969. In 1972, the Renwick Gallery was opened, and in 1974, the Hirshhorn Museum and Sculpture Garden was dedicated. To celebrate the American bicentennial, the National Air and Space Museum was opened in June 1976. There was a brief pause in this frenetic museum building on the National Mall; the next building was dedicated eleven years later, in 1987. The National Museum of African Art and the Arthur M. Sackler Gallery opened in a new underground museum. There was another pause, and then the National Museum of the American Indian was dedicated in 2004. The National Museum of African American History and Culture was built and opened in 2016. (That is a lot of museum building.)

The Tut to Till tension is reflected in these stories in that they contained powerful impulses from the first period of museum building *and* impulses to radically transform the work of the earlier period. These tensions are vividly embodied in the story of the National Museum of American History. It started as a home for fairly miscellaneous collections of history and technology that didn't quite fall under the rubric of "natural history." Some of the remnants of the original collection of the Smithsonian that hadn't made it into the National Museum of Natural History (NMNH) and some materials that *were* in the NMNH were the foundation of the collection for the new museum of technology and history. The new name only lasted from 1964 to 1980, when it became the National Museum of American History (NMAH). It's somewhat of a surprise that the name lasted that long, given that the air and space museum, which is so fully a museum of technology, opened in 1976. But the history and technology name reflects how the early collections were amassed and an abiding interest in the materiality of history.

The National Museum of American History building, dedicated in 1964, is the last building designed by the esteemed architecture firm McKim, Mead & White. The firm, which had been building neoclassical and Beaux-Arts edifices intended to convey permanence and confidence since it designed the Harvard Club of New York in 1894, knew how to express significance. The building is a smart updated play on the white-pillared museum. Instead of pillars, the massive rectangular building is distinguished by huge limestone panels, set slightly apart from the building itself, that replicate the effect of pillars—without including the pillars. And this is a pretty good metaphor for a lot of what has happened inside the museum—a struggle between the impulse to replicate and the impulse to reject the logics and practices of the first golden age. A quick look at a series of key exhibits in this period illustrates this struggle.

The *Nation of Nations* exhibit ran from 1976 to 1991 and included more than five thousand objects. According to the museum, "This exhibition documented the diversity of people who came to America over the centuries and affirmed that America is linked to other nations by an intricate web of cultural ties." It took up many aspects of American life and points of connection in a diverse society. It was relatively complex in its thinking. A section on education was introduced in the exhibit catalog as follows: "Public education has been a major contributor to the blending of the population of the United States, as well as the catalytic agent for other 'Americanizing' social forces."[18] It stressed the importance of teaching values in American public education, noting, "'To diffuse the principles of virtue and patriotism' was an intention of Educators from the mid-nineteenth to the mid-twentieth century," and included impassioned language from Teddy Roosevelt on the subject:

> There is no room in this country for hyphenated Americanism. When I refer to hyphenated Americans, I do not refer to naturalized Americans...But a hyphenated American is not an American at all. This is just as true of the man who puts "native" before the hyphen as of the man who puts German or Irish or English or French before the hyphen. Americanism is a matter of the spirit and of the soul. Our allegiance must be purely to the United States. We must unsparingly condemn any man who holds any other allegiance. But if he is heartily and singly loyal to this Republic, then no matter where he was born, he is just as good an American as any one else.[19]

Also of note was the section on the military, titled "Military Uniformity," in which the tension between the uniformity required by the military and the diversity of the background of the soldiers was stressed in a reconstructed Army barracks. A favorite feature of the exhibit was a reproduction of an Italian American home from the 1920s. In a sense, this early and important exhibition in the museum reflects the modification of the pillars on the exterior of the building in that it was very much a celebration of collectivities—it was making an argument about the nation for the nation that celebrated a nation—that was dedicated to respecting and celebrating difference and distinction rather than sticking to a singular narrative about triumphant whiteness. Opened in the same year that the Tut exhibit started traveling, it was an exhibit that would not require a booklet about why Tut, in Egypt in 1323 BC, was likely European.

A More Perfect Union opened in 1987 as part of the bicentennial celebration of the United States Constitution. This exhibit did a radical thing: it celebrated the Constitution by looking at one of its darkest hours, and it put the struggle for racial justice at the center of the story of who we are in the United States at the national history museum. It was a history of the internment of Japanese Americans during the Second World War. It was told with carefully reconstructed barracks from the camps where Japanese Americans were held from 1942 to 1945. The objects in the exhibition were collected at community centers and in individual homes across the West Coast. They included family photographs, high school diplomas issued by the Bureau of Indian Affairs, which oversaw the bureaucracy of the camps, and elements of the structures of the camps themselves. In 1987, most Americans were not particularly aware of the internment of Japanese Americans during the war, and the exhibition was both startling for those who did not know the story and a bold political move on the part of the museum. It didn't fit anywhere into a narrative of a racialized movement from savagery to civilization because it was explicitly critical of race-based policies and ideologies.

The big image at the entrance to the exhibition was a Dorothea Lange photograph of two very young Japanese American girls dutifully, and hopefully, holding their hands over their hearts as they said the Pledge of Allegiance to the flag in their San Francisco school a few days before they were sent to the camps. (We will come back to this photo in the next chapter.) Curator Tom Crouch told the *Washington Post*, "This is a tough show, we have to let visitors know up front."[20] Museum director Roger Kennedy defended the exhibit, saying, "This is about as unabashedly patriotic a display as you're going to see this year, maybe this decade.... The difference between American culture and most others is we have a long tradition of self-correction, a long tradition that I believe from the beginning distinguished us from tyrannical systems."[21] As a review in the *Public Historian* tellingly concludes, "Although doubts and opposition were voiced at first about this controversial show, the only persistent objections come from a handful of reactionaries who would have us believe that relocation, like the Holocaust, was justified. The evidence proves otherwise. The American public's education in its own history is well served by this exhibit."[22]

Field to Factory also opened in 1987. Like *A More Perfect Union*, it told a story that had not been frequently represented in American museums and certainly had not been represented in a national history museum: the story of the great migration of African Americans in the first part of the twentieth century from the fields of the South to the factories of the North. It included two particularly memorable elements. First, at the entryway to the exhibition, a Klan robe hung just above reach in the middle of the first gallery. It was shocking, and it was shocking that it was shocking. By this, I mean that encountering this explicit weapon of white supremacy inside a museum in a way that was critical of white supremacy—even in the late 1980s—was surprising. This is not to say that visitors would have expected explicit statements of white supremacy in a national museum in the United States in the 1980s, but a direct confrontation with the mechanisms of violence that have maintained white supremacy was a surprise to see in a museum. Visitors felt, somehow, as though the rules were being violated; the unspeakable was being spoken.

The other particularly memorable element was a doorway from a train station that was split between an entryway with a sign above it that read "Whites" and an entryway with a sign above it that read "Colored." This was also shocking. It required visitors to make a choice that was not easy for any visitor. Choosing, whatever your race, to walk through the "Whites" door was in a sense choosing to acknowledge complicity; and choosing to walk through the "Colored" door could have been a gesture of compliance or an ally, or it could have felt like ceding to the power of the racial logic. Neither choice was satisfying; neither choice felt good. The choice was always arresting and required wrestling with every time. (I worked in the museum while this exhibition was up and so had occasion to be in there often, and I never found the choice easy, even when I was busy and preoccupied.) *Field to Factory* was a relatively small exhibition—it took up a tenth of the space of the *Nation of Nations* exhibition—but its impact was profound. Like *A More Perfect Union*, it inspired a generation of young scholars to want to work in museums, and in a sense, it changed the range of possibilities for what could be done in a museum. (It moved the needle from Tut to Till.)

Around this same time, another shift was happening in the federal museum landscape. The Native American Graves Protection and Repatriation Act was enacted. As I have noted, this law requires federal entities or institutions that receive federal funds to return Native American remains and cultural objects to the descendants of those who produced the objects. This was a huge step forward. The act has proved challenging to enforce, but it also powerfully moved the needle from Tut to Till.

A 1995 exhibit about World War II, however, seemed like a step too far from the work that museum had long done, and there was a dramatic backlash. Like the Vietnam Veterans Memorial, less than a mile away on the National Mall, *Field to Factory* also made some people nervous about changes underway in cultural infrastructure in the United States and the implications of those changes. Two years after the opening of *A More Perfect Union* and *Field to Factory*, this World War II exhibit wanted to push (gently) on the boundaries of what was sayable inside a national museum in the United States. Curated by Tom Crouch, who had curated *A More Perfect Union*, this exhibit, titled *Enola Gay*, was to feature the plane that dropped atomic bombs on Hiroshima and Nagasaki. It was intended to explore the technology and, to a much lesser extent, the politics and values connected to that event. Instead, the *Enola Gay* exhibit stirred up a national firestorm: veterans' organizations, politicians, and talk radio jockeys all got in on the action, and there was plenty of outrage to go around. The fundamental problem that those who were outraged had with the exhibition was that it questioned the morality of dropping an atomic bomb on a densely populated city. Such questioning was interpreted in 1995 as an act of disloyalty to the American troops who had served in the Second World War.

The American Legion and Newt Gingrich joined forces to express their outrage at the questioning of American soldiers in World War II, although they didn't actually say much about the dropping of the bomb. They protested the implication that American GIs in the war had not been infallible. In response to the exhibit, Senator Nancy Kassebaum, a respected moderate Republican, introduced a Senate Resolution that railed against any exhibit that might question the heroism of American soldiers in World War II.[23] This is a powerful demonstration of the intensity of feeling about what could be said about that war and heroism—and about what it meant to be an American—in a museum.

Lots has been written about this controversy; what is important to know here is that what was said in the museum seemed to matter to many people and powerful interest groups and that the politics of the curators was untenable for these interest groups. They were able to seriously delay the exhibit's opening and rewrite the story it told. Following quickly on the heels of *Field to Factory* and *A More Perfect Union*, this successful censorship had a significant chilling effect—chilling, but ultimately not entirely successful.

The National Museum of the American Indian (NMAI) is clear evidence of this and of the evolution of the Smithsonian as an institution. The NMAI was created by legislation introduced in 1989, two years after *Field to Factory* and *A More Perfect Union* opened at NMAH, by Senator Daniel Inouye. The museum was built on just about the most high-profile real estate there is in Washington D.C., and it marked a seismic and indelible shift in American museums as cultural infrastructure. It was a dramatic shift toward Till, if you will.

It is on the National Mall, directly across from the East Building of the National Gallery of Art and adjacent on its western side to the Air and Space Museum. It is just down the hill from the Capitol Building. According to the NMAI website, "Since the passage of its enabling legislation in 1989 (amended in 1996), the NMAI has been steadfastly committed to bringing Native voices to what the museum writes and presents....The NMAI is also dedicated to acting as a resource for the hemisphere's Native communities and to serving the greater public as an honest and thoughtful conduit to Native cultures—present and past—in all their richness, depth, and diversity."[24] The enabling legislation promised to create an institution with an unparalleled capacity to tell the story of native people: to create "a living memorial to Native Americans and their traditions."[25] It also promised to return human remains, sacred objects, and illegally "collected" objects to the indigenous communities from which they came. (It is a rare museum that starts with returning objects—think *Black Panther*.) It is the first national museum in the United States devoted to Indigenous Americans, and its design works hard to make a series of compelling points about museums and Indigenous people.

Dedicated in 2004, the building is designed to express a set of ideas that likely could not be expressed with the architectural vocabulary of official Washington. The building's design is not a violent rejection of the neoclassical, but it's not a subtle subversion of it, either. It is a very, very high-profile suggestion that there is a different way to understand culture, museums, who we are as a nation, and what authority is and can look like. I know this is an awful lot for the exterior design of one building to do, but NMAI is located amid a sea of the neoclassical. It was designed by native architects in a dialogic process that involved consultation with the Blackfoot, Cherokee/Choctaw, Oneida, and Hopi Nations. It is not angular, and it is not uniform. It is curvilinear and designed to look windswept—as if it was made by natural forces over a very long time. It is made to look a little like Navajo dwellings carved into hillsides. Maybe the most interesting thing about it, in relation to the neoclassical architecture surrounding it, is that it doesn't cede power—it offers a suggestion of power coming from a different place.

Inside, the museum was designed to be something other than the typical museum. It "was meant to 'museum different,'" as the founding director, Rick West, often asserted. And everything from the design of the building (a striking architectural achievement with organic, undulating walls that contrast with the neoclassical and brutalist structures that surround it), to the curvilinear layout of the exhibit halls, to the community-based curatorial methodology used for the three initial permanent galleries ("Our Universes," "Our Peoples," "Our Lives") typified the "museum different" vision. As historian C. Joseph Genetin-Pilawa writes, the curators had an "expansive vision," and "the NMAI mission also charged the museum to be a center for learning and cultural expression, a space for the living communities whose ancestors created the things displayed throughout."[26] Without even delving into the complexity of how this has played out—sometimes brilliantly—in the interior space and the collections, it is easy to see that the NMAI makes a profound statement about museums as racial cultural infrastructure. And, importantly, it does not reject the museum as a tool; it just sets about reimagining the uses to which that tool is put. (It made a start in the process of museums making themselves unrecognizable.)

In 2004, the Smithsonian also tacked back hard toward Tut. *The Price of Freedom* opened at the National Museum of American History. It is explicitly part of the pushback against new frameworks for thinking about museums. It is a massive exhibition, probably the most significant exhibit undertaken in the museum since the *Nation of Nations* exhibit, and it is a response to the political turn in the museum that produced *A More Perfect Union* and *Field to Factory*. It is a corrective for those exhibits in the way that the World War II Memorial and the Korean War Memorial are correctives to the Vietnam Veterans Memorial. *The Price of Freedom: Americans at War* is a very thinly veiled effort to restore certain logics and power dynamics to the museum. It is a sprawling exhibition on the history of American wars. It is fascinating in that it is never historically inaccurate in the details yet is able to tell a story that is fundamentally untrue. The title of the exhibit and its fundamental logics and organization did not come from the curatorial staff at the museum as those of *A More Perfect Union* and *Field to Factory* had. Rather, they came from a single donor who gave $80 million to be able to restore the museum to the kind of patriotic institution that he thought a national historical museum should be. His name was Kenneth Behring, and the whole museum now bears his name. His generous donation, enabled by his success as a mall developer, was not simply a gift given in the name of education or "the increase and diffusion of knowledge." Like people such as J.P. Morgan and other museum founders of the first golden age of museums in the United States, Behring donated a portion of his fortune to the museum so that he would be able to determine the kind of story it told about who we are in the United States, who we have been, and, crucially, who belongs and who doesn't. Behring was emphatic about his demands of the museum and this exhibition in particular, and despite the fact that he did not fully make good on his financial promises, he got what he wanted, at least with *The Price of Freedom*.[27]

War, in the exhibit's title and at every turn throughout the exhibit, is conflated with the noble pursuit of "freedom." The exhibit is driven by a blind and sweeping narrative that connects the Indian Wars to the Vietnam War to the "conflict" in Iraq and all wars in between to an ill-defined idea of "freedom." (Only occasionally—in reference to the Second World War, for example—is the relationship between a war and the idea of freedom made explicit.) The exhibit is able to do this because it holds a tight focus, literally and rhetorically, on the faces of the fighting men and (occasionally) women in these wars. "The heart of the story," the exhibit text tells us, "is the impact of the war on citizen soldiers." And while millions across the globe might disagree, *The Price of Freedom* uses the trope of the common fighting man (the beloved GI, the individual sacrificing for the greater good) to whitewash the costs and the consequences of "America's wars." (The same story was being played out on the war memorials on the Mall in this period.) The exhibit uses this soldier to justify and romanticize the wars the United States has fought and is fighting regardless of what they actually did in the world. The celebration of the citizen-soldier trumps, in the exhibit and for the kids on their way to buy dog tags in the gift shop, the terms that have compelled citizens to fight, the deeply racialized politics of many of these wars, and the compound objectives of the various wars. It is hard to deny that this exhibit marked a return to the racial logics of an earlier era, but the story was nowhere near over at NMAH. (Think of the bullet riddled Till sign.)

The National Museum of African American History and Culture (NMAAHC) was making its long journey to a site on the National Mall as the National Museum of American History was doubling down on this old model and its work as racial cultural infrastructure in the United States. The NMAAHC building was dedicated and opened in 2016, but the fight to build it, to carve out a place on the National Mall to tell a national story of the place of African American history and culture in the history of the United States, goes back at least forty years. In the 1980s and 1990s, various pieces of legislation were introduced to support the building of a national African American museum, and various strategies were used by elected officials who were quite explicit about their desire to avoid creating such an institution. In the early 1990s, for instance, the House passed a bill in support of the museum, but Senator Jesse Helms successfully blocked a Senate vote on the bill, effectively killing it. Helms blocked the legislation because "the Smithsonian already has two related museums—the Anacostia Museum and the African Art Museum"[28] The reference to the Anacostia Museum does make a little sense, although he clearly failed to see that it was a local museum that was part of the Smithsonian and that the push was for a national museum that did not exist. But the reference to the African Art Museum reveals a telling level of ignorance and willingness to state the ridiculous in public. A United States senator could not distinguish between a museum dedicated to art produced by *African* people and a museum dedicated to the history and culture of *African American* people? Really? He also expressed concern about the possible involvement of "the Nation of Islam and other radical 'black separatist' groups."[29] So, in Helms's mind, we already had museums with the word *African* in their titles, and another one was not worth the risk of the ideas—about race and national belonging—that it might include.

In 2001, two decades into the struggle to build a museum on the Mall, Representative John Lewis managed to finally get the legislation passed, and a new phase of work on the museum began. In 2005, founding director Lonnie Bunch, now the fourteenth secretary of the Smithsonian Institution, was hired. Bunch, who credits the work of his fellow curator Spencer Crew on *Field to Factory* as a source of inspiration for shaping the museum, was well into a celebrated career in museums and knew as well as anyone the terrain he had to navigate.[30] Everything about the design and the execution of the museum, from the development of the collections to the architecture of the building, was thoughtfully structured to emphatically respond to the conversations and tensions in the history of museums in the United States. There is a huge amount to be said and written about this new museum. Some of that work has begun, and much more will come in the future. For the purposes of my arguments here, there are two particularly useful points to take up. The first involves the exterior architecture of the building, and the second involves the collection and display of Emmett Till's casket.

Architect David Adjaye, working with Bunch and the museum's board, developed a stunning and pointed design for the building. It is museum architecture that has something important to say about the long reign of the neoclassical and the message it has conveyed. On the National Mall, sandwiched between the National Museum of American History with its pseudo neoclassical facade, the Washington Monument, the Lincoln Memorial, and the White House, the National African American Museum of History and Culture could hardly be in a more freighted symbolic space, and it could hardly be more surrounded by high-stakes neoclassical architecture. Adjaye and Bunch responded to this site with a museum that is not white, does not have pillars, does not have grand stone steps leading into dramatically oversized front doors. It is bronze-clad and three-tiered. As the museum website describes it,

> From one perspective, the building's architecture follows classical Greco-Roman form in its use of a base and shaft, topped by a capital or corona. For our Museum, the corona is inspired by the three-tiered crowns used in Yoruban art from West Africa. Moreover, the building's

FIGURE 8   The National Museum of African American History and Culture

main entrance is a welcoming porch, which has architectural roots in Africa and throughout the African Diaspora, especially the American South and Caribbean. Finally, by wrapping the entire building in an ornamental bronze-colored metal lattice, Adjaye pays homage to the intricate ironwork crafted by enslaved African Americans in Louisiana, South Carolina, and elsewhere.[31]

In other words, it is almost a close-up of the top of a classical column, shown in detail to reveal the craftsmanship of people of African descent in the United States, *and* a gesture to Yoruba artistic tradition, all rolled into one. But you don't need to know this to get a profound hit of meaning from the building. The dark metalwork and the unfamiliar shape of the building do a great deal of work very quickly. They convey that this is not business as usual and that there is more than one kind of authority. They promise to revise how a museum might operate as cultural infrastructure. (See Figure 8.)

The other element of the museum that is crucial for this story is the casket of Emmett Till. This is the endpoint of the "Tut to Till" narrative for museums in the United States in this second golden age. This narrative, I have argued, shows uneven and inconsistent change. It moves from a moment in which the Metropolitan Museum of Art would issue a booklet explaining, with a strange awkwardness, that people in Egypt were likely European, to a moment in which the casket of a young man, murdered fifty years before George Floyd, becomes an important touchstone for a national museum.

Museum Director Lonnie Bunch knew that Till's mother, Mamie Mobley, very much wanted to keep the memory of her son alive—for all Americans. When Bunch learned that the casket in which Till was first buried was stored in a shed with raccoons, he worked with Till's family to bring it to the new museum. And while putting any casket on display in a museum—even Tut's—is complicated, exhibiting the Till casket was freighted but not terribly fraught. This is because it had been so important to Mobley, in 1955, for people to see what had happened to her son. She wanted an open casket, and she wanted his brutalized face to be seen. She wanted people to see what had happened to her child—to see what the maintenance of white supremacy actually looks like. While it is very carefully displayed, and there are nearly always lines to view it, putting Till's casket on the Mall was a radical gesture in the history of rethinking museums. It not only makes ignoring the long, brutal history of white supremacy more, rather than less, difficult, but it also uses the authority of cultural infrastructure to make a new argument about who we are and who we have been.

James Madison's plantation, Montpelier, was being transformed as the NMAI and the NMAAHC were being built. It is a compelling site for serious transformations that were happening at museums and historic sites beyond the Smithsonian. It could do this work in part because it is a plantation with an unusual history. While the plantations of other former United States presidents had been kept in their families or rescued by ladies' organizations in the nineteenth century, James Madison's plantation was sold to the DuPont family, who made their fortune on gunpowder and chemicals. The DuPonts held onto the plantation into the 1980s. At the request of Marion DuPont, upon her death in 1983, the plantation was transferred to the National Trust for Historic Preservation. A few years later, The National Trust established, with $10 million from Marion DuPont, a foundation to restore and care for Montpelier going forward. This is worth noting because it created a different perspective for imagining and developing a plantation site for twentieth and twenty-first century viewers. In other words, unlike Mount Vernon, Montpelier was never controlled by patriotic ladies' associations and didn't experience the same long-sustained effort to suppress the memory of slavery at the site. This has made Montpelier a fascinating example of how to rethink the historic site and reimagine historic sites of cultural infrastructure that do not convey the same ideas about race that the other plantation sites work so hard to convey. Curators and the leadership at Montpelier have worked very carefully over a long period of time with descendant communities of the one hundred people who were enslaved there. Their dialogic relationship with these descendants and their investment in trying to understand how to make the historic site a place that had meaning for them and that included the stories of their ancestors as foundational to the stories of the plantation is quite remarkable.

In 2021, Montpelier was on the verge of doing something no other institution has done. It is not just consulting with descendants: it is being run by descendants. The institution agreed to a proposal from descendants requesting co-equal leadership. The board reversed this decision in March of 2022, but by May 2022 they had elected eleven new members, creating parity between descendants and others on the board. (This is a long way from a once a day slavery tour at Mount Vernon.)

This site deserves much more space than it can have here. But one effort on the part of the leadership at Montpelier to reimagine the museum offers a powerful, indelible story—little fingerprints in the bricks—about what it looks like to reimagine sites that have been places for the articulation of white supremacist logic for a very long time.

Part of the work that the folks at Montpelier took up from the beginning was an effort to excavate the site where the slaves' quarters had stood and find whatever evidence they could of the experience of the people enslaved there. They quickly found bricks made by slaves on the plantation, including lots of chips or broken bits of bricks, and they observed that many of these bricks contained fingerprints. On the plantation, eight- or nine-year-old boys were the brickmakers, and therefore the small fingerprints on the bricks they found around the plantation were a particularly visceral kind of evidence. The folks at Montpelier wanted to include these children in the story of the place. They commissioned a mosaic titled *E Pluribus Unum*, which depicts an African American child, composed of chips of these bricks. (See Figure 9.)

FIGURE 9 *E Pluribus Unum* by Rebecca Warde

Kat Imhoff, Montpelier's president, explains, "As a cultural institution engaged in the interpretation of slavery, we must have a more holistic conversation about freedom, equality and justice." She goes on, "Without understanding slavery and its resulting impacts, we do not understand the true roots of the establishment of our country. An essential part of understanding slavery and its legacy was engaging the descendants of the enslaved people here at Montpelier to help us interpret slavery in its most real terms."[32] The fingerprints in the bricks are pretty real. (They are a big move toward Till.)

E Pluribus Unum is a remarkable work of art. It is also a fantastic, painful metaphor for thinking about museums in this period. The mosaic literally uses the imprints these laboring children made on the buildings to represent their presence there. Still, the child represented looks distinctly wary. For good reason.

So, the basic principles for understanding the cultural work that museums and historic sites do, in broad terms, emerged pretty clearly in this second golden age. First, *they are powerful*: museums continued to take up significant civic space, and advocates for all kinds of museums fought hard for more of this civic space. Second, *they have been built and run by powerful people with big ideas to express*: Congress, the American Legion, and powerful donors stepped up to censor exhibits that they did not like, and Nixon and Kissinger threw their muscle behind exhibits they *did* like. Third, *architecture matters*: the design of the National Museum of the American Indian inspired the design of the National Museum of African American History and Culture, which may have inspired the "Making Federal Buildings Beautiful Again" executive order. Fourth, *they are doing their best work when they seem to fit seamlessly into the landscape; when they stop being noticeable, their job is done*: if you don't notice that it is odd for the Met to want to make it clear that Tut was not Black, racist cultural infrastructure is working. And when the Yoruba- and Greek-inspired National Museum of African American History and Culture building no longer feels like a disruption in the sea of neoclassical buildings in Washington, it will have succeeded. Fifth, *they are not neutral. Ever*: meticulously restoring Montpelier and the wariness of the child in the mosaic of brick fingerprints is a good shorthand for this. And sixth, *museums have used a few basic and familiar conventions to make their points*: for instance, they naturalize, in art and science and history, a progression from savagery to civilization by repeating it with quiet but weighty authority—and upending this narrative has proved to be an enormous undertaking.

These principles, as they played out, make answering the key questions about them pretty straightforward.

1. When was it built? If it was founded between 1965 and 2020, we know that it was part of the fraught second golden age of American museums and was likely driven by either Tut or Till impulses.
2. By whom was it built? In this period, it was either the work of ambitious, wealthy industrialists interested in public education, tax breaks, and self-aggrandizement *or* African American, Chinese

American, Native American (and, later, Japanese American, Latino, and Arab American) civic associations and local community organizations.

3. What does it look like? The architectural vocabulary of museums in this period both repeated the neoclassical, out-sized, stone, pillared authority of the early period and tried to, sometimes literally, turn it on its head.

4. How is it organized? Most museums in this period were more narratively explicit, if still pretty bound to conveying confidence about their authority with big, definitive gestures.

5. How has its point of view been sustained, and how has it been challenged? These are big questions with relatively easy answers. Their point of view has been sustained by repetition, longevity, and the power of the authority they express. (Think of the investment in King Tut from the days of *Downton Abbey* into the Nixon Administration.) This perspective has been challenged for decades by scholars, activists, and people working in museums. And, again, while it may seem strange to add his name to the pantheon of museum history—Peale, Goode, Frick, Mellon, J. P. Morgan— George Floyd has opened up new space for a bigger conversation about how to challenge this authority.

THE SUMMER OF 2020

The summer of 2020 stirred up conversations in every kind of museum, either coming from the museum or being pushed by outside forces about complicity in the project of white supremacy in response to the Black Lives Matter movement and the murder of George Floyd. The conversations were often about diversifying staff and collections—both important, but neither enough. Understanding how museums operate as racist cultural infrastructure requires moving well beyond diversifying. Scholars Silvia Domínguez, Simón E. Weffer, and David G. Embrick suggest that "Museums, as colonized projects, are one example of White sanctuaries. Although many nationally recognized museums serve the purpose of reinforcing White supremacy, not all of these White sanctuaries operate in the same way. Sociohistorical context matters. Thus, museums, as White sanctuaries, are created, curated, and maintained in ways that are dependent on the racial histories of place, over time."[33] They see museums as spaces in which "White lives are considered to be more valuable than their non-White counterparts. White logics, rationales, and intellect are considered to be more superior compared with non-Whites." They argue that "within White dominated spaces there are White sanctuaries, or specifically safe white spaces that allow Whites to reaffirm their dominant position in society," and they conclude that museums are "refuges for Whites who feel threatened by the (real or imagined) perception that Whites are becoming the minority and will soon lose their heritage, culture, or even status in society."[34] They also conclude that "museums, as White sanctuaries, are created, curated, and maintained in ways that are dependent on the racial histories of place, over time."[35] They are not wrong, even if their rhetoric is pitched pretty high.

Curator and critic Maurice Berger created something of a stir in the art world thirty years ago when he published an article titled, "Are Art Museums Racist?" But really, the question could hardly have come as a surprise—then or now.[36] Two years after Berger's stir, noted psychiatrist Robert Coles published a moving account of how Black children respond to museum field trips, entitled, "Whose Museum?" that also stirred a lot of conversation. In a way, what is surprising is that either article could have surprised anyone. (Think *Black Panther*.) "Who are the patrons of art, the museum board members, the collectors?" Coles asked. "Who is the audience for high culture? Who is allowed to interpret culture? Who is asked to make fundamental policy decisions? Who sets the priorities? Is the art world merely mirroring social changes or can art institutions actually play a role in challenging the conditions of institutional racism in America?"[37] We are still asking Berger's and Coles' questions but the work that museums are doing is also undeniably changing.

So while the idea of the museum as a "white sanctuary" might seem a little overwrought, the history we have walked through here demonstrates both that the boy in the mosaic still has reason to be wary and also that the white sanctuary might not be the future of museums. (Think the Till sign next to the flag. It hurts that we have reason to celebrate this brutal object of violence nearly 70 years after Till's death, but that is where we are and we should celebrate it. Also, Kenneth Behring's name is coming off our national history museum in 2027.)

SECTION III

PATRIOTIC PRACTICES

THE FIRST THING YOU are likely to notice about Dorothea Lange's 1942 photograph of kids at Raphael Weill Public School in San Francisco is just how cute these girls are. In their sweet faces is a funny mix of serious business and play. Certainly, whatever they are up to, they are into it. Smiling. Heads thrown back. The second, immediate thing that is likely to strike viewers is that these girls are taking part in a familiar American cultural ritual. Most people in the United States will quickly recognize that they are saying the Pledge of Allegiance to the flag. A little more information about the photograph complicates it in ways that make it a useful starting point for a conversation about patriotic practices in the United States—not only as elements of American cultural infrastructure but also as elements of racist cultural infrastructure. (And, again, naming these practices as racist is not intended to be hyperbolic or dramatic and totalizing. It is intended to be part of an earnest effort to understand how painful structures of inequity have been maintained across time by people who find such joy in the idea of "liberty and justice for all.") (See Figure 10.)

Remember that this book is shaped by a few basic observations. The first is that it takes a tremendous amount of work to make the patently untrue seem natural. (The proud assertion that the United States is "the land of the free" despite all of the active mechanisms of inequality, for

FIGURE 10   San Francisco, California, April 1942. Children of the
Raphael Weill Public School

instance.) The second is that cultural infrastructures are powerful tools.
(The same people who describe the practice of standing and saluting for
the national anthem as benign will go to *extraordinary* lengths to prevent
any variation in the practice.) The third is that all infrastructure is cultural.
(It is made by people who have a point to make.) The fourth observation
builds on these. It is that we are surrounded by cultural objects and practices that don't necessarily seem to have anything to do with race but that
work every day to tell us who we are; and, crucially, much of this telling,
in the infrastructure that is obviously cultural and the infrastructure that
is less obviously cultural, has been about racial hierarchies and has been
stunningly effective in maintaining structures of inequity. As our explo-
rations of memorials and museums have revealed, cultural infrastructure
does not have to be explicitly racist, or even specifically about race, to be
actively doing the work of maintaining structures of inequity.

The Pledge these girls are saying is certainly not an explicit racist
statement. On the contrary, it is a statement about liberty and justice for

all. It gives every generous heart a reason to soar—look at their faces! (I bet even the most cynical or angry American can recall a bit of that happy, aspirational feeling.) But a little more information about this photograph begins to reveal some of the ways in which the Pledge and the context in which the girls in the center, Mary Ann Yahiro and Helene Nakamoto, are saying it are more complicated.

This photograph was taken by Lange in April 1942 at a public school on O'Farrell Street in San Francisco. In December 1941, the Japanese had attacked Pearl Harbor, and the United States had entered World War II. In February 1942, President Franklin Roosevelt had issued Executive Order 9066 requiring Japanese Americans to be removed from their homes and sent to live in internment camps for the duration of the war. Lange took the photograph as part of her work for the War Relocation Authority, the government entity created to carry out the order. She was hired to document the process, just as she had been hired by the US government to document conditions of rural poverty during the Depression. When she visited the Raphael Weill School in April, the diversity of the kids she encountered was striking. By the end of May 1942, all of the Japanese American children had been relocated to camps—many of them to "converted horse stalls at Tanforan Race Track in San Mateo County."[1]

Immediately and obviously, there is something heartbreaking about these girls throwing themselves into the Pledge to the flag that stood for liberty and justice just a few days before they were rounded up and locked in camps for three years. But that isn't what makes this photograph a useful place to start thinking about patriotic practices as racist cultural infrastructure. (The context of the internment just functions to heighten the stakes for the story.)

What makes this photograph of these girls saying the Pledge useful is that it demonstrates the successes of a long-term, multifaceted effort to create and normalize rituals of American citizenship, what I am calling *patriotic practices*, that have always had mixed impulses and have often participated in the creation and maintenance of structures of inequity. There are complicated questions about intent in the stories of all the elements of patriotic rituals in the United States, but it is hard to tell the stories, hard to understand the history, without seeing the powerful through-line of the development of patriotic practices as tools for creating and maintaining social order—a particular kind of social order—that has almost always been linked in some way to thinking about race and the maintenance of racial hierarchy.

And again, to avoid sounding overwrought, cultural practices that work to maintain social order are not necessarily a bad thing. They are essential for a functioning society. A feeling of shared investment, or a spiritual principle or an imagined community, if you will, is crucial for the functioning of a nation. And as we have seen, something has to be invented to be shared—to be made to seem eternal and like a natural result of "the progress of man." So, what we need to track is *what* is made to seem natural and eternal and the impact it has had—and continues to have. The history of the development of these practices in the United States is usefully revealing on this point, and it is not, as we will see here, a one-note story or an overly simple history. It is a complicated, heartbreaking mix of the aspirational and an insistent investment in particular, race-based hierarchies. (Think of the joy on the faces of the little girls at the Raphael Weill School. The Pledge of Allegiance was not written to crush them, but it is part of a system that enabled their confinement.)

Patriotic practices, broadly defined, include songs, holidays, remembrances of soldiers, and, most fervently, all kinds of practices related to the flag—flying the flag, treatment of the flag, saluting the flag, and pledging allegiance to the flag. For the purpose of this book, I will focus here on the *practices*—songs, events, rules, and expectations—related to the flag. The flag is a useful focus because while there are many disparate kinds of patriotic practices, they nearly all have some relationship to the flag.

A quick working definition of *patriotism* is helpful here, too. As Brookings Institute political scientist Walter Galston defines it, *"Patriotism* denotes a special attachment to a particular political community, although not necessarily to its existing form of government. *Nationalism*, with which patriotism is often confused, stands for a very different phenomenon—the fusion, actual or aspirational, between shared ethnicity and state sovereignty. The nation-state, then, is a community in which an ethnic group is politically dominant and sets the terms of communal life."[2] This makes a decent start, but it is too easy in its separation of patriotism and nationalism. While Galston is right that patriotism is about something beyond the particulars of government, it is not distinct, as we shall see, from the fusion of ethnicity and the idea of the state. And, as his final idea here suggests, in the United States, the "nation-state," the idea of the nation to which people connect, is indeed "a community in which an ethnic group is politically dominant and sets the terms of communal life." Patriotic practices are one important way the politically dominant in the United States have, and continue to, "set the terms of communal life."

It is also important to note here, again, that these practices are, indeed, blunt instruments—they are not subtle, but they are also not always the inventions of rabid and explicitly racist patriots. Their success relies on a long game and a requirement of fealty, loyalty.

The girls in the photograph are reciting a pledge, written by a Christian socialist in 1892, to a flag, the design of which was inspired by the seventeenth-century flag of the East India Trading Company, at a public school, intended to instill in them "a sense of duty toward their society and the state."[3] They are enacting "terms of communal life" that have a hodge-podge history in a moment of intense fear and patriotism, and they are about to learn in the most visceral terms that the family defined by the *patri* does not necessarily include them. This seemingly fragmentary history of practices functions quite powerfully to "set the terms of communal life."

PATRIOTIC PRACTICES BASICS

A few basic principles, to build on this heightened moment and these fragmentary practices, will make understanding patriotic practices easy. First, *they are powerful.* Second, *they are doing their best work when they seem to fit seamlessly into the landscape; when they stop being noticeable, their job is done.* Third, *they were developed by people who felt strongly that they had something very important to say.* Fourth, *they are not neutral. Ever.* Fifth, *they are usually inspired by anxiety, not the confidence their soaring lyrics and rigorous practice might seem to project; they always come from an unsettled moment.* And, sixth, *they use a few basic and familiar conventions to make their points.*

Each of these principles deserves a little fleshing out.

First, they are powerful. This seems like it hardly needs elaboration. Lange's photograph is sweet without the context and then powerful when the betrayal of the willingness of these girls to give themselves to the Pledge is revealed by the context. The power of the photograph is in its pathos; it hurts because it reveals the potency of the Pledge. The girls are caught in a moment of being swept up in the pleasure of a swelling feeling of collectivity in a practice that was designed, in part, to produce a social order in which they were seen, as the children of immigrants and as children who are not white, as something of a threat. (It gets even more powerful when you learn that Mary Ann Yahiro was separated from her mother in the confusion of the relocation and didn't see her again "until she was lying in a casket, after dying in camp at age 51."[4]) And, of course, the story of Colin Kaepernick is where this book began. His decision to kneel rather than stand during the playing of the national anthem has successfully set the culture on fire; his rejection of the "set terms of communal life" demonstrated, in the most vivid terms, the power of these practices. If they didn't really, really, really matter, no one would have cared what Kaepernick was doing on the sidelines at a preseason game.

Second, they are doing their best work when they seem to fit seamlessly into the landscape; when they stop being noticeable, their job is done. Like most rituals, rituals of citizenship are intended to naturalize what is not necessarily natural. Kaepernick created such a stir because he called attention to something that was not supposed to be noticed. His refusal to participate revealed a mechanism that was intended to go unnoticed: the requirement of fealty. The problem was that he called out the mechanism. He insisted that he could not honor the flag when the violence of inequity was still so alive in the culture: that he couldn't keep participating as if everything was okay, as if the aspirations of the anthem and the flag matched the world he lived in when they did not. When historian Wilfred McClay writes, in *National Affairs*, "There is a naturalness to patriotism, reflecting a healthy love for what is one's own, gratitude for what one has been given, and reverence for the sources of one's being," he is describing just what patriotic practices hope to achieve—naturalness and a sense of inevitability.[5] When McClay continues, "Such dispositions are more visceral than intellectual, being grounded in our natures and the basic facts of our natality," he doubles down on the value of both the "innate" and the natural, biological nature of patriotism. It comes, in his understanding, from birth. When he goes on, "Yet their power is no less for that, and they are denied only at great cost. A disposition toward gratitude nourishes the roots of our most important moral sentiments," he underscores all of the above—roots that will only be denied at great cost. But even the most cursory look at the history of a practice like the Pledge reveals the extent to which the "natural" narrative is patently false.

Even before Franklin Roosevelt signed the 1942 "Flag Code" law that mandated it, the saying of the Pledge in schools had a long legal history including the first of many hearings before the Supreme Court of the United States. These very public and deeply fraught legal battles reveal a lot—but mostly, they reveal that "a naturalness to patriotism" is a fiction.

Third, they were developed by people who felt strongly that they had something very important to say. The Pledge of Allegiance was written at the end of the nineteenth century for school children in Chicago at the Chicago World's Fair of 1893 who were being instructed in the celebration of the quadricentennial of Columbus's discovery of America. It was, in part, a marketing scheme to sell more flags to schools and sell more copies of the magazine *The Youth's Companion*. The editors of the magazine commissioned educator Francis Bellamy to write the Pledge in a moment when big waves of immigration, migration to cities, and expanding public schools created anxiety about what it meant to be American, and a resultant "Americanization" movement sought to use schools to define and enforce particular ideas about who was included. Most of the people forging the public practices mandated in the schools were not Julian Carrs, people publicly delighting in the pleasures of publicly whipping a Black woman. They were people like Francis Bellamy, who understood themselves to be patriots and who were worried, to varying degrees, about being overrun by foreign elements. (They were slowly simmering as opposed to frothing at the mouth.) But they still had business to attend to, an idea of who people in the United States were and what the terms of communal life should be. In 1942, some of the concerns of the folks in Chicago were still alive, as they continue to be today. But they also held new meanings. In the first year of the war, patriotic spirits ran high—they did not need to be inflamed, but their terms needed to be clarified in a way that was cruel for these beautiful little girls.

President Trump's 1776 Commission, established by executive order, sought to do something similar: to use public schools to instill a particular form of patriotism. His order was a response to a report he commissioned, which concluded that "identity politics, and its influence on history studies, [foster] resentment by trying to divide people into separate, protected classes based on race and other characteristics."[6] As *Education Week* reports, the 1776 report contends that "schools and others who have roles to play in sharing the nation's history should focus on providing a 'patriotic education' that celebrates America's ideals, its progress, and what unites its citizens, even as people are taught about the nation's flaws and mistakes. That will help lead to a restoration of American education and a 'national renewal.'"[7] *Education Week* continues, "The 1776 Commission's report blames a variety of factors and actors for what it says is the degradation of historical studies, including the 1619 Project, a *New York Times Magazine* collection of essays about the influence of slavery on America, and what it calls the 'anti-American' attitude of many in academia."[8] President Biden didn't waste time reversing this order; he did it on the second day of his term. However, we can't but conclude that the teaching of patriotism and the practices that this includes still really matter, because powerful parties still have something important to say about them.

Fourth, they are not neutral. Ever. As the investment of both Trump and Biden in the stakes of the 1776 Commission report reveals, neutrality isn't part of the story of patriotic practices. Both Trump and Biden have serious investments in shaping patriotic practices. If they were neutral, there would be no interest in them. This almost feels too obvious to bother stating; but it needs to be said because part of the magic of these practices is that they work so hard to be "natural" and "neutral" and "natal" and "inevitable" that it takes a little work to see them as something else. Before Kaepernick's modest-but-wildly-provocative protest, it might have seemed incongruous to find a history of the national anthem on the National Basketball Association's official website. It certainly would have seemed strange to find an article titled "National anthem is inseparable from politics: History shows how Francis Scott Key's poem from 1814 is inherently political." But as this 2018 post points out, correctly, the poem that became the anthem had a stanza that is not much sung now that goes like this: "No refuge could save the hireling and slave / From the terror of flight or the gloom of the grave, / And the star-spangled banner in triumph doth wave / O'er the land of the free and the home of the brave." Key was likely expressing frustration at the slaves who chose the freedom offered to them by the British for their service in the War of 1812 and "hireling" could well have been a reference to Indigenous soldiers fighting for the crown. This was personal for Key, who held slaves and whose wife's family's wealth was built on slaveholding. And while this stanza has largely been dropped from the anthem since it was officially adopted in 1931, it is not unimportant. In a way, it's just another example of what historians find to be a truism of American history: almost everywhere you look in the American past, you find racial thinking, if not Julian Carr–style racism. (Although it is worth noting that Key is getting close to Carr here—threatening the lives of people fighting for their release from enslavement.) But certainly, this stanza embodies the contradictions that historians also find everywhere. The same poem that has been so passionately repeated as the ultimate expression of the aspirations of American freedom was originally written, in part, to threaten Black and brown people who chose freedom. The very idea of the land of the free that most of us have sung about at some time or another, with full hearts, was predicated on a violent denial of freedom and, worse, a racial logic that enabled the two ideas to occupy the same stanza without seeming contradictory to Key. (Think of the girls in the Lange photograph.) Putting aside the fact that we chose as our national anthem a song about war that is a call to arms, we also chose a song that specifically calls out enslaved people for punishment—"terror of flight or the gloom of the grave"—for choosing their freedom, *and* one that celebrates "the land of the free and the home of the brave." Certainly there is nothing neutral about this. In a sense, Key wrote into the anthem itself the contradiction in US national culture that so frustrated Kaepernick—it is all right there and plain as day. As the NBA.com post concludes, "Didn't mean to go all history professor tweed jacket on y'all. I'm just trying to make a point. The anthem itself is political. So was the man who wrote it."[9] Even after Kaepernick, this writer felt it was necessary to state the very obvious: that the anthem is political. This is certainly potent evidence that these practices are not neutral. Ever.

Fifth, they are usually inspired by anxiety, not the confidence their soaring lyrics and rigorous practice might seem to project; they always come from an unsettled moment. We didn't have an official national anthem in the United States until 1931—more than 150 years into national life. And why did we finally adopt an official anthem in 1931? Because when we were going to hell in a handbasket—2,294 banks failed, losing $1.7 billion in deposits; 28,285 businesses failed; unemployment rose to 16 percent; and the US nominal GDP fell by more than 8 percent for the third consecutive year—more mechanisms of social cohesion, more clear "terms for communal life," suddenly seemed like a very good idea. If Bellamy and the editors at *The Youth's Companion* and the hundreds of public school administrators since had been confident in the naturalness of patriotism, they wouldn't have bothered with the Pledge. Nature, it would seem, has always needed a good deal of assistance.

And, finally, sixth, these practices use a few basic and familiar conventions to make their points. These conventions are different from the ones we have encountered so far in this book because they are not buildings or structures. They are less physical but equally present and consequential forms of cultural infrastructure. They are ubiquitous. And the conventions that they share are pretty straightforward. They are very often connected to schools; they are very often connected to the flag; and they are very often produced by citizens' organizations and then eventually mandated in one way or another by the state, local, or federal government. As the timeline ahead will demonstrate, these practices were developed in a fairly consistent manner. They were mostly, originally, the work of patriotic organizations formed around the turn of the nineteenth century, and they were, mostly, later taken up by the federal government, which has become increasingly involved in setting the "terms for communal life."

Taken together, these principles make the work of understanding patriotic practices relatively straightforward. They set up a clear set of questions to ask of any patriotic practice: (1) When was it introduced as a practice? (2) By whom was it introduced? (3) What was unsettled about the time in which it was made? (4) What point did the instigators want to make? (5) How, in what forms, did they try to make their point? (A song? A school requirement?) (6) And, finally, what happened to the practice in the summer of 2020? (Has there been any pushback?)

Because the first question, "When was the practice introduced?" is so key, a timeline for the development of patriotic practices in the United States is a crucial tool. And while this timeline does not try to be absolute or definitive, it is possible to characterize the impulses that drove the development of patriotic practices in a given period, and these characterizations can offer a very useful shorthand for understanding the work that a given practice was intended to do.

The two chapters in this section take up key periods in the building of patriotic practices as follows. Chapter Five takes up the periods 1776–1865 and 1866–1916, and Chapter Six takes up the periods 1917–1976 and 2001–2021. 1776–1865 was the first century of American life before the Civil War, during which there was a struggle to figure out what an American patriotic culture might be. 1866–1916 was the post-war period in which there was a struggle to find a collective sense of national identity after the Civil War and to respond to huge waves of immigration. 1917–1976 was a period when patriotic practices went from being somewhat idiosyncratic, ground-up, and citizen-led to being federally mandated; and 2001–2021 was a period of intense post-9/11 patriotism and war and reckoning.

5

ALLEGIANCE GOT PLEDGED

1776–1865: A FRAUGHT BEGINNING

1776–1865, the first century of American life, was a period during which there was a serious struggle to figure out what an American patriotic culture might be, a period of what historian Cecilia O'Leary has called "embryonic cultural nationalism."[1] Remember that people in the United States at this time were *creating* a nation and a *concept of national unity*, or cohesion, from whole cloth. They had little history and few symbols to work with. Early on, especially, they were much more likely to identify with their state than with the idea of the nation. Thomas Paine is typically referred to as one of the first to articulate and try to activate a particularly American sense of identity—and he worried both that "the Continental belt is too loosely buckled" and about "the force of local prejudice."[2]

Historian Phil Deloria has deftly demonstrated that participants in the Boston Tea Party, certainly an early moment of colonists distinguishing themselves from the British, struggled to figure out the right symbolic vocabulary with which to make their emergent American point. And they landed on, consequentially and logically, dressing up like Indians as a way to create an identity that was distinct from the British traditions, which also involved dressing up, that they hoped to be rejecting. This impulse, one strand of the helix of American cultural DNA, has been potent and insistent and durable. It has not only continued in many different forms as a practice but also successfully made racial thinking inextricably bound to American patriotism. Playing Indian wasn't really about Indigenous people. (Think of the problem of inauthentic Indians at the centennial exhibition.) It emerged as, and has been sustained as, a practice of rejecting European forms of cultural cohesion through the assertion of white colonial domination of Indigenous people. It tries to do two things simultaneously: reject monarchy and articulate white dominance. And, again, this may sound a little overwrought, but even the most cursory glance at the most basic statistics about Indigenous life in the United States in the twenty-first century has to give anyone willing to write off the power of this gesture some pause.

Early Americans, casting around for symbols, also looked to Rome for a symbolic vocabulary, with mixed results.[3] As O'Leary tells us, "In search of symbols for the new nation, early leaders looked to ancient Rome for idealized...models."[4] We certainly used Roman models for civic architecture but beyond that, Romans and their togas have had little more appeal. An 1841 Horatio Greenough figure of a bare-chested, toga-wearing Washington was eventually removed from the Capitol grounds because a naked, seated Washington did not convey the virility its commissioners had wanted.

Maybe the most important point to make about this early period is that "the growth of a unifying national culture in the United States proved to be unusually slow."[5] As O'Leary describes it, "Conditions of disunity prevailed: weak central government; persistent local and regional ties; a heterogeneous population made more diverse with each new arrival of immigrants; the absence of threatening neighbors; divisive partisan politics; and the dynamics of a population on the move." The lack of "blood heritage" was also perceived as a problem for the creation of national feeling.

This problem—a reticence to think in national patriotic terms—is likely hard for most twenty-first century Americans to square with their experience of a constant drumbeat of celebratory exceptionalist rhetoric and feeling. Early Americans were suspicious of a standing federal Army? In 1787, James Madison told the Constitutional Convention in Philadelphia, "The means of defence against foreign danger, have been always the instruments of tyranny at home. Among the Romans it was a standing maxim to excite a war, whenever a revolt was apprehended. Throughout all Europe, the armies kept up under the pretext of defending, have enslaved the people."⁶ They were more identified with their states than the nation? The first American government, defined by the Articles of Confederation, was a collection of sovereign states—and it was hard to convince early Americans to give up this model. (Think *Hamilton*.) They felt that too much nationalist sentiment was too European, too Old World? (Think the political, not to mention the aesthetic, objections to Washington in the toga.)

Fourth of July celebrations are probably the most recognizable early patriotic practices. By the 1780s, many communities did something to celebrate the anniversary of the Declaration of Independence. And while much of this is now familiar—speeches, parades, picnics—Americans in the 1780s were not all celebrating the same ideas about independence, and they were not all celebrating in the same ways. As O'Leary describes it, "The variety of celebratory styles, from Sabbath-like rituals, middle-class self-restraint, and private observances to festivals of fireworks, working-class exuberance, and public beer drinking, also demonstrated how different regions and social groups interpreted the day's significance."⁷ By the 1820s, this range of kinds of celebrations and ideas to be celebrated had become both a little less varied and a little more pointed. Nativists in the North and white Southerners and abolitionists and "labor associations, temperance activists, evangelical preachers, and women's suffrage advocates all tried to use July Fourth for their reformist campaigns."⁸ This was all more than a hundred years before the day became a federally recognized holiday, and the practices were still quite idiosyncratic; these celebrations were locally organized and came from the ground up rather than being federally mandated.

The American flag was the most commonly shared national symbol in this early period, but it would be a mistake to think that it was either universally embraced or particularly sacralized. It was something, however, as "The paucity of national symbols left the flag as the main physical representation of the early republic" but, "Rallying around the flag, the ritualistic core of the modern patriotic movement, was slow to develop."⁹ Before the Civil War, the flag was hardly sacred. The flag itself was first developed by the Sons of Liberty, a loose early collection of revolutionaries, in 1767, in response to the Stamp Act of 1765. It evolved without a lot of thought or debate, driven by circumstances. Essentially, white stripes were added to the red field of the British ensign (a flag flown to identify the national origins of a boat) so that the earliest American flag could be made easily by adding stripes to existing flags. (This is not quite as odd as it seems: for many rebellious colonists, the British flag was itself used as an act of rebellion—not as a statement of allegiance with the British government *but* as one of rebellion against the British monarchy because claiming the power to use the flags for their own devices was an affront to the traditions of the monarchy.)[10] This design idea was likely stolen from the British East India Company flag. In 1777, the first flag act was passed, declaring simply, "*Resolved*, That the flag of the thirteen United States be thirteen stripes, alternate red and white; that the union be thirteen stars, white in a blue field, representing a new constellation."[11] The important thing to note here is that the idea of a national flag, so ubiquitous around the world now, didn't exist as such. Flags had much more naval significance than symbolic significance when the republic was forming.

(But it does seem worth noting that the American flag was likely inspired by the flag of the most powerful company in the world at the time. The British East India Company was a relatively small band of British men who were trading tea and slaves and had managed to rule a large and diverse population of multiethnic and multilingual Indians across disparate territories on the subcontinent. It doesn't make sense to make too much of this, but it is odd soil for the roots of so much rhetoric about freedom to be sown in.)

The War of 1812 started to change the significance of flags. The physical Star Spangled Banner, the actual flag that inspired Francis Scott Key to write the poem that would become the national anthem, was made to fly over Fort McHenry, near Baltimore, in 1813. And while most Americans have heard this story a hundred times before they are ten years old, in August 1814, the British reached Washington D.C. and burned the Capitol Building and the President's Mansion. So, when they moved against Fort McHenry, the stakes were very high. Key was being detained in a ship in the Baltimore harbor, and what he saw "by the dawn's early light" of September 14, 1814, was the American flag flying above the fort, a sign that the Americans had held onto the fortification. (I had always imagined, to the limited extent I thought about it as a kid, Key as a soldier in danger, in a foxhole, and was somewhat let down to discover that he was a civilian lawyer safe on a ship. Somehow the fact that he was an observer rather than a participant was a disappointment.) And while it took some time for

Key's lyrics to circulate broadly, the attack on Washington and the United States' ultimate victory created what historians used to call the "era of good feeling." (There is nothing like an attack to inspire national feeling.)

As historian Matthew Dennis writes, "'Victory' in the War of 1812 unleashed a wave of American patriotism after 1815, ironically emphasizing the triumph of the American Revolution more than the split decision of the 'Late War.' The glories of the latter struggle—such as they were—were rendered indistinct as the war was subsumed by Revolutionary memory. The years 1812–1815 seemed to ratify the popular memory of 1776 and 1783, igniting new nationalism, expressed in politics, festive commemorations, architecture, arts, and literature."[12] The war unleashed patriotic feeling in a new way, and this time there was history to turn to and remember as a shared national past. Dennis suggests that "American public memory was transformed in these years in two significant ways—it was diversified and democratized to include common soldiers and sailors and to emphasize heroic maritime achievements largely absent during the Revolution."[13] In the end, the most significant relics of patriotism of this period are certainly the flag and the song that celebrated it in new terms.

Francis Scott Key's "The Star-Spangled Banner" is most famous, perhaps, for the lyrics about "the land of the free and the home of the brave." This aspirational language has been stunningly powerful across two centuries. This has been a good thing. Can you imagine if Key could see the impact he has had? One short poem and millions and millions of waves of real emotion? It almost feels like a cheap shot to stand on the lyrics that are less aspirational—almost, but not quite. They were mostly dropped by 1931, but they have been brought to light many times since; and in 2020, a wave of critiques of Key and the racism in the "The Star-Spangled Banner" were part of the post-Floyd reckoning.

"No refuge could save the hireling and slave" is pretty hard to defend. When journalist Jefferson Morley claims that "veneration of the piece is rooted in white supremacist thinking," he is drawing not only on these few lines but also on research into Key's thinking and his life beyond the song.[14] Not only was Key an enslaver, but he advocated, across his career, for the rights of slaveholders and publicly expressed ideas such as that African Americans are "a distinct and inferior race of people, which all experience proves to be the greatest evil that afflicts a community."[15] Key, it is worth adding, also advocated on behalf of some slaves during his career. Like many of his era, he held positions that seem contradictory to observers now. But ultimately he believed runaway slaves deserved the death penalty, and his beloved song threatens the enslaved with violence.

Morley and others have taken the position that "the assumption of White supremacy and Black slavery was integral to Key's patriotism" because Key worked hard to make this clear right up until his death in 1843.[16] Others have suggested that it is time to get rid of the anthem altogether, that it is simply too hard to disaggregate Key's original, racist ideas of bravery and freedom from the song, and that these ideas are too far out of alignment with American ideals now.[17]

In June 2020, Lawrence Johnson of Salt Lake City circulated a petition to change the anthem to "America the Beautiful."[18] Johnson made a familiar argument: "1. The 'Star Spangled Banner' contains 'racism,' elitism and even sexism embedded in its third and fourth stanzas. These sentiments have no place in the national anthem of a democracy that claims that all men (and women) are created equal." And he added a new, compelling argument: "2. The only ideal or national priority the 'Star Spangled Banner' spells out is military strength and victory. Nowhere in the anthem is brotherhood, national unity (E Pluribus Unum, Out of Many, One) or even a JUST and ETHICAL use of military power proposed."[19] (Think Jimi Hendrix's furious guitar argument with the anthem.) Johnson didn't get much traction with his petition, but it reflects a pretty good sense of the issues.

The problem with Johnson's first argument, and with too much emphasis on Key's awful third verse, is that it was dropped—it was there in the song, and we need to remember that, but it has long been out of use, and we need to remember that too. Singers of the song have not carried it forward across time. Jonson's second argument is potent and has not been part of contemporary debates about the anthem. The anthem's more pressing problem in our moment has not been so much about the lyrics but about the requirement to stand for them.

Flag worship evolved slowly in this early period. In 1818, when Congress passed a second flag act to set up a process for adding stars as new states were added to the union while keeping the number of stripes at thirteen to honor the original thirteen colonies, it was noted that even the Capitol building itself was flying multiple versions of the flag. So, while consistent flags and flag practices took quite a long time to develop in the United States, there was some increasing investment in the flag as a national symbol—and a military symbol—before the Civil War.

In the Mexican-American War of 1846, the American flag was carried into combat, and "The association of patriotism with military expansion, masculinity and the flag resonated broadly."[20] By 1847, mass production of flags was required to meet rising demand, and the Annin Flagmakers, still operating today, was founded in Manhattan. (Unsurprisingly, the company added new production facilities in both 1918 and 2001.)

The flag gained the nickname "Old Glory" in 1862 when a former sea captain reminiscing about his days of adventure *and* reflecting on his determination to fly the flag in his home in Tennessee during the war wrote, "It has ever been my staunch companion and protection. Savages and heathens, lowly and oppressed, hailed and welcomed it at the far end of the wide world. Then, why should it not be called Old Glory?"[21]

During the Civil War, "Old Glory" came to have a new depth of meaning for Northerners. Walt Whitman, in an April 1864 letter to his mother, captured some of this when he wrote, "Mother, you don't know what a feeling a man gets after being in the active sights & influences of the camp, the Army, the wounded &c.—he gets to have a deep feeling he never experienced before—the flag, the tune of Yankee Doodle, & similar things, produce an effect on a fellow never such before—I have seen some bring tears on the men's cheeks, & others turn pale, under such circumstances."[22] He goes on,

> It was taken by the secesh (secessionists) in a cavalry fight, & rescued by our men in a bloody little skirmish, it cost three men's lives, just to get one little flag, four by three—our men rescued it, & tore it from the breast of a dead rebel—all that just for the name of getting their little banner back again—this man that got it was very badly wounded, & they let him keep it—I was with him a good deal, he wanted to give me something he said, he didn't expect to live, so he gave me the little banner as a keepsake—I mention this, Mother, to show you a specimen of the feeling.[23]

"A specimen of feeling" actually becomes a pretty good phrase to describe this developing idea about the flag.

The Confederate flag was created at the beginning of the war out of necessity: a new nation required a new flag. The first Confederate flag, the Stars and Bars, was a variation on the American flag that reduced the number of stripes to three and the number of stars to seven, to represent the seven original states that formed the Confederacy: South Carolina, Mississippi, Florida, Alabama, Georgia, Louisiana, and Texas. Those charged with designing this flag sought public comment and were very much surprised to find themselves overwhelmed with calls not to abandon "the old flag."[24] Flag Committee Chairman William Porcher Miles was outraged, writing, "There is no propriety in retaining the ensign of a government which, in the opinion of the States composing this Confederacy, had become so oppressive and injurious to their interest as to require their separating from it. It is idle to talk of 'keeping' the flag of the United States when we have voluntarily seceded from them."[25] He did, however, compromise with this impulse in the design of the first Confederate flag, which was essentially a simplified version of the US flag.

But this first Confederate flag never captured the imagination of secessionists and their descendants the way the second flag of the Confederacy did. The second flag was developed, in part, because the similarities between the first Confederate flag and the American flag were dangerous, especially when there was no wind on the battlefield. After the first battle at Bull Run, it became clear that another battle flag was necessary, and this flag is the one that has continued to live in the dreams and nightmares of the American popular imagination. This second flag, called the "Stainless Banner," was composed of a blue X, or saltire, with white stars on a red field. But unlike versions that you might see today, the official flag in 1863 placed the red field in the upper-left corner of the flag—and the rest of the flag was white. William T. Thompson, an editor of the *Savannah Morning News* and a possible designer of an early version of the flag, claimed that the white background was important because "As a people we are fighting to maintain the Heaven-ordained supremacy of the white man over the inferior or colored race."[26] (Did you get that? Despite all the claims of neutrality made in defense of this flag, one of the likely designers of the flag could not have been more explicit about its relationship to white supremacy. He said, "we are fighting to maintain the Heaven-ordained supremacy of the white man over the inferior or colored race.") This flag, it is worth noting, also caused concern about problems on the battlefield because all the white could be read as a sign of surrender. (History has proved that worry to be unmerited. The people who love this flag haven't surrendered even 150 years after the end of the war.)

After the war, both flags took on new meanings. The US flag was embraced more fully as a national symbol, and more Americans seemed to have deeper national identifications. (Think Whitman's letter to his mother.) And plenty of public actors of all stripes jumped in to take advantage of this. Infamous abolitionist and Massachusetts senator Charles Sumner reflected this when he addressed New York's Young Men's Republican Union, telling them,

> There is the National Flag. He must be cold indeed, who can look upon its folds rippling in the breeze without pride of country. If he be in a foreign land, the flag is companionship and country itself, with all its endearments. Who, as he sees it, can think of a State merely? Whose eyes, once fastened upon its radiant trophies, can fail to recognize the image of the whole Nation? It has been called "a floating piece of poetry"; and yet I know not if it have an intrinsic beauty beyond other ensigns. Its highest beauty is in what it symbolizes. It is because it represents all, that all gaze at it with delight and reverence.[27]

He goes on, "It is a piece of bunting lifted in the air; but it speaks sublimely, and every part has a voice....And all together, bunting, stripes, stars and colors, blazing in the sky, make the flag of our country, to be cherished by all our hearts, to be upheld by all our hands."[28] Gone is the reticence to embrace federal symbols or the overly florid expression of national feeling.

In the South, the Confederate flag also kept flying. As John Coski, a historian at the American Civil War Center at Historic Tredegar, tells it, "The history of the flag since 1865 is marked by the accumulation of additional meanings based on additional uses. Within a decade of the end of the war (even before the end of Reconstruction in 1877), white Southerners began using the Confederate flag as a memorial symbol for fallen heroes." He continues, "By the turn of the 20th century, during the so-called 'Lost Cause' movement in which white Southerners formed organizations, erected and dedicated monuments, and propagated a Confederate history of the 'War Between the States,' Confederate flags proliferated in the South's public life."[29] And he makes it plain that "Far from being suppressed, the Confederate version of history and Confederate symbols became mainstream in the postwar South."[30] He adds, crucially, "What is remarkable looking back from the 21st century is that, from the 1870s and into the 1940s, Confederate heritage organizations used the flag widely in their rituals memorializing and celebrating the Confederacy and its heroes, yet managed to maintain effective ownership of the flag and its meaning."[31] In fact, this would be true well beyond the 1940s. (Think Caroline Holiman and Herman Nelson in 2020 claiming it as heritage that hasn't got "a thing to do with race or racism.")

The military service that Whitman and Coski and Holiman and Nelson connect so tightly to practices around the flag is—understood as a practice itself—neglected in histories of patriotism. It is almost as if military service is something else, somehow beyond the pedestrian business of patriotic feeling. But it is not. Military service—willingness to serve or unwillingness to fight—is essential to understanding how nationalism works and how patriotism works. To paraphrase Benedict Anderson, maybe the most compelling theorist of nationalism, the greatest mystery of nations is not the willingness of so many to kill for them but the willingness of so many to *die* for them. During the Civil War, 2.75 million men served: 2 million for the North and 750,000 for the South. (A very few women served, and only when they passed as men.) According to historian Bell Wiley, "The average Yank or Reb was a 'white, native-born, farmer, protestant, single, between 18 and 19.' He stood about 5 feet 8 inches tall and weighed about 143 pounds."[32] Roughly 5 percent of those who served were drafted, and 6 percent were paid by draftees to serve (and die) in their place.[33] (Yes, more American men paid someone to serve in their place than were drafted and served. It is also the case that the descendants of those who served for draftees have often not been welcome in the United Daughters of the Confederacy. So, yes, again, if you are the relative of someone who was paid to serve, you likely can't join a hereditary organization; if you are the descendent of someone who paid someone else to serve, you can.)

All of which is to say that millions willingly risked their lives for the idea of a nation in the Civil War. And while most of the letters they wrote home were about the food they were or were not eating and about how much they missed their mothers, they were killing each other and dying for conflicting ideas about the nation, which were, of course, ideas about race.

So, patriotic practices emerged in this early period in an uneven, if increasingly impassioned, process. It is useful to know that what seem now like the eternal and somehow preordained attachments of particular ideas to objects and rituals are neither: they were invented in an uneven process, and their meanings were fought over, but in the end, they were worth dying for.

It could come to seem like a too-easy party trick to show a practice and then show its (not necessarily intuitive) roots in racism and racial logics. But first, who wants to go to that party? And, second, isn't this too obvious? The United States was founded on settler colonialism that displaced and killed millions, and it was built by a system of race-based slavery. So, how could any of this be a surprise? It is a surprise because the country was also founded on the promise of the expansion of liberties for all—and we have been in a long tug of war between the material realities of settler colonialism and slavery and the aspirational language that has been part true aspiration and part shield. If Colin Kaepernick is, in some ways, the true north of this book, his protest showed how obvious and violent racism is alive in the patriotic practices we have inherited. His was not a total, abject rejection of the practice of singing the national anthem—he was, in fact, calling our attention to its failure to live up to its aspirations. He was trying to show us that adoring the freighted flag unquestioningly in the face of continued harsh inequity enables obvious structural racism to go unchecked and be maintained.

So, the basic principles for understanding the cultural work that patriotic practices do, in broad terms, emerged pretty clearly in this first period. First, *they are powerful*: think Whitman's friend dying for a scrap of a banner and every man and woman who has died for the flag since then. Second, *they are doing their best work when they seem to fit seamlessly into the landscape; when they stop being noticeable, their job is done*: it does not seem wildly counterintuitive to us that Whitman's friend should have died for the scrap, and it probably should. Third, *they were developed by people who felt strongly that they had something very important to say*: the designs of the Confederate flags, for instance, reflect a mix of practicality and ambition for what these symbols might do. (Recall the claim that the original white background was important because it expressed the "Heaven-ordained supremacy of the white man.") Fourth, *they are not neutral. Ever:* the point of patriotic practices is to stir national feeling—forging a "a floating piece of poetry" from cloth requires something other than neutrality. The surge of national feeling that Francis Scott Key captured in 1813 was a new kind of civic emotion, the joy of the steadfastness of a nation almost lost—a feeling that has been used in many different, and conflicting, ways since. Fifth, *they are usually inspired by anxiety, not the confidence their soaring lyrics and rigorous practice might seem to project; they always come from an unsettled moment:* Key wrote about a victory for the land of the free and the home of the brave, and in the same stanza he threatened the "hireling and the slave" fighting for the British with the "gloom of the grave."[34] And, sixth, *they use a few basic and familiar conventions to make their points:* "a reticence to think in national patriotic terms" required hard work over a long period of time to overcome, however odd that might seem to us now; it has been accomplished with the forging of a mix of national symbols from moving fictions, often skirting around the military, loss, and race.

These principles, as they played out before 1865, make answering the key questions about them pretty straightforward:

1. When was it introduced as a practice? If it was produced before 1865, it was likely somewhat experimental, developing rather than reiterating what national patriotic practices might look like.
2. By whom was it introduced? The producers of these early practices were a somewhat mixed bag of volunteers: songwriters and flag sewers and poets and idiosyncratic, local campaigners of all kinds. (They were mostly not big national organizations or the federal government.)
3. What was unsettled about the time in which it was made? The whole idea of what patriotism might be, maybe more so than the terms of the social order it might create.
4. What point did the instigators want to make? They were trying to figure this out. National sentiments were stirred around various ideas of belonging—especially in martial and racial terms.
5. How, in what forms, did they try to make their point? (A song? A school requirement?) These patriotic practices were most often

forms of culture that could circulate easily and didn't require significant institutional support: songs, picnics, "radiant trophies," "rippling in the breeze."

6. And, finally, what happened to the practice in the summer of 2020? (Has there been any pushback?) Yes. Plenty.

1866–1916: PATRIOTISM FROM THE GROUND UP

1866–1916, the post-war period, was a time of struggle to find a collective sense of national identity after the Civil War and in response to huge waves of immigration. This was a period of intense interest in different forms of *patriotism from the ground up*. There were some traditions to build on—veterans' organizations, increasing adoration of the flag that took hold in schools—and national holidays to celebrate. But in this period, this patriotic work was still very much the work of local citizens' organizations rather than the federal government, and those local groups were still collections of various voices and opinions—a passionate cacophony rather than a singular voice. And this period is defined by the end of the Civil War and the start of World War I. Of course, these wars were hugely consequential, but the reason the war years shaped this period is more about the cultural shifts they stirred than the wars themselves. It is formed by the post–Civil War needs of veterans and nativists worried about immigration, and then it ends abruptly with the specter of a war in Europe that will require a new, federally produced form of patriotic culture. So, this period is shaped by the need to care for the soldiers from one war and the need to recruit bodies for another.

The Grand Army of the Republic was one of the patriotic organizations that emerged powerfully in this period. Even before the organizations that formed to build memorials across the South and the North came into being, the Grand Army of the Republic (GAR) was founded, in 1866. (You might remember that the Sons of the American Revolution, the Daughters of the American Revolution, and, most crucially, the United Daughters of the Confederacy were formed around 1890.) GAR membership "was limited to honorably discharged veterans of the Union Army, Navy, Marine Corps or the Revenue Cutter Service who had served between April 12, 1861 and April 9, 1865."[35] By 1890, the GAR had four hundred thousand members, more than 25 percent of surviving veterans.

As the organization of the "sons" of these intrepid veterans tells it, "With the advances in the care and movement of the wounded, many who would have surely died in earlier wars returned home to be cared for by a community structure weary from a protracted war and now also faced with the needs of widows and orphans. Veterans needed jobs, including a whole new group of veterans—the colored soldier and his entire, newly freed, family. It was often more than the fragile fabric of communities could bear."[36] They continue, "State and federal leaders from President Lincoln down had promised to care for 'those who have borne the burden, his widows and orphans,' but they had little knowledge of how to accomplish the task. There was also little political pressure to see that the promises were kept."[37] As O'Leary tells us, "Patriotic culture emerged from war deeply fractured and ambivalent. In the ideological battle over meanings of mass allegiance that followed, the veterans themselves became a critical force."[38] "Ultimately," she says, "the Grand Army's adoption of a specifically militaristic conception of patriotism, backed by its demand that the nation economically reward its citizens-soldiers, had far-reaching consequences for future generations."[39]

The GAR was both a local and national organization—local "posts" were connected by regular national "encampments"—and while membership sagged in the economically tense 1870s, it boomed through the 1880s and 1890s. (This was a period of robust interest from Americans in joining organizations of all kinds—a "golden age of fraternity." Forty percent of the male population belonged to at least one group by 1900.[10]) Reunions and brotherhood were the lifeblood of the organization, but it had its greatest impact as a lobbying organization in two arenas: pushing to expand pensions for veterans and, crucially here, pushing for patriotic education in schools.

It is also worth noting that the GAR was a racially complicated organization. It did not easily fit into the now-familiar historical narrative that all veterans of the great war, in an effort to find a national idea with which to move forward, embraced an idea of the shared suffering only of white soldiers—what historian David Blight has called "racialized reconciliation." Instead, the white veterans of the GAR were surprisingly willing to include Black veterans; and while most veterans' activities in this period held the color line—the 1865 Grand Review of Union soldiers after the war was the first but certainly not the last all-white celebration of a fighting force that was not all white—the GAR at least aspirationally sought "to create an organization where veterans of every race, creed, or ethnicity could come together as comrades."[41] The GAR welcomed Black members but had a pretty abstract notion of equality in relation to the emancipation they seem proud to have helped enable. So, the GAR was complicated and powerful, and racial thinking shaped its activities and impulses.

The Woman's Relief Corps (WRC) was the ladies' auxiliary organization for the GAR, which precluded women members because it required military service from which women were barred. It was formed in 1883 by women anxious to contribute to the rising tide of patriotic activities. They wanted to express their allegiance to the United States, and teaching patriotism was central to their mission. Like the women in the DAR and UDC in this same period, they worked within the confines of expectations of women in this period—they could be moral leaders and educators. They could lead as "auxiliary" and in the context of children. And while these were pretty tight limitations, these women made a big impact within these confines.

This was an age of dramatic growth of public education in the United States. The 1840s saw a revolution in public education and the expansion of access and expectations for attendance, and by the end of the decade, more than half of American children under fourteen attended school for some period. (This was a stunning change.) By the 1880s, a growing number of states had compulsory schooling laws and formally trained teachers. There were national models and organizations and deeply shared ideas about what public education should accomplish. By 1900, thirty-four states had compulsory education, and only four of them were in the South, so this was largely a Northern phenomenon. There was a kind of natural confluence here—a rising tide of educational and patriotic impulses.

As well as patriotism in schools, the WRC gave us Memorial Day. Memorial Day has multiple origins, going back to the 1860s, but Memorial Day as a broadly shared national holiday owes much to the advocacy of the WRC. Most early Memorial Day activities were the work of Southern women in local organizations who buried the dead and then tended gravesites. By the time the WRC was starting to have influence as an organization, the women of the North were unhappy that the women of the South were claiming Memorial Day for their purposes, and they set to work to claim Memorial Day as a *national* holiday and to make it a "holy day" rather than a day of amusement.[42] They were successful for a time, but their greatest success was getting more patriotism into classrooms.

The GAR and the WRC had their biggest moment at the Chicago World's Fair of 1893, when they introduced the Pledge of Allegiance. As noted, the Pledge was commissioned for the fair and was written in 1892 by Francis Bellamy. The original version, thirty-two words, read, "I pledge allegiance to the Flag and to the republic for which it stands—one nation indivisible—with liberty and justice for all."[43] It was inspired by Union veteran Colonel George Balch, who worried "that national unity was threatened by the huge influx of immigrants to whom the Patriotic sacrifices of the Civil War meant little."[44] Balch attended an event at a New York City school in 1888 that moved him, and a prominent GAR leader—Charles Homer—who was with him, greatly. It involved a student solemnly parading the flag before his classmates. Homer was inspired to present a flag to the City College of New York a few months later in a ceremony at which students were told, "Whatever nation you belong to by birth, whatever tongue your mother taught you, whatever your color or your race, no matter, there is only one flag....Come and gather under its blessed folds. Let us be tangled in the stars and covered with the stripes."[45] (Note the egalitarian, aspirational terms of belonging here—Homer's vision was dramatically inclusive.)

Accounts of this event stirred more passions, and at the 1889 national meeting of the GAR, members were urged to present the American flag to local public schools. This set off a decade-long push from the GAR to get flags into schools—by giving flags, passing legislation requiring schools to fly flags, and promoting the idea in the magazine that had the largest circulation of any magazine at the time: *The Youth's Companion*.[46] *The Youth's Companion* entered into the campaign with some misgivings. It offered flags with subscriptions but also warned, "Our boys and girls are already very patriotic. What they now need is to be taught the duties we all owe to such a country as ours—to keep it pure and good."[47] But within a year, *The Youth's Companion* was all in. It ran an essay contest titled "Patriotic Influence of the American Flag When Raised over the Public Schools" and, by 1890, declared its ambition to see the nation commemorate the 400th anniversary of the discovery of America by Columbus "by raising the US flag over every public school from the Atlantic to the Pacific."

A few years later, *The Youth's Companion* proposed to use a pledge as part of its educational activities at the Chicago fair. Balch wrote the first version, which read, "We give our heads and hearts to God and our country; one country, one language, one flag!" But Bellamy, a writer at the magazine, found that to be too simplistic and undignified. Bellamy, a Christian socialist who had been recently relieved of his duties at his church because his deep sympathies with the poor and economically oppressed rubbed his parish the wrong way, wrote a new version. He was well aware that the language of this pledge was aspirational. (And certainly, many a conservative patriot in the twentieth century might be shocked to find that the pledge for which they were so often fighting was written by a socialist.) It is clear that circumstance, and maybe chance, produced a pledge inspired by mixed impulses. The big idea was not just to stir patriotic feelings among the youth but also to require them. At the same time, it wasn't about giving yourself to God and your country on any terms, as Balch's had been. It was, is, about loyalty to a republic defined by liberty and justice for all. (Think of the girls in the Lange photograph.)

As Bellamy argued, "The state fosters the school; it is the school's business to make for the state a substantial bottom of citizenship....All the centuries have been praising the patriotic soldier, the patriotic statesman; the twentieth century must be above all the age of the patriotic school-master."[48]

Bellamy included a salute in his vision of saying the Pledge of Allegiance. It was, unfortunately, a kind of salute that is very easy to call to mind because it was the straight-armed Nazi salute. At the turn of the century, the "Bellamy salute" was practiced widely by school children. As he describes it in *The Youth's Companion*,

> At a signal from the Principal the pupils, in ordered ranks, hands to the side, face the Flag. Another signal is given; every pupil gives the flag the military salute—right hand lifted, palm downward, to align with the forehead and close to it. Standing thus, all repeat together, slowly, "I pledge allegiance to my Flag and the Republic for which it stands; one Nation indivisible, with Liberty and Justice for all." At the words, "to my Flag," the right hand is extended gracefully, palm upward, toward the Flag, and remains in this gesture till the end of the affirmation; whereupon all hands immediately drop to the side.[49]

(This salute was mandated—by law—in 1942 to be replaced by "standing with the right hand over the heart." Who knew that we put our hands to our hearts to avoid seeming to copy Hitler Youth?)

But this is not to say that those pushing patriotism did not have a pretty clear agenda. As Ewert has it, "Although white middle- and working-class women made up a majority of the nation's teaching force, texts crafted by elite reformers required they teach a version of patriotic education that reiterated Anglo-Saxon manhood's cultural dominance."[50] They understood patriotic education "as a vital aspect of a nationwide project of regeneration. In working toward this goal these advocates inundated school curricula and popular patriotic practice with their own assumptions about gender, race and ethnicity, religion, and America's superior place among other nations." Further, "Proponents of patriotic education aimed to unite the nation under a common set of ideals, symbols, rituals, and a shared past. Similarly, they lauded America as a naturally superior nation in terms of its institutions, racial and ethnic makeup, and history."[51] Certainly they were right that schools were powerful sites to do this work. (Again, think of the girls in the Lange photograph.)

"In 1895," Ewert tells us, "the Illinois state legislature passed a law mandating the United States flag's mandatory presence atop all schools, courthouses, and state prisons and charities. Soon thereafter, several groups decried this legislation's specifics. One offending aspect directly addressing schools demanded that 'all colleges and educational institutions of every description in this State, whether State, county, municipal, district, sectarian or private...provide United States national flags.'"[52] This push moved beyond the exterior of school buildings, as well. Around the same time, the perhaps ironically named Nebraska Superintendent Melville Beverage Cox True proclaimed, "An American child should no more be allowed to read an adverse criticism of American institutions, and of American social conditions, than he should be allowed to read an adverse criticism of his family. His historian should be en rapport with the American people, and with their efforts to push their civilization to higher planes." True felt historians could not be "true citizens of the nation without presenting a favorable assessment of American history."[53] In other words, he easily linked the mandate to fly the flag to the need to teach without a critical lens. (Think of the 1776 Commission.)

But while True expressed a vision of what patriotism in the schools meant to many, this perspective was never totalizing. It is worth remembering that the celebration of Columbus and the anniversary of his arrival, for instance, had an egalitarian impulse that might be hard for contemporary observers to see. In the 1890s, Italian Americans were struggling for access to full citizenship because their southern European origins did not have the kind of Anglo purity that many associated with the ideal American. So, celebrating Columbus represented an expansion of the idea of who really counted as an American. And although the Chicago fair was everywhere about whiteness and racial hierarchy, accepting an Italian as a founder felt to some like a magnanimous gesture.

The first celebration of Columbus Day was in 1892, initiated by a presidential declaration from Benjamin Harrison, in part as a response to the lynching of eleven Italian Americans in New Orleans and the tension with the Italian government and Italian Americans across the country that this stirred up. In the twenty-first century context, it's hard to evoke the name Columbus without thinking of conquest, displacement, and the murder of indigenous people. It was a different story in the 1890s—the question of the legacies of settler colonialism was very much alive at that moment—but for most Americans, Columbus had a different resonance than his legacy has now.

Despite all of these competing urges and intentions, it is clear that the GAR and the WRC were hugely successful in "bringing about a massive political and cultural transformation in which identification with and devotion to the national would take precedence over all other forms of group, ethnic and regional loyalties."[54]

And what they started in the 1890s exploded over the next two decades with new purpose as American immigration patterns shifted. When Bellamy wrote the Pledge, the divisions that he and *The Youth's Companion* were seeking to bridge were North/South and Irish/Anglo in nature. Until 1885, the vast majority of immigrants to the United States came from northern Europe: Ireland, Scotland, and Germany. Ten years later, three-quarters of immigrants to the United States came from southern and eastern Europe, and they were Catholic and Jewish. These populations raised nativist anxieties and inspired the desire to teach a more pointed kind of patriotism.

Americanization campaigns, which often taught this more pointed kind of patriotism, built on the work of the GAR, WRC, and UDC but placed a greater emphasis on learning how to be American than on simply inspiring *feelings* of loyalty and fidelity. In a 1916 article in the *New York Times* about the distribution of a new "Citizenship Syllabus," the author explains the necessity for such a thing:

> We have so long left to chance and to the principle of survival of the fittest the Americanization of our great foreign-born population that we cannot now by any single measure deal adequately with the situation we have created. What the situation is needs no exposition here: the headlines of the last six months, the history of strikes among foreign-born colonies in munitions factories and elsewhere, the catalogs of newly-formed "leagues" and "societies," the radical meetings programs and resolutions are a sufficient index. What America is facing now is not simply the economic problem of giving immigrants a chance as a piece of benevolent paternalism; in the large number of assimilated groups in our factories and towns we are facing a vast social problem involving our national unity, the preservation of a uniform ideal of citizenship, the maintenance of industrial peace, and the conservation of a social ideal based on the use of the English language, and a regard for American citizenship and American standards of living.[55]

These Americanization efforts flourished in the years just before the United States entered the First World War. They, like the flags in school and the Pledge, were blunt instruments. They defined belonging in particular, often in racially limited terms, and they—unlike memorials or museums—were *actions, practices* that were mandated by citizen groups. This does not mean they were uncomplicated or not born of mixed impulses, but that the requirement to participate—by saluting or pledging or conforming in various ways—was also a fairly simple and blunt way to maintain social control. There is racist language to excavate everywhere in these stories, but eventually that seems beside the point. Compulsory patriotism ends up requiring a positive statement that the United States is a republic that stands for liberty and justice for all, even when that statement, despite its heart-thrilling aspirations, is simply patently untrue.

In the 124 years between the publication of Bellamy's Pledge and Kaepernick's refusal to participate in uncritically celebrating the anthem, there were a whole lot of compulsory affirmations of untruths. It isn't so much the details of the Americanization programs or the number of flags flown at schools, before or after they were required by law in all fifty states, that matter but the efforts to require compulsory affirmation that we need to note.

The other key point about this period, between the Civil War and World War I, is that these practices largely came from citizens and were citizen-driven rather than state-driven. The First World War would change all of that. As O'Leary describes it,

> Between the Civil War and World War I, the cultural politics of patriotism were by no means fixed, definitive, or saturated with jingoism. There was considerable motion and flux regarding who possessed sufficient authority to speak for the nation and which memories, icons, and rituals could represent the nation's symbolic meanings. On one side stood the emancipatory and democratic tradition, which saw the state as the potential guarantor of rights and freedoms. On the other side stood the militaristic tradition, which emphasized a faithlike loyalty to the nation as the highest form of allegiance.[56]

So, here are the basic principles for understanding the cultural work that patriotic practices do, in broad terms, in the period between the wars. First, *they are powerful*: stop, if you will, some morning at 9:00 a.m. and imagine the cacophony of *millions* of young voices saying the Pledge as they start their school days. Second, *they are doing their best work when they seem to fit seamlessly into the landscape; when they stop being noticeable, their job is done*: the fact that we don't often think about the reality that nearly all American children begin their days with an oath of loyalty pretty much says it all. Third, *they were developed by people who felt strongly that they had something very important to say*: the members of the GAR and the WRC emerged from the war determined that the nation they sacrificed for would be maintained across future generations. Fourth, *they are not neutral. Ever*: think of the battles to keep the Pledge in the classroom. Fifth, *they are usually inspired by anxiety, not the confidence their soaring lyrics and rigorous practice might seem to project; they always come from an unsettled moment*: the success of the idea of a pledge—a fealty oath—in this period speaks well to the anxieties about how a post-war racial order and immigration might change the nation. And, sixth, *they use a few basic and familiar conventions to make their points*: it required hard work to overcome "a reticence to think in national patriotic terms," however odd that might seem to us now; in this period this was accomplished, mostly, with the muscle of veterans' organizations and willing teachers.

These principles, as they played out between 1866 and 1916, make answering the key questions about them pretty straightforward:

1. When was it introduced as a practice? In the post–Civil War period, there was a surge of the production of practices that have had *remarkable staying power*—in fact, they have likely, in some way, shaped the contours of the experience of most readers—in schools, on holidays, and, of course, at football, baseball, and basketball games.

2. By whom was it introduced? If it was produced in this period between the wars, it was likely the work of a veterans' organization or of educators inspired by them.

3. What was unsettled about the time in which it was made? Both the problem of postwar reunion and the tide of immigration shaped this period in ways with which we are still contending.

4. What point did the instigators want to make? First, that some national feeling was a good thing. And then, that it had potential to be used to great effect.

5. How, in what forms, did they try to make their point? The flag, the Pledge, and the content of civic education.

6. And, finally, what happened to the practice in the summer of 2020? (Has there been any pushback?) The changes started a few years before 2020 but exploded startlingly in ways we will track in the next chapter.

6

ALLEGIANCE GOT PAID FOR

1917–1976: FEDERALLY MANDATED PATRIOTISM

The most important story of patriotic practices in this period is that they went from being somewhat idiosyncratic, ground-up, citizen-led practices to being federally mandated. With the onset of the First World War, the federal government took on the business of producing and sustaining patriotic culture in the United States. This was a significant and consequential change, and the reasons the federal government got into the business of patriotism are fairly straightforward and easy to understand.

As the war approached, one out of three Americans was foreign-born or the child of a foreign-born parent. Of those thirty-two million, ten million came from enemy countries. This posed serious problems for the prospect of getting the millions of Americans needed to enlist to fight this war; and it doesn't account for the huge number of recent immigrants from Ireland—at least five million—who were not likely to be interested in fighting and dying for the British empire.

Faced with this very real dilemma, and impressed by the persuasive powers of emerging visual tools like the cinematic love letter to the Ku Klux Klan, *The Birth of a Nation*, President Wilson decided to get the federal government into the business of stirring public opinion. He created the Committee on Public Information and changed American patriotism forever.

The Committee on Public Information (CPI) was announced in a wry April 14, 1917 story in the *New York Times* that reads, "The American censorship question was settled today when President Wilson created by executive order a Committee on Public Information to combine the two functions of censorship and publicity and named George Creel, a magazine writer and former newspaperman, as executive chairman of the committee." The *Times* quotes a letter from the White House: "America's great present needs are confidence, enthusiasm, and service and these needs will not be met completely unless every citizen is given the feeling of partnership that comes with full frank statements concerning the conduct of the public business."[1] The letter continues, "It is our opinion that the two functions—censorship and publicity—can be joined in honesty and with profit, and we recommend the creation of a committee of public information. The chairman should be a civilian, probably some writer of proved courage, ability, and vision able to gain the understanding co-operation of the press."[2] Creel, a journalist and reformer and gifted publicist, proved an able leader, and the committee set right to work on a multidimensional campaign that was most pressingly focused on encouraging enlistment and discouraging draft dodging. The work of the committee involved sending out more than twenty thousand "four minute men"—volunteers across the country—to descend on movie showings and other public gatherings to give short speeches to drum up support for the war. The committee also sent stories to the press and distributed vivid color posters, radio broadcasts, and films. (Think a stern but benevolent Uncle Sam pointing his finger and saying, "I Want You.")

Historian Christopher Capozzola captures this sea change, writing, "In the years before the war, voluntary associations—clubs, schools, churches, parties, unions—organized much of American public life. Such groups provided social services, regulated the economy, policed crime, and managed community norms. Schooled in this world of civic volunteerism, Americans formed their social bonds—and their political obligations—first to each other and then to the state."[3] He continues, "Now, these private obligations were suddenly fundamental to war mobilization in a moment of crisis, prompting state intervention into American bedrooms, kitchens, and congregations, places where the federal government hadn't always been before."[4] Americans in this new context, Capozzola tells us, "were, therefore, obliged to volunteer in a culture of coercive volunteerism. A paradoxical notion, to be sure, but one that President Woodrow Wilson clearly articulated when he introduced America to The Selective Service Act in a May 1917 proclamation, 'It is a new manner of accepting and vitalizing our duty to give ourselves with thoughtful devotion to the common purpose of all of us.'" He quotes Wilson continuing, "'It is in no sense a conscription of the unwilling; it is, rather, selection from a nation which has volunteered in mass.'"[5] But not all were willing, as Capozzola describes it: "Americans did not always do their utmost. Some of this was subtle resistance to an unpopular war. Given federal legislation such as the Espionage and Sedition Acts, which criminalized anti-war speech, many challenges to the politics of obligation took the form not of words, but of surreptitious actions or inactions."[6]

Americanization campaigns from the nineteenth century started to look more innocent as they gave way to 100 percent Americanism and the hand of the state became heavy indeed. Uncle Sam's wagging finger wasn't just public relations; it was a stern redefinition of the relationship between citizens and the state—between the wielders of blunt instruments and those the instruments were intended to work on. As Capozzola puts it, "As the needs of modern war blurred the lines between state and society, between mobilization and social control, the war made private coercions into public interests through the language of political obligation. When Uncle Sam said 'I want YOU,' he invoked a culture of obligation at the same time that he threatened to enforce it."[7]

And while there certainly was plenty of resistance, the big story of Wilson and the creation of the CPI is how wildly successful it was. By the end of the war, more than 2 million men and women had volunteered for military service, and more than 2.8 million had been drafted, with only 350,000 cases of draft resistance. Given the number of German Americans and Irish Americans and the sharp limitations put on African American military service—and the thin logics that sparked the war in the first place—this is a pretty remarkable outcome. The federal government discovered that blunt instruments could work very well in state hands, and the United States was set on a new course.

The work that the GAR and the WRC had been doing in schools was taken up with increased zeal by the CPI. As Cody Ewert describes it, "Patriotic education developed parallel to an unprecedented surge in state-sponsored educational reform and shifting popular opinions of war, expansionism, and citizenship."[8] He writes, "The outburst of nationalist excitement that the World War I era witnessed should be understood not merely as a reaction to the wartime state's immediate demands, but also a manifestation of the patriotic curriculum many Americans had received for decades. The patriotic ideals articulated in the late-nineteenth century took root in school textbooks, lesson plans, and rituals, creating a standardized form of national expression and entrenching it in the public schools."[9] And the legacy of the CPI and the federal involvement in patriotic practices reached well beyond the war.

The Works Progress Administration (WPA) and other New Deal programs, especially the Farm Security Administration, put these new instruments to work to great effect. Franklin Roosevelt faced, as Wilson had, both a material crisis and the need to rally support for responses to it, which were likely to be unpopular. To gain support for all of his expensive New Deal programs, Roosevelt relied on federal public relations campaigns to sell them to a population that was not eager to spend in the midst of a severe economic crisis. Most famously, and most successfully, his Farm Security Administration (FSA) set out to sell the need to support suffering farmers with photographs of dust bowl misery and dignity. To justify the agricultural programs, the FSA hired some brilliant documentary photographers and sent them out to capture the experience of those suffering. These photographs appeared in national magazines and newspapers and in government materials. They had a broad audience and a dramatic impact. Many people in the United States can still easily call up these images from ninety years ago. (Think Dorothea Lange's "Migrant Mother"). And the photographs' success in selling depression-era programs led to their use to sell the Second World War.

Much has been written about these powerful images, but an important point to make is the emphasis on white subjects in the published images. White suffering sold the programs when it was feared that Black or brown suffering, which was, of course, ongoing and very real, would not. As critic Sarah Boxer describes it, the FSA "openly worried that too much racial honesty might sink [the] ship."[10] These were not Machiavellian efforts at masterful, masked manipulation; they were pretty straightforward images—distributed in new, vivid reproductions and at new scales enabled by developments in publishing technologies.

However, the simplicity of these images does not mean their audience, the American people, were unsophisticated or fully compliant targets of this propaganda. These campaigns were seriously successful, but there was plenty of critique and pushback, especially about the Office of War Information, where the stakes were somewhat higher than with the FSA.

The Office of War Information (OWI) was created by President Roosevelt in 1942 as he pivoted from selling WPA programs to selling World War II. Inspired by the success of the CPI, the OWI was charged with fighting propaganda with propaganda—and with selling the war to a weary population. Executive Order 9182, signed in June 1942, charges the OWI director to "Formulate and carry out, through the use of press, radio, motion picture, and other facilities, information programs designed to facilitate the development of an informed and intelligent understanding, at home and abroad, of the status and progress of the war effort and of the war policies, activities, and aims of the Government."[11]

The War Relocation Authority (WRA), the arm of the government charged with overseeing the internment of 110,000 Japanese Americans during the war, hired Dorothea Lange to photograph the process just days after it was formed on March 18, 1942.[12] On March 22, she was on the streets of San Francisco. A month later, she took the picture of Mary Ann Yahiro and Helene Nakamoto. But while they are certainly part of the legacy of the CPI, the FSA, and the OWI—not to mention the GAR and the WRC—Lange's internment photos had a different trajectory.

First, the photograph of the girls, taken for the WRA, had a different fate than the photographs taken for the FSA and the OWI. The earlier photographs were published early and often. They were taken to be shared and to do the work of cultivating patriotic feelings in the moment. The logics that drove the taking of the WRA photographs are less well documented and less well understood. We know they were not published or made available to the public for fifty years after they were taken. They were quietly buried in the National Archive—stamped with the word "IMPOUNDED"—and went unseen until historians stumbled on them and reintroduced them into the public iconography.[13] Does this reveal a sense of the limitations of these government propaganda photographs as blunt instruments? Did it come to seem like a bad idea to show the public the faces of these beautiful children who were about to be stripped of all the rights of which Americans had been so proud? Certainly the Japanese attack on Pearl Harbor changed what Roosevelt needed from an Office of War Information. Patriotic sentiment was fired up, and Roosevelt didn't face the same kind of challenges that Wilson had in 1917. Still, the OWI was busy for the duration of the war: directing public sentiment, recruiting 6 million volunteers, and successfully helping draft 10 million more soldiers. (That makes 16 million in the service by 1945, when the US population was 140 million.)

Interesting recent scholarship contends that New Deal spending and war-era spending inspired significant patriotism. "It turns out," writes Torsten Bell, "that what your country was willing to do for you had a significant link to what you were willing to do for your country. People in the areas of the US that benefited most from the New Deal were much more likely to engage in 'patriotic' acts, such as buying war bonds. They also put their lives, not just their cash, on the line, being more likely to volunteer to fight and to do the kind of brave/dangerous things in battle that get you a medal."[14] This is compelling and reveals something about the fickle nature of public sentiment.

Finally, it's important to say something about race and these new federal efforts to do the work voluntary organizations had done in the eighteenth and nineteenth centuries. Federal engagements with patriotic culture were neither colorblind nor shaped by Julian Carr–style violent and racist rhetoric. But that does not mean they didn't have an important impact on racial thinking in the United States. Even though the photographers took remarkable photographs of Black and brown people, the FSA photographs that were published were more often of white suffering, for the explicitly stated reason that Black suffering would not stir the same kind of support for the programs. The wartime propaganda was also mostly white.

Moreover, the OWI did not respond to the sharp racial propaganda of the Axis Powers with a celebration of an American ideal of racial equality. It was relatively mute on the subject.

In the end, the most significant contribution of federal patriotic practices to the long story of racialized cultural infrastructure might be connected to the easy acceptance of segregation—in the military and in civilian life—in the context of old arguments made about freedom and equality by the CPI and the OWI. From World War I through World War II and beyond, a gaping hole in the logic of American patriotism was sustained and naturalized. We seemed to try to be the people bringing freedom and democracy to the world without acknowledging the limits of freedom and democracy at home. (Think of the Lange photograph of the girls, buried in the National Archives.) In the context of federal enthusiasm for steering sentiment and the sharp limitations on access to military service and both freedom and democracy for African Americans, the second-class status of Black Americans is naturalized as a part of what freedom and democracy mean, and this becomes, in the years after the war, a serious and sustained problem.

The Pledge of Allegiance re-entered the conversation about patriotic practices in the post-war period. In 1954, after a campaign by the Knights of Columbus, Congress added the words "under God" to the Pledge. The Pledge was now both a patriotic oath and a public prayer. And the role of the Knights of Columbus in making this happen conveys something of the increased status of Catholic Americans and their civic devotion—they had civic muscle to flex in this period, and they flexed it. It also captures something of the post-war mood. (Lange's girls would not have had to pledge to God, but their daughters would.)

Finally, another modest centennial came and went in this period. The American bicentennial resembled the American centennial in many ways. 1976, like 1876, hit during a hard economic downturn and a moment of serious cultural insecurity, as I have noted. The deeply unpopular Vietnam War had just ended, President Richard Nixon had just been impeached and resigned, the economy was caught in a nightmare of "stagflation," and we were newly dependent on oil from the Middle East that we did not control. New York City was trying to declare bankruptcy, social mores were stirred up, and Black and brown Americans still had to fight for full legal, economic, and social citizenship. You get the idea. There was not a huge appetite for patriotic pomp and circumstance. Patriotism was for most, save Nixon's "silent majority," out of style and would stay that way—with some exceptional moments of nostalgia during the "Reagan Revolution"—for the rest of the twentieth century. A recent exhibit at the Gerald Ford Presidential Library on the bicentennial celebrations that seemed to consist mainly of handmade polyester macramé in red, white, and blue is a pretty good summary of the modest affair; there didn't seem to be much appetite.

However, a federal need for patriotism would sharply define the next period of interest in it. The Vietnam War had been so unpopular, and the draft had been such a particularly unfair and painful point of contention, that in 1974, the draft—which had been more or less in place since 1917—was ended. This, of course, meant the military had to rely entirely on volunteers. You don't need to be a public relations genius like George Creel to realize that this was going to require both old and new mechanisms for inspiring enlistment. Financial and educational incentives were the first and easiest carrots on offer, and they mostly kept the military adequately staffed in the relative peacetime between 1975 and 2001. (The CPI-inspired ad campaigns that might still rattle around in your head, like "Be All That You Can Be," were also helpful.)

A few basic principles for this first era of federalized patriotism should make understanding these patriotic practices easy. First, *they are powerful*: we all recognize the Uncle Sam poster, and it inspired millions to risk their lives. Second, *they are doing their best work when they seem to fit seamlessly into the landscape; when they stop being noticeable, their job is done*: we tend to accept Uncle Sam as a genial patriarch, while early Americans would have seen an awful lot of King George in him. Third, *they were developed by people who felt strongly that they had something very important to say*: not only did Woodrow Wilson love *The Birth of a Nation*, but it inspired him to use film and photography and a whole new PR tool kit to pitch patriotism from the White House. Fourth, *they are not neutral. Ever*: the terms for pitching patriotism from the White House were set, in part, by a love letter to the Klan. Fifth, *they are usually inspired by anxiety, not the confidence their soaring lyrics and rigorous practice might seem to project; they always come from an unsettled moment*: recruiting young men to risk death or maiming is about as hard a sell as there is. And, sixth, *they use a few basic and familiar conventions to make their points*: the federally mandated patriotism that began with the CPI used all the means for public relations the federal government had or could invent—and in the last forty years, it has continued to be inventive, as we shall see.

These principles, as they played out between 1917 and 1976, make answering the key questions about them pretty straightforward:

1. When was it introduced as a practice? If it was introduced between the start of World War I and the end of the Vietnam War, it is likely to have been produced and pushed by some part of the federal government.

2. By whom was it introduced? The federal government likely produced it, and the success of the efforts to win support for World War I and New Deal programs is excellent evidence that they worked.

3. What was unsettled about the time in which it was made? Enough that enforcement of patriotism came to seem like a good idea.

4. What point did the instigators want to make? First, that some national feeling was a good thing. And then, after World War I, that the federal government should require the production of that national feeling.

5. How, in what forms, did they try to make their point? As in the earlier period, the flag, the Pledge, the content of civic education, and a massive decades-long public relations campaign.

6. And, finally, what happened to the practice in the summer of 2020? Think Colin Kaepernick.

2001–2021: PAID PATRIOTISM AND OUTRAGEOUS REFUSAL

The planes that hit the twin towers in Manhattan and the Penatgon in Virginia and crashed in Shanksville, Pennsylvania, on September 11, 2001, were not filled with thousands of American flags. But it's easy to understand why one might recall that. In the days and months after the attack, it seemed that American flags were suddenly everywhere and had exploded across the landscape. On bumper stickers, on car antennas, on houses, in shops, on television—on television—on television—like confetti landing everywhere. The surge of collective American national feeling was omnipresent.

Even people who had not ever felt it had surges. Poet and musician Sekou Sundiata describes just such a surge in "The 51st (dream) State" when "he began sifting through what he calls his 'troubled love' for a country he had often critiqued."[15] Describing himself standing at Ground Zero in New York, staring into the hole in the ground, he writes, "Woman to my right worried a flag / the size of a handkerchief / the kind you get at the fairgrounds / And little Emmett Till came to me / a face that long ago cured / my schoolboy faith in that lyric / So that I could no longer sing / With the voice of praise / As if it was my own / O Beautiful for spacious skies." Sundiata walks his reader through a short history of patriotic practices, from Bellamy in school to the world he had to weigh against its promises, embodied by a "visit" from Till that "cured" him of the longing for belonging to which he had responded as a boy. (Again, think of the girls in Lange's photograph.) He wrenchingly captures the ache of longing to be part of the collective while refusing its terms.

Suddenly patriotic culture was everywhere, and in this period, it took particular forms. There were the flags immediately, and then, right on the heels of the US invasion of Afghanistan in October, there were signs everywhere reading "Support our troops." It is worth noting here that the signs didn't say "Win in Afghanistan" or, two years later, "Win in Iraq." They focused on the troops and only on the troops, not on what the troops were doing in the world.

As historian John Bodnar has it, as people who had lived outside the boundaries of patriotic inclusion strained to lean into it, an ugly form of patriotism also blossomed in this period; "Belligerent Patriots have been on the march since 9/11."[16] He writes, "Loyal Americans who love their country more than many of the people in it have been pledging their allegiance through outbursts of anger and bigotry. In their aggressive worldview myths prevail; painful truths are ignored. They cast the nation itself in a glow of grandeur in order to avoid coming to terms with its most pressing problems. Intolerance and violence become weapons deployed by forceful loyalists intent upon inflicting their will on national and international life."[17] (Think January 6, 2021.) Somewhere in between these strains of patriotism was what seemed a middle ground in which not just patriotism but fealty was as ubiquitous as oxygen and so successfully naturalized that most Americans were likely genuinely startled at the idea that anyone might have a reason to push back.

The NFL played a role in this suddenly saturated patriotic landscape. It had been involved since the end of World War II, but it stepped up its game in this period. It was part of the great success of efforts that continued to come directly from the federal government—now from the Department of Defense—to further stir up patriotic feeling and recruit people willing to die for it. Can you imagine a professional game without a playing of the anthem and some miscellaneous callout to veterans?

The "earliest documented performance" of "The Star-Spangled Banner" at a ball game was on May 15, 1862, during the "opening game played at Union Base Ball and Cricket Grounds in Brooklyn, New York."[18] The *New York Times* covered the first game of the 1918 World Series as follows:

> Far different from any incident that has ever occurred in the history of baseball was the great moment of the first world's series game between the Chicago Cubs and the Red Sox, which came at Comiskey Park this afternoon during the seventh-inning stretch. As the crowd of 19,274 spectators...stood up to take their afternoon yawn...the band broke forth to the strains of "The Star-Spangled Banner." The yawn was checked and heads were bared as the ball players turned quickly about and faced the music. Jackie Fred Thomas of the U.S. Navy was at attention, as he stood erect, with his eyes set on the flag fluttering at the top of the lofty pole in right field. First the song was taken up by a few, then others joined, and when the final notes came, a great volume of melody rolled across the field. It was at the very end that the onlookers exploded into thunderous applause and rent the air with a cheer that marked the highest point of the day's enthusiasm. The mind of the baseball fan was on the war. The patriotic outburst following the singing of the national anthem was far greater than the upheaval of emotion which greeted Babe Ruth, the Boston southpaw, when he conquered Hippo Him Vaughn and the Cubs in a seething flinging duel by a score of 1 to 0.[19]

The wartime joy these baseball fans found in this playing of the anthem is contagious. And it is worth noting that this able reporter is describing what seems like a spontaneous event.

"The Star-Spangled Banner" officially became the national anthem in 1931, and by the time the Second World War was underway, as more and more stadiums could use sound systems to play recordings of the anthem, baseball teams came to play it regularly during the seventh-inning stretch. But its use was still pretty casual. It wasn't until the end of World War II, after Japan surrendered, that NFL Commissioner Elmer Layden called for all of the league's teams to play "The Star-Spangled Banner" at their games. He told the *New York Times* in an August 23, 1945, story—one week after V-J Day—that "The National Anthem should be as much a part of every game as the kick-off. We must not drop it simply because the war is over. We should never forget what it stands for."[20] He also told the *Times* that "He will instruct all teams to make the playing of 'The Star-Spangled Banner' a permanent part of every game."[21] All of this seems pretty innocent compared to the relationship between professional sports and the Department of Defense that developed after 2001.

A dramatic 2015 joint oversight report issued by Senators John McCain and Jeff Flake begins, "In 2013, a roaring crowd cheered as the Atlanta Falcons welcomed 80 National Guard members who unfurled an American flag across the Georgia Dome's turf. Little did those fans—or millions of other Americans—know that the National Guard had actually paid the Atlanta Falcons for this display of patriotism as part of a $315,000 marketing contract."[22] It continues, "This unfortunate story is not limited to professional football, but is repeated at other professional and college sporting events around the nation. In fact, these displays of paid patriotism are included within the $6.8 million that the Department of Defense (DOD) has spent on sports marketing contracts since fiscal year 2012."[23] The report laments the implications of the practice, concluding that

> By paying for such heartwarming displays like recognition of wounded warriors, surprise homecomings, and on-field enlistment ceremonies, these displays lost their luster. Unsuspecting audience members became the subjects of paid marketing campaigns rather than simply bearing witness to teams' authentic, voluntary shows of support for the brave men and women who wear our nation's uniform. This not only betrays the sentiment and trust of fans, but casts an unfortunate shadow over the genuine patriotic partnerships that do so much for our troops, such as the National Football League's Salute to the Service campaign.[24]

They add, giving the league some wiggle room, "While well intentioned, we wonder just how many of these displays included a disclaimer that these events were, in fact, sponsored by the DOD at taxpayer expense." And they conclude, "Even with that disclosure, it is hard to understand how a team accepting taxpayer funds to sponsor a military appreciation game, or to recognize wounded warriors or returning troops, can be construed as anything other than paid patriotism."[25] This seems to be letting the league—which would come to hold others to a much higher standard—off the hook a bit, yes?

In 2015, when the report was released, the NFL took in $1 billion in revenue. One *billion* dollars.[26] Yet the league was taking money to trot wounded warriors, who were making around $20,000 a year and risking their lives, out onto the field.

Maybe the most surprising part of the report is that while Department of Defense found $5.4 million that had been inappropriately spent, it "still cannot fully account for the nature and extent of paid patriotism activities. In fact, more than a third of the contracts highlighted in this report were not included in DOD's list; instead, our offices discovered the additional contracts through our own investigative work. In the end, two-thirds of the contracts found by our offices or reported by DOD contained some form of paid patriotism."[27] This reveals two things: first, this could well be just the tip of the iceberg; and second, neither the DOD nor the teams pocketing money for putting on patriotic shows were willing to come forward with the details about how much money was exchanged or over how long a period this had gone on.

It feels like there is a pretty significant distance between the crowd standing at a Cubs/Sox game in 1918 and a paid-for-in-secret series of military flyovers, flag unfurlings, emotional color guard ceremonies, enlistment campaigns, and national anthem performances almost one hundred years later. All those tear-jerking moments—and they do move people—were faked. They were not genuine expressions of patriotism. They really, truly, were not. They were a cynical cash grab for which the NFL and the other leagues have not fully accounted.

The paid "salutes" and "celebrations" included an "on-field color guard, enlistment and reenlistment ceremonies, performances of the national anthem, full-field flag details, ceremonial first pitches and puck drops." More specifically,

- The Air Force paid the Los Angeles Galaxy for "recognition of five high ranking officers of the Air Force" in 2012 as well as four sets of sideline season tickets.
- The National Guard paid the Seattle Seahawks in 2014 for a ceremony that allowed "up to 10 soldiers to re-enlist pregame on the field."

- The National Guard paid the Indianapolis Colts for the use of a suite, autographed items, field visits, and appearances by cheerleaders.
- The National Guard bought an eighteen-person luxury box from the Indiana Pacers and an "executive-view" suite for twenty-five people on Military Appreciation Night.[28]

So, the Seattle Seahawks took money to hold a ceremony in which soldiers re-enlisted pregame on the field? And the Pacers took cash to host a Military Appreciation Night that the team probably proudly advertised as if it were a genuine expression of gratitude? The National Guard "paid NFL teams nearly $7 million for marketing and advertising contracts, including $675,000 to the New England Patriots, which included the team's 'True Patriot' promotion, in which the team honored Guard soldiers during home game half-time shows"?[29] Really?

In May 2016—four months *before* Colin Kaepernick's first protest—the NFL announced that it was "reimbursing U.S. taxpayers more than $720,000 in so-called 'paid patriotism' money that the teams took from the military to allow things like color guard displays and video tributes at pro football games."[30] In a November 2015 letter to Flake and McCain, NFL Commissioner Roger Goodell boasts about the patriotism of the NFL and denies knowing anything about any paid patriotism. He writes, "The National Football League deeply values the dedication and sacrifice of the men and women who serve our country. For many decades, at home and abroad, the league and our individual clubs have offered respect, appreciation, and support for the U.S. military and our veterans."[31] He continues, "The military has also separately engaged individual NFL clubs to promote recruitment efforts, using multiple platforms to maximize the reach of their message, such as ads placed in game programs and on scoreboards or recruitment kiosks in our stadiums. These efforts are intended to be separate and apart from the NFL's long-standing recognition of the service members and their families who have dedicated their lives to serving this great country."[32] But, of course, Flake and McCain were not concerned about recruitment kiosks. Goodell wrote to them again in May 2016 with the same word-for-word boasting about patriotism but then did own that "an audit uncovered that over the course of four seasons $723,734 may have been mistakenly applied to appreciation activities rather than recruitment efforts."[33]

So, the sports and patriotism marriage that was so insistent and ubiquitous after 9/11 was a money grab. Period. And the full story has yet to be revealed. As *Sports Illustrated* reports, "Before 2009, the anthem was played while NFL players prepared for games in their respective locker rooms. Beginning in 2009, the league opted to play the anthem while players were on the field." They continue, "This seemingly minor change in presentation was made in coordination with television networks and league sponsors, including the National Guard."[34] It is not clear if there was some financial arrangement, but given what followed, it would certainly not be a surprise—and it can't be impossible to discover. Isn't it worth a closer look?

A spokesman for the NFL, Brian McCarthy, told NBC News in August 2016, with some considerable nerve, that the league did not have a policy regarding players and the anthem before 2009 because they were in the locker room while it was played, but that, "As you know, the NFL has a long tradition of patriotism. Players are encouraged but not required to stand for the anthem."[35] As *Think Progressive* puts it, "It's unclear whether the policy change was implemented as a direct result of any Defense Department contracts," but, again, that would hardly seem like a stretch.[36] ESPN commentator Stephen A. Smith cut through the evasive language about the switch and said it happened "because it was seen as a marketing strategy to make the athletes look more patriotic."[37]

There is no doubt that there was money to be made. McCain and Flake reported "that all military branches reported spending $53 million on marketing and advertising contracts with professional sports organizations between 2012 and 2015. More than $10 million of that went to the NFL, MLB, NHL, NBA and Major League Soccer."[38] The gravy train was slowed down in 2016 because Senators Richard Blumenthal, John McCain, and Jeff Flake "filed an amendment to the National Defense Authorization Act for Fiscal Year 2016 that prohibits the Department of Defense from spending taxpayer dollars to honor American soldiers at sporting events. The amendment also encourages professional sports organizations that have accepted taxpayer funds in exchange for military tributes to return those profits as a charitable contribution to organizations that support members of the U.S. armed forces, veterans, and their families."[39] (Think any of the money was returned?)

According to a Blumenthal press release, "Football fans across America learned last month that several NFL teams were honoring U.S. service members not out of a sense of patriotism, but for profit in the form of millions of dollars from the U.S. Department of Defense." It continues, "Our amendment would put an end to this practice, and ask professional sports leagues like the NFL to donate to charities supporting American troops, veterans and their families. In a time of growing threats to our nation's security, we can't afford to give scarce defense dollars to wealthy sports teams, and fans should have confidence that their hometown heroes are being honored on Sundays because of their honorable military service, not as an NFL marketing ploy." It went on to say one more very revealing thing: "In a government oversight report released last month, Senator McCain highlighted $49 million that the Army National Guard spent in 2014 on marketing and advertising with pro sports organizations despite the fact that the Guard was facing serious budget shortfalls in the accounts used to pay and train soldiers."[40] And these people lost their minds when Kaepernick took a knee? Maybe this is why? Maybe they were protecting a piece of their $1 billion income stream rather than the flag? (That is a really blunt instrument.)

These are blunt instruments in a couple of ways. First, they are like memorials in that they are performing a sleight of hand—they are pretending to be something they are not, and the lives of young people are at stake. How is that not deeply disgusting? How do these people—Roger Goodell, in particular—think they get to take the high ground and punish and critique athletes like Kaepernick when they protest? When Kaepernick took a knee, the business of paid patriotism had been public for more than a year. Is the pretense of the league, the cynical trading of dollars for recruited bodies, more respectful than kneeling on the field?

As you may remember, in August 2016, Colin Kaepernick hit a breaking point regarding the contradiction between the language, Key's language, of the anthem he was being required to stand for and the murder of innocent Black men, women, and children (a gross but until recently barely acknowledged inequity very much alive in the culture). You will recall that he told reporters, "I am not going to stand up to show pride in a flag for a country that oppresses Black people and people of color. To me, this is bigger than football, and it would be selfish on my part to look the other way. There are bodies in the street and people getting paid leave and getting away with murder."[41]

The NFL responded, "The national anthem is and always will be a special part of the pre-game ceremony. It is an opportunity to honor our country and reflect on the great liberties we are afforded as its citizens. In respecting such American principles as freedom of religion and freedom of expression, we recognize the right of an individual to choose to participate, or not, in our celebration of the national anthem."[42] This statement has something of different resonance when you know that the anthem was a big moneymaker for the NFL. It insists with quiet authority that "this is how we do things," and it asserts, with remarkable tone-deafness, that the point of the anthem is to "reflect on the great liberties we are afforded as…citizens" without seeming to understand how ridiculous and offensive this might sound to people frustrated by living in a culture in which some people are empowered to kill any Black people—in front of a billion witnesses—at will.

In 2016, Kaepernick was respectful and clear. "Once again, I'm not anti-American," Kaepernick said. "I love America. I love people. That's why I'm doing this. I want to help make America better."[43] He started kneeling during the anthem after talking to Retired Army Green Beret Nate Boyer. "We sort of came to a middle ground where he would take a knee alongside his teammates," Boyer told HBO's *Real Sports*. He explained, "Soldiers take a knee in front of a fallen brother's grave, you know, to show respect."[44]

For the NFL, in 2016, the only options were flag or no flag. Given the league's recent hand-slapping from Congress, it was remarkably bold and unwilling to yield. There was no acknowledgment that there might be a bigger problem, no conception that those liberties might be inequitably distributed, no awareness that the anthem and the act of standing for it were part of a system that enables some Americans to deeply believe they live in an egalitarian society despite the obvious fact of the deaths of Martin, Brown, Garner, and many more.

This first position taken by the NFL was followed over the next four years by some wild swings. It was much milder and more generous than the league's position would come to be as more athletes joined Kaepernick and the President of the United States got involved, telling crowds, "You have to stand proudly for the national anthem or you shouldn't be playing, you shouldn't be there, maybe you shouldn't be in the country."[45] Trump stepped in and threw down this barely veiled racial gauntlet. Trump loved trashing Kaepernick on the campaign trail; he told adoring crowds that he didn't belong and that owners should "get that son of a bitch off the field right now."[46] After the election, he bragged both that "he was responsible for NFL owners' not signing Kaepernick, a free agent at the time, because they feared a public rebuke from [him]," and that Kaepernick was "a very winning, strong issue for me....This one lifts me."[47]

How do you *not* conclude that some of this is about race and social control? How can you understand the difference between the reaction to the NFL lying about patriotism and spending taxpayer dollars illegally to manipulate soldiers who have served in the military and the reaction to Kaepernick taking a knee? Isn't this what the requirement of a particular kind of loyalty creates? But as we have witnessed, the flag and the requirement to stand for it are not only "made things"—mechanisms put in place to create and protect ideas about who we are and who belongs—but also *recently* made things. It is also important to remember that the desire of the forgers of these practices for permanence reflects the vulnerability of their ideas. They have needed, across two hundred years, to work to make the patently untrue seem natural because the patently untrue is not natural. Kaepernick's refusal to unquestionably celebrate what was in his lived experience, and the lived experience of millions and millions of Americans, a lie, was so threatening because the lie was so big and had been so important for so long.

The NFL changed its tune in 2020 after the murder of George Floyd and the dramatic expansion of the Black Lives Matter movement, although Kaepernick has yet to play again. In June 2020, Commissioner Goodell issued an apology in which he said, "We, the NFL, condemn racism and the systematic oppression of Black People." He continued, "We, the NFL, admit we were wrong for not listening to NFL players earlier and encourage all to speak out and peacefully protest....We, the NFL, believe Black Lives Matter."[48] In August, he apologized to Kaepernick, saying, "I wish we had listened earlier, Kaep, to what you were kneeling about and what you were trying to bring attention to." He went on, "It is not about the flag. The message here, and what our players are doing, is being mischaracterized." He tried to demonstrate his understanding by saying, "These are not people who are unpatriotic, they're not disloyal, they're not against our military. In fact, many of those guys were in the military, and they're a military family. What they were trying to do was exercise their right to bring attention to something that needs to get fixed. That misrepresentation in who they were and what they were doing was a thing that really gnawed at me."[49] (Do you believe this?)

By the start of the 2020 season, the old playbook had been thrown out. The same folks who had been so outraged by Kaepernick and so confident that their defense of military families would silence him were singing a whole new tune. Players wore armbands reading "Black Lives Matter." End zones read "End Racism" and "It Takes All of Us." "Lift Every Voice and Sing," the unofficial Black national anthem, was played during pre-game ceremonies.[50] At the Super Bowl, helmets read "Breonna Taylor" and "Ahmaud Arbery." The league promised to donate $250 million toward social justice initiatives. And, maybe most surprisingly, the NFL has a video of Derek Chauvin murdering Floyd posted just a few clicks off of its home page.[51] (All of this was shocking change in 2021, and most of this was *not* visible at the 2022 Super Bowl.)

The authenticity of Goodell's personal transformation or the extent to which the league is responding to a changing tide of public opinion or the players union flexing some political muscle may be beside the point here. In the span of a few months, the use to which patriotic practices were being put was transformed. This was a moment of change. Even NASCAR banned the flying of the Confederate flag at its races.

Understanding how the patently untrue is made to seem natural—how clear, basic, obvious untruths like the supremacy of white people or men are sustained in a culture as often unspoken givens—is vital to creating a more just society. Kaepernick; Black Lives Matter leaders Alicia Garza, Patrisse Cullors, and Opal Tometi; and many others who have been willing to step into the fray have revealed a bit about how this process works. And while it might seem like lunacy to be celebrating NASCAR's rejection of the Confederacy 150 years after the Confederates lost their crusade to keep Black people enslaved, that is, in fact, where we are in 2022.

Cultural infrastructure is a long game. Making its mechanisms explicit, however, helps us to better understand how the patently untrue is made to seem natural. Again, this book is shaped by a few basic observations. The first is that it takes a tremendous amount of work to make the patently untrue seem natural. (The bald, insistent assertion that Confederate soldiers gave their lives to preserve an innocent, race-neutral American heritage, for instance.) The second is that cultural infrastructures are powerful tools. (The same people who describe the monuments as benign will go to extraordinary lengths to prevent their removal.) The third is that all infrastructure is cultural. (It is made by people who have a point to make.) The fourth observation builds on these. It is that we are surrounded by cultural objects that don't necessarily seem to have anything to do with culture or values or ideology (like a science museum) but that work every day to tell us who we are—and, crucially, that much of this telling, in the obviously cultural infrastructure and the less obviously cultural infrastructure, has been about racial hierarchies and has been stunningly effective in maintaining structures of inequity.

CONCLUSION

Remaking a Made Thing

KEHINDE WILEY'S *RUMORS OF WAR* puts a young Black man in a hoodie and Nikes on a muscular mid-stride horse on a plinth just off Monument Avenue in Richmond, Virginia. Wiley does much of the work that "White Lies Matter, Inc.," described in the introduction to this book, is trying to do. He flips a familiar convention to reveal the work that the convention is doing. Wiley makes the heroic memorial figure a young, twenty-first-century Black man. He makes the heroic, celebrated soldier who is thrust into battle this man and asks us to see that his struggle is to defend himself. (See Figure 11.)

You can feel this even in the young man's posture, as his head is twisted warily to see what is coming his way. The title, *Rumors of War*, borrowed from Matthew 24:6 ("You will hear of wars and rumors of wars, but see to it that you are not alarmed. Such things must happen, but the end is still to come"), doubles down on the figure as a warrior but also wants to promise that "the end is still to come." It is a very effective bit of cultural infrastructure. It is a war memorial that calls for an end to this long cultural war.

And it is a powerful reminder that cultural infrastructure matters.

This book is a tool to help readers identify, contextualize, and name elements of our everyday landscapes and cultural practices that are designed to seem benign or natural but that, in fact, work tirelessly to tell vital stories about who we are, how we came to be, and who belongs. As we

FIGURE 11 *Rumors of War* by Kehinde Wiley

have seen, these are stories about who has power in the culture and who doesn't. They are also almost always stories about race.

We have looked at three categories of cultural infrastructure: memorials and monuments, museums, and everyday patriotic practices. Each of these has been very much in the news for most of the twenty-first century.

More intense, riotous, fraught attention has been paid to them in the last twenty years than in most of the first two hundred years of American life. And yet, they are seldom looked at together or understood explicitly as tools used by particular people in particular times and places to shape the culture in particular ways.

Cultural infrastructures enable the circulation of knowledge, meaning, and power in a national context. In fact, it is the very circulation of knowledge, meaning, and power they enable that creates the nation itself. In the United States, these systems have been and will continue to be preoccupied with negotiating white supremacy. Understanding what cultural infrastructure is and its deep and broad impact is crucial to understanding how structures of inequity are maintained and how they might be dismantled.

Two observations seem worth standing on here. First, cultural infrastructure isn't going anywhere. It will always be around in one form or another; useful tools don't get abandoned, and human societies require some social cohesion. Second, it is possible to remake a made thing. In other words, Kehinde Wiley's *Rumors of War* offers a path forward. He uses the oldest tool in the cultural infrastructure toolkit to make a new point.

Wiley started by subverting the meanings of the conventions of European oil painting by using them to paint portraits of twenty-first century Black Americans. He then took on the conventions of the man on a horse on a plinth.

Rumors of War is alive and exciting. It explicitly seeks to reframe the workings of the maintenance of structures of inequality. It works to naturalize a new version of who we are, and it is a model we should follow. There is so much work to be done—conventions to rethink, plinths to repopulate, institutions to reimagine—and Wiley offers a powerful vision of what this work can be.

ACKNOWLEDGMENTS

THE FIRST PEOPLE I want to thank for enabling this book are the Americans of every stripe who have taken to the streets and op-ed pages and dull municipal meetings to try to reshape our shared cultural infrastructure to make it a more egalitarian expression of who we are and who we can be. Like so many observers, I have been humbled and amazed by the numbers and by the wit and by the bravery and by the tenacity of these folks.

I also want to thank the scholars whose work has been helping me to think about these issues for a couple of decades. They include David Blight, John Bodnar, Christopher Capazzola, Karin Cox, Benjamin Filene, David Kieran, Daniel Kim, Meredith Lair, Ed Linenthal, Melanie McAlister, Tiya Miles, Frank Mitchell, Cecilia O'Leary, Fath Ruffins, Andrew Shanken, Fred Wilson, and Mabel Wilson. Karin Cox deserves special thanks for insisting that we all keep our eyes on the UDC. And Cecilia O'Leary deserves a shout out for having mapped out so much of this so clearly. Special thanks also to Ed Linenthal for an early conversation about this book and to Daniel Kim for the much-needed tough love and the wicked smart feedback on my first attempt to describe it. Thanks Benjamin for your smart notes. Thank you, Tiya, for reading a draft. And Frank, all the faults in this book are mine, but it feels like the latest version of a thirty-year conversation that I have been blessed to have with you.

I was lucky to meet Frank in the 1980s at the Smithsonian when people like Spencer Crew and Lonnie Bunch were starting on the work that would shape the story this book starts to tell. I had the great good fortune to meet them and to work for Pete Daniel and Charlie McGovern. I also was lifetime lucky to meet Deirdre Cross then. Thank you, Deirdre, for reading a draft.

I also want to thank my colleagues at the University of Michigan. Sheri Sytsema-Geiger and Audrey Becker stepped up for me when I was deep in this book. The folks in the Department of American Culture have shaped my thinking about just about everything. Special thanks to Sara Blair, William Calvo-Quirós, Greg Dowd, Julie Ellison, Larry La Fountain-Stokes, Sandra Gunning, June Howard, Mary Kelley, and Alex Stern. I was thrilled to use the scholarship of AC PhD Liz Harmon in this book. Peggy McCracken helped jump-start my thinking about the shape of this book. Mark Clague gave me useful Francis Scott Key feedback. And lastly, thanks to University of Michigan Museum of Art Director Tina Olsen for listening and encouraging me through this process and for transforming our museum.

Also, huge thanks to Danielle LaVaque-Manty. Your help was invaluable. Thanks too to Cordelia Ko, Lillian Ku, and the students in AC 103 during Fall 2021 at the University of Michigan.

Thank you, Gayatri Patnaik, for taking on this project and helping me realize its promise. Thanks also to Ruthie Block, Janet Vail, Tiffany Taylor, and the rest of the Beacon Press team.

I am seriously grateful to my pals who read drafts, especially Coco Catallo, Jean Mandel, Dahlia Petrus, Sioban Scanlon, and Ann Stevenson. Thanks to Curt for the great cocktails at various stages of the process. Thanks to my family—to my dad for talking through all of this with me and to my mom for all the love. Thanks to Tom and Brenda, too. And thanks especially to Libby and Riva, who helped me when I was gutted.

Lastly, thanks to Cameron, Finn, Cole, and Haze. You guys are the best part of everything—always.

NOTES

INTRODUCTION

1. Jefferson Davis, *Jefferson Davis: The Essential Writings*, ed. William J. Cooper (New York: Modern Library, 2004), 136.

2. Michael Levenson, "After Threats to Turn It Into a Toilet, a Confederate Monument Is Recovered," *New York Times*, April 11, 2021, https://www.nytimes.com/2021/04/11/us/jefferson-davis-chair-white-lies-matter.html.

3. Cindy Boren, "A Timeline of Colin Kaepernick's Protests Against Police Brutality, Four Years After They Began," *Washington Post*, August 26, 2020, https://www.washingtonpost.com/sports/2020/06/01/colin-kaepernick-kneeling-history.

4. Department of Justice, "Department of Justice Report Regarding the Criminal Investigation into the Shooting Death of Michael Brown by Ferguson Missouri Police Officer Darren Wilson," March 25, 2015, https://www.justice.gov/sites/default/files/opa/press-releases/attachments/2015/03/04/doj_report_on_shooting_of_michael_brown_1.pdf.

5. "'I Can't Breathe': Eric Garner Put in Chokehold by NYPD Officer—Video," *The Guardian*, December 4, 2014, https://www.theguardian.com/us-news/video/2014/dec/04/i-cant-breathe-eric-garner-chokehold-death-video.

6. Ashley Southall, "Daniel Pantaleo, Officer Who Held Eric Garner in Chokehold, Is Fired," *New York Times*, August 19, 2019, https://www.nytimes.com/2019/08/19/nyregion/daniel-pantaleo-fired.html.

7. Boren, "A Timeline."

8. Tadd Haislop, "Colin Kaepernick Kneeling Timeline: How Protests During the National Anthem Started a Movement in the NFL," *Sporting News*, September 13, 2020, https://www.sportingnews.com/us/nfl/news/colin-kaepernick-kneeling-protest-timeline/xktu6ka4diva1s5jxaylrcsse.

9. "Infrastructure," *Cultural Anthropology*, accessed May 19, 2021, https:// journal.culanth.org/index.php/ca/catalog/category/infrastructure.

10. Executive Office of the President, "Promoting Beautiful Federal Civic Architecture," *Federal Register*, December 23, 2020, https://www.federalregister .gov/documents/2020/12/23/2020-28605/promoting-beautiful-federal-civic -architecture.

11. Executive Office of the President, "Promoting Beautiful Federal Civic Architecture."

12. Executive Office of the President.

13. Executive Office of the President.

14. "Not Just Hitler and Mussolini: Neo-Nazis Love Neo-Classical Ar- chitecture, Too," *Pharos: Doing Justice to the Classics*, February 20, 2020, http:// pages.vassar.edu/pharos/2020/02/20/not-just-hitler-and-mussolini-neo-nazis -love-neoclassical-architecture-too.

15. "Not Just Hitler and Mussolini."

16. Kriston Capps, "Why Trump's 'Beautiful' Federal Building Order May Be Here to Stay," *Bloomberg CityLab*, December 23, 2020, https://www.bloom berg.com/news/articles/2020-12-24/trump-s-beautiful-building-order-is-here -to-stay.

17. Ernest Renan, "What Is a Nation?" Foundation for Economic Educa- tion, accessed May 20, 2021, https://fee.org/articles/what-is-a-nation.

18. Renan, "What Is a Nation?"

19. Joe Biden Speech Condemning Capitol Protest Transcript, https:// www.rev.com/blog/transcripts/joe-biden-remarks-condemning-capitol-protest -transcript.

20. Maria Cramer, "Confederate Flag an Unnerving Sight in Capitol," *New York Times*, January 9, 2021, https://www.nytimes.com/2021/01/09/us/poli tics/confederate-flag-capitol.html.

21. Kim R. Holmes, "The Problem of Nationalism," The Heritage Foun- dation, December 13, 2019, https://www.heritage.org/conservatism/commen tary/the-problem-nationalism.

22. Holmes, "The Problem of Nationalism."

23. Richard Wolffe, "Democracy or the White Supremacist Mob: Which Side Is the Republican Party On?" *The Guardian*, February 3, 2021, https://www.theguardian.com/commentisfree/2021/feb/03/democracy-white -supremacist-mob-republican-party.

24. Michael German, "Hidden in Plain Sight: Racism, White Supremacy, and Far-Right Militancy in Law Enforcement," Brennan Center for Justice, August 27, 2020, https://www.brennancenter.org/our-work/research-reports/ hidden-plain-sight-racism-white-supremacy-and-far-right-militancy-law.

25. Jemele Hill, "Donald Trump Is a White Supremacist…" Twitter, September 11, 2017, https://twitter.com/jemelehill/status/907391978194849793.

26. Ta-Nehisi Coates, "The First White President," *The Atlantic*, October 2017, https://www.theatlantic.com/magazine/archive/2017/10/the-first-white-president-ta-nehisi-coates/537909.

27. Coates, "The First White President."

28. Coates.

29. Coates.

30. john a. powell, Hasan Kwame Jeffries, Daniel Newhart, and Eric Stiens, "Towards a Transformative View of Race: The Crisis and Opportunity of Katrina," PN: Planners Network, April 26, 2006, https://www.plannersnetwork.org/2006/04/towards-a-transformative-view-of-race-the-crisis-and-opportunity-of-katrina.

31. Amanda Kolson Hurley, "How the Critics Covered the NMAAHC," *Architect*, October 17, 2016, https://www.architectmagazine.com/design/how-the-critics-covered-the-nmaahc_o.

32. Eric Hobsbawm, "Introduction: Inventing Traditions," in *The Invention of Tradition*, eds. Eric Hobsbawm and Terence Ranger (New York: Cambridge University Press, 1988) 14.

33. Hugh Trevor-Roper, "The Invention of Tradition: The Highland Tradition of Scotland," in *The Invention of Tradition*, eds. Eric Hobsbawm and Terence Ranger (New York: Cambridge University Press, 1988) 15.

34. Matt Mathers, "Proud Boys MAGA DC March Kilts Made by LGBTQ-Owned Company That Has Since Removed Them from Sale," *Independent*, December 15, 2020, https://www.independent.co.uk/news/world/americas/proud-boys-maga-dc-march-kilts-lgbtq-b1774329.html.

35. Ceili Doyle, "'Heritage Not Hate': Why Some Rural Ohioans Say They Fly Confederate Flag," *Columbus Dispatch*, June 21, 2020, https://www.dispatch.com/story/news/local/2020/06/21/lsquoheritage-not-hatersquo-why-some-rural-ohioans-say-they-fly-confederate-flag/112772304.

36. Doyle, "Heritage Not Hate."

37. Khary Polk, *Contagions of Empire: Scientific Racism, Sexuality, and Black Military Workers Abroad, 1898–1948* (Chapel Hill: University of North Carolina Press, 2020), 5.

SECTION I. MEMORIALS

1. For more on this, see Kristin Ann Hass, *Sacrificing Soldiers on the National Mall* (Berkeley: University of California Press, 2013).

2. For the purposes of this book, *monuments* and *memorials* are interchangeable terms. Some have tried to refine distinct definitions of the two, but because they are mostly used to mean the same thing in common usage, such definitions are not terribly useful.

3. "About the Ronald Reagan Legacy Project," The Ronald Reagan Legacy Project, Americans for Tax Reform, accessed May 26, 2021, http://www.ron aldreaganlegacyproject.org/about.

4. "About the Ronald Reagan Legacy Project."

5. William Sturkey, "Carr Was Indeed Much More Than *Silent Sam*," *The Herald Sun*, October 31, 2017, https://www.heraldsun.com/opinion/article181 567401.html.

6. Antonia Noori Farzan, "'Silent Sam': A Racist Jim Crow Era Speech Inspired UNC Students to Topple a Confederate Monument on Campus," *Washington Post*, August 21, 2018, https://www.washingtonpost.com/news/morning -mix/wp/2018/08/21/silent-sam-a-racist-jim-crow-era-speech-inspired-unc -students-to-topple-a-confederate-monument-on-campus.

7. "Park Statistics," *Little Bighorn Battlefield*, National Park Service, accessed May 26, 2021, https://www.nps.gov/libi/learn/management/statistics .htm.

8. Tony Perrottet, "Little Bighorn Reborn," *Smithsonian Magazine*, April 2005, https://www.smithsonianmag.com/travel/little-bighorn-reborn -79240914.

9. "Indian Memorial at Bighorn Finally Dedicated," Indianz.com, June 6, 2003, https://www.indianz.com/news/2003/002868.asp.

10. Perrottet, "Little Bighorn Reborn."

11. John Troesser, "The Spirit of Sacrifice, aka, the Alamo Cenotaph," *Texas Escapes Online Magazine*, accessed Mary 26, 2021, http://www.texases capes.com/SanAntonioTx/The-Alamo-Cenotaph.htm.

12. Jan Ross P. Sakian and David Martin Davies, "What Is the History Behind the Alamo Cenotaph & Why Is It So Controversial Today?" Texas Public Radio, August 13, 2018, audio, https://www.tpr.org/show/the-source /2018-08-13/what-is-the-history-behind-the-alamo-cenotaph-why-is-it-so -controversial-today.

13. For a more detailed version of this story, see Hass, *Sacrificing Soldiers*.

14. "442nd Regional Combat Team," Go for Broke, accessed May 26, 2021, https://www.goforbroke.org/learn/history/military_units/442nd.php.

15. "About the Foundation," NAJMF, accessed on May 26, 2021, https:// www.njamemorial.org/about.

16. For much more on this, see Hass, *Sacrificing Soldiers*.

CHAPTER 1. THE LOST CAUSE WON

1. Kieran J. O'Keefe, "Monuments to the American Revolution," *Journal of the American Revolution*, September 17, 2019, https://allthingsliberty.com/2019/09/monuments-to-the-american-revolution. Used with the permission of the author; thank you, Kieran O'Keefe.

2. O'Keefe, "Monuments."

3. For more on this, see Kristin Ann Hass, *Sacrificing Soldiers on the National Mall* (Berkeley: University of California Press, 2013).

4. For more on this, see Jeffery Smith, *The Rural Cemetery Movement: Places of Paradox in Nineteenth-Century America* (Lanham Maryland: Lexington Books, 2017).

5. James A. Hijiya, "American Gravestones and Attitudes toward Death: A Brief History," *Proceedings of the American Philosophical Society* 127, no. 5 (1983): 339–63, https://www.jstor.org/stable/pdf/986503.pdf.

6. Colleen McDannell, *Material Christianity: Religion and Popular Culture* (New Haven: Yale University Press, 1995): p. 107, https://www.google.com/books/edition/Material_Christianity/9qxO-FadNckC?hl=en&gbpv=1&dq=%E2%80%9CPicturesque+landscapes+purified+the+sentiments+of+visitors,+while+monuments+to+the+dead+evoked+a+sense+of+history,+continuity,+and+patriotism&pg=PA107&printsec=frontcover.

7. For more on this, see Hass, *Sacrificing Soldiers*.

8. Myron Magnet, "How Private Philanthropy Saved the Founders' Homes," *City Journal*, August 2014, https://www.city-journal.org/html/how-private-philanthropy-saved-founders%E2%80%99-homes-13689.html.

9. For more on this, see Caroline E. Janney, *Burying the Dead but Not the Past: Ladies' Memorial Associations and the Lost Cause* (Chapel Hill: University of North Carolina Press, 2008).

10. "Why the Ladies' Aid Societies, Ladies' Memorial Associations, Daughters of the Confederacy?" *Confederate Veteran* 24, no. 3 (March 1916): 110.

11. For more on this, see Simon Wendt, *The DAR and Patriotic Memory* (Gainsville, FL: University Press of Florida, 2020).

12. "History of the UDC," United Daughters of the Confederacy, accessed May 26, 2021, https://hqudc.org/history-of-the-united-daughters-of-the-confederacy.

13. Aaron O'Neill, "Life Expectancy (from Birth) in the United States from 1860–2020," Statista, February 3, 2021, https://www.statista.com/statistics/1040079/life-expectancy-united-states-all-time.

14. "History of the UDC."

15. Linda Edwards, "Statement from the President General," United Daughters of the Confederacy, accessed May 26, 2021, https://hqudc.org/.

16. Edwards, "Statement from the President General."

17. Kevin Sack and Alan Blinder, "No Regrets from Dylann Roof in Jailhouse Manifesto," *New York Times*, January 5, 2017, https://www.nytimes.com/2017/01/05/us/no-regrets-from-dylann-roof-in-jailhouse-manifesto.html.

18. The Southern Poverty Law Center identifies at least thirty-one neo-Confederate groups active in 2020, but this is the tip of the iceberg in terms of use of the Confederate flag, https://www.splcenter.org/fighting-hate/extremist-files/ideology/neo-confederate.

19. Edwards, "Statement from the President General."

20. Washington-Williams spoke publicly of her attempts. I have been trying to get information about her application from the UDC for a decade.

21. Edwards, "Statement from the President General."

22. Edwards.

23. Edwards. Trademark included.

24. Edwards.

25. J. Edward Hackett and Walter Isaac, "Refuting the Four Legs of Southern Confederate Memorial Defenders' Arguments," *Essays in the Philosophy of Humanism* 27 (2019): 63, http://americanhumanist.org/wp-content/uploads/2019/12/art-4-Hackett-Refuting-the-Four-Legs-of-Confederate-Monument.pdf.

26. Hackett and Isaac, "Refuting the Four Legs."

27. "Social Divisions in Antebellum North Carolina," Anchor, accessed May 27, 2021, https://www.ncpedia.org/anchor/social-divisions-antebellum.

28. Chris Carola, "Civil War 'Silent Sentinels' Still on Guard in North, South," AP, April 18, 2015, https://apnews.com/article/7fd4944b673e48c9b98c12257fb8e007.

29. Joe Killian, "UNC-Chapel Hill Board of Trustees votes to remove white supremacist names from buildings," *The Pulse* NC Policy Watch, https://pulse.ncpolicywatch.org/2020/07/29/unc-chapel-hill-board-of-trustees-votes-to-remove-white-supremacist-names-from-buildings/#sthash.IfNJK8Lk.4WtvzlCR.dpbs.

30. Hilary N. Green, "Julian Carr's Speech at the Dedication of Silent Sam," accessed May 27, 2021, https://hgreen.people.ua.edu/transcription-carr-speech.html.

31. Green, "Julian Carr's Speech."

32. Green.

33. Green.

34. Cole Villena, "Maya Little Isn't Done Fighting White Supremacy at

UNC," *Indy Week*, December 18, 2018, https://indyweek.com/news/northcar
olina/maya-little-white-supremacy-unc.

35. Julia Jacobs and Alan Blinder, "Chancellor Explores New Spot for
'Silent Sam,'" *New York Times*, August 31, 2018, https://www.nytimes.com/20
18/08/31/us/north-carolina-silent-sam-moving.html.

36. Jacobs and Blinder, "Chancellor Explores New Spot."

37. Green, "Julian Carr's Speech."

38. Green.

39. Speech by Mary Lyde Williams at the unveiling of the monument,
printed in the *Wilmington Morning Star*, 15 June 1913, https://exhibits.lib.unc
.edu/files/original/3333889eb89e79aabbeb85298a8960db.pdf.

40. Williams.

41. Williams.

42. Williams.

43. Green, "Julian Carr's Speech."

44. Karen L. Cox, "The Whole Point of Confederate Monuments Is to
Celebrate White Supremacy," *Washington Post*, August 16, 2017, https://www
.washingtonpost.com/news/posteverything/wp/2017/08/16/the-whole-point
-of-confederate-monuments-is-to-celebrate-white-supremacy.

45. "Whose Heritage," Southern Poverty Law Center, accessed May 27,
2021, https://www.splcenter.org/data-projects/whose-heritage.

46. "Whose Heritage."

47. Archer Anderson, "Dedication of the Monument to General Robert E.
Lee," Lee Family Digital Archive, accessed May 27, 2021, https://leefamilyar
chive.org/reference/addresses/anderson/index.html.

48. Anderson, "Dedication of the Monument."

49. Thessaly LaForce, Zoë Lescaze, Nancy Hass, and M. H. Miller, "The
25 Most Influential American Works of Protest Art Since World War II," *New
York Times Style Magazine*, October 15, 2020, https://www.nytimes.com/2020
/10/15/t-magazine/most-influential-protest-art.html.

50. Ned Oliver, "In Lee Monument Lawsuit, Judge Rules It's No Longer
Public Policy in Virginia to Honor Confederacy," *Virginia Mercury*, October
27, 2020, https://www.virginiamercury.com/blog-va/in-lee-monument-lawsuit
-judge-rules-its-no-longer-public-policy-in-virginia-to-honor-confederacy.

51. Oliver, "In Lee Monument Lawsuit, Judge Rules."

52. Bénédicte Deschamps, "'The cornerstone is laid': Italian American
Memorial Building in New York City and Immigrants' Right to the City at the
Turn of the Twentieth Century," *European Journal of American Studies* 10, no. 3
(2015): 2.

53. Deschamps, "'The cornerstone is laid,'" 3.

54. "From Italians to America," *New York Times*, July 9, 1890, https://times machine.nytimes.com/timesmachine/1890/07/09/103251830.pdf.

55. "From Italians to America."

56. "Columbus Memorials," *New York Times*, June 13, 1892, https://times machine.nytimes.com/timesmachine/1892/06/13/104135789.pdf.

57. "Columbus Memorials."

58. Brock Read, "UNC Will Give Silent Sam to a Confederate Group— Along With a $2.5-Million Trust," *The Chronicle of Higher Education*, December 1, 2019, https://www.chronicle.com/article/unc-will-give-silent-sam-to -a-confederate-group-along-with-a-2-5-million-trust.

59. Michael Levenson, "Toppled but Not Gone: U.N.C. Grapples Anew With the Fate of Silent Sam," *New York Times*, https://www.nytimes.com/2020 /02/14/us/unc-silent-sam-statue-settlement.html.

60. North Carolina General Statutes §100: Monuments, Memorials, and Parks, accessed May 27, 2021, https://www.ncleg.gov/EnactedLegislation/Stat utes/PDF/ByChapter/Chapter_100.pdf.

CHAPTER 2. THE LOST CAUSE KEEPS WINNING

1. Andrew M. Shanken, "Planning Memory: Living Memorials in the United States During World War II," *The Art Bulletin* 84, no. 1 (March 2002): 130.

2. Smithsonian Art Museum, "Viquesney, E. M., 1876–1946, Sculptor," Art Inventories Catalogue, accessed June 2, 2021, https://siris-artinventories.si.edu /ipac20/ipac.jsp?session=U614792W64P39.174&source=~!siartinventories&pr ofile=ariall&page=2&group=0&term=Viquesney%2C+E.+M.%2C+1876-1946 %2C+sculptor.&index=AUTHOR&uindex=&aspect=Browse&menu=search& ri=1&ts=1614792064537&deduping=.

3. Karen Gardner, "The History Behind the Doughboy," Emmitsburg Area Historical Society, accessed June 2, 2021, http://www.emmitsburg.net/ar chive_list/articles/history/stories/doughboy.htm.

4. As quoted in Jennifer Wingate, "Over the Top: The Doughboy in World War I Memorials and Visual Culture," *American Art* 19, no. 2 (Summer 2005): 27.

5. Wingate, "Over the Top," 30.

6. Shanken, "Planning Memory," 130.

7. Shanken, 130.

8. New York City Department of Parks and Recreation, "World War I

Monuments," accessed June 2, 2021, https://www.nycgovparks.org/about/histo ry/veterans#world-war-I.

9. "Touring the New Victory Highway," *Concrete Highway Magazine*, April 1924, https://archive.org/details/concretehighwaymooportrich/page/94/mode /2up?view=theater.

10. New York City Department of Parks and Recreation, "World War II Memorials," accessed June 2, 2021, https://www.nycgovparks.org/about/histo ry/veterans#world-war-II.

11. New York City Department of Parks and Recreation, "World War II Memorials."

12. Victoria Wolcott, *Race, Riots, and Roller Coasters: The Struggle over Seg- regated Recreation in America* (Philadelphia: University of Pennsylvania Press, 2012), 1.

13. Martin Luther King Jr., "Letter from Birmingham Jail," August 1963, https://www.csuchico.edu/iege/_assets/documents/susi-letter-from -birmingham-jail.pdf.

14. For more on this, see Richard Rothstein, *The Color of Law* (New York: Liveright, 2017), and Thomas Sugrue, *The Origins of the Urban Crisis* (Prince- ton: Princeton University Press, 1996).

15. This is a very short summary of the arguments of my books *Carried to the Wall* (Oakland: University of California Press, 1998) and *Sacrificing Soldiers on the National Mall* (Oakland: University of California Press, 2013).

16. For more on this, see Hass, *Sacrificing Soldiers*.

17. Dell Upton, *What Can and Can't Be Said: Race, Uplift, and Monument Building in the Contemporary South* (New Haven: Yale University Press, 2015), 14.

18. Upton, *What Can and Can't Be Said*.

19. Southern Poverty Law Center, "Civil Rights Memorial," accessed June 2, 2021, https://www.splcenter.org/civil-rights-memorial.

20. Kayla Epstein, "This Emmett Till Memorial Was Vandalized Again. And Again. And Again. Now, It's Bulletproof," *Washington Post*, October 20, 2019, https://www.washingtonpost.com/history/2019/10/20/this-emmett-till -memorial-was-vandalized-again-again-again-now-its-bulletproof.

21. Upton, *What Can and Can't Be Said*.

22. Doug Stanglin, "Fact Check: Black Lives Matter Protesters Did Not Deface Vietnam Memorial in Washington," *USA Today*, September 18, 2020, https://www.usatoday.com/story/news/factcheck/2020/09/18/fact-check-blm -protesters-did-not-deface-vietnam-memorial-dc/3479002001.

23. Ethan Kytle and Blain Roberts, "Take Down the Confederate Flags, but Not the Monuments," *The Atlantic*, June 25, 2015, https://www.theatlantic

.com/politics/archive/2015/06/-confederate-monuments-flags-south-carolina
/396836/.

24. Southern Poverty Law Center, "SPLC Reports Over 160 Confederate Symbols Removed in 2020," February 23, 2021, https://www.splcenter.org/presscenter/splc-reports-over-160-confederate-symbols-removed-2020.

25. Southern Poverty Law Center, "SPLC Reports Over 160."

26. Southern Poverty Law Center.

SECTION II. MUSEUMS

1. Donna Haraway, "Teddy Bear Patriarchy: Taxidermy in the Garden of Eden, New York City, 1908–1936," *Social Text* no. 11 (Winter, 1984–1985): 20, https://doi.org/10.2307/466593.

2. Sumaya Kassim, "The Museum Will Not Be Decolonised," Media Diversified, November 15, 2017, https://mediadiversified.org/2017/11/15/the-museum-will-not-be-decolonised.

3. Robin Pogrebin, "Roosevelt Statue to Be Removed from Museum of Natural History," *New York Times,* June 21, 2020, https://www.nytimes.com/2020/06/21/arts/design/roosevelt-statue-to-be-removed-from-museum-of-natural-history.html.

4. I-Chun Chen, "Met Museum Attendance Up 6 Percent in 2016, Natural History Museum Attendance Holds Steady," *New York Business Journal,* June 2, 2017, https://www.bizjournals.com/newyork/news/2017/06/02/met-museum-attendance-up.html.

5. Pogrebin, "Roosevelt Statue to Be Removed."

6. Terence Washington (panelist), "Future of Art Institutions: Rebuild or Repair?" UMMA, February 22, 2021, https://umma.umich.edu/events/5623/future-art-institutions-rebuild-or-repair.

7. Bob Mondello, "A History of Museums, 'The Memory of Mankind,'" NPR, November 24, 2008, https://www.npr.org/templates/story/story.php?storyId=97377145.

8. Giuliana Bullard, "Government Doubles Official Estimate: There Are 35,000 Active Museums in the U.S.," Institute of Museum and Library Services, May 19, 2014, https://www.imls.gov/news/government-doubles-official-estimate-there-are-35000-active-museums-us.

9. Statista Research Department, "Museums in the U.S.—Statistics & Facts," Statista, February 5, 2021, https://www.statista.com/topics/1509/museums/#dossierKeyfigures.

10. Karl Meyer, *The Art Museum: Power, Money, Ethics: A Twentieth Century Fund Report* (New York: Morrow, 1979), 24.

11. Bonnie Pitman, "Muses, Museums, and Memories," *Daedalus* 128, no. 3 (1999): 1, https://www.jstor.org/stable/20027565.

12. Pitman, "Muses, Museums, and Memories."

13. Executive Office of the President, "Promoting Beautiful Federal Civic Architecture," Federal Register, December 18, 2020, https://www.federalregis ter.gov/documents/2020/12/23/2020-28605/promoting-beautiful-federal-civic -architecture.

14. Executive Office of the President, "Promoting Beautiful Federal Civic Architecture."

15. Alice Stevenson, "Egyptian Archaeology and the Museum," Oxford Handbooks Online, February 2015, https://doi.org/10.1093/oxfordhb/978019 9935413.013.25.

16. Alice Stevenson, "Egyptian Archaeology and the Museum."

17. Neil Harris, "Museums and Controversy: Some Introductory Reflections," *The Journal of American History* 83, no. 3 (1995): 1102, https://doi.org /10.2307/2945115.

18. Coco Fusco, "The Couple in the Cage," Coco Fusco, accessed June 4, 2021, https://www.cocofusco.com/the-couple-in-the-cage.

19. Leticia Robles-Moreno, "'Please, Don't Discover Me': On the Year of the White Bear," *Walker Reader*, July 19, 2018, https://walkerart.org/magazine/ guillermo-gomez-pena-and-coco-fuscos-the-year-of-the-white-bear.

20. Carol Duncan, *Civilizing Rituals: Inside Public Art Museums* (New York: Routledge, 1995), 8.

21. Carol Duncan, "Art Museums and the Ritual of Citizenship," in *Exhibiting Cultures: The Politics and Poetics of Museum Display*, eds. Ivan Karp and Steven D. Lavine (Washington, D.C.: Smithsonian Books, 1991), 88–103, https://pages.ucsd.edu/~bgoldfarb/cocu108/data/texts/Duncan.pdf.

22. Duncan, "Art Museums and the Ritual of Citizenship," 88.

CHAPTER 3. WHITE TEMPLES EMERGED

1. Ellen Sacco, "Racial Theory, Museum Practice: The Colored World of Charles Willson Peale," *Museum Anthropology*, 20-2 (1996): 25, https:// anthrosource-onlinelibrary-wiley-com.proxy.lib.umich.edu/doi/epdf/10.1525/ mua.1996.20.2.25.

2. Ellen Sacco, "Racial Theory, Museum Practice."

3. Silvia Dominguez, Simón E. Weffer, and David Embrick, "White Sanctuaries: White Supremacy, Racism, Space, and Fine Arts in Two Metropolitan Museums," *American Behavioral Scientist* 64, no. 14 (2020): 2028–2043, https://doi.org/10.1177/0002764220975077.

4. Dominguez, Weffer, and Embrick, "White Sanctuaries."

5. Dominguez, Weffer, and Embrick.

6. Stuart Hall, "Whose Heritage? Un-settling 'The Heritage', Re-imagining the Post-Nation," *Reading the Periphery.org*, accessed Jun 4, 2021, https://readingtheperiphery.org/hall2.

7. Steven Conn, *Museums and American Intellectual Life, 1876–1926* (Chicago: University of Chicago Press, 1998), 4.

8. "About the Museum," The Charleston Museum, accessed June 4, 2021, https://www.charlestonmuseum.org/support-us/about-the-museum.

9. Conn, *Museums and American Intellectual Life*, 37.

10. Conn.

11. G. Brown Goode, *Museum-History and Museums of History* (New York: The Knickerbocker Press, 1889), https://babel.hathitrust.org/cgi/pt?id=hvd.32044072249097&view=1up&seq=12.

12. Ellen Sacco, "Racial Theory, Museum Practice," 31, https://anthrosource-onlinelibrary-wiley-com.proxy.lib.umich.edu/doi/epdf/10.1525/mua.1996.20.2.25.

13. "A Museum of Art and Culture," Peabody Essex Museum, accessed June 3, 2021, https://www.pem.org/about-pem/museum-history.

14. Walter Muir Whitehall, Clifford K. Shipton, Louis Leonard Tucker, and Wilcomb E. Washburn, "History of Museums in the United States: Report of a Session of the American Historical Association 28 December, 1964," *Curator* 8, no. 1 (1965): 5, https://doi.org/10.1111/j.2151-6952.1965.tb00850.x.

15. Walter Muir Whitehill, *The East India Marine Society and the Peabody Museum of Salem: A Sesquicentennial History* (Salem, Mass: Peabody Museum, 1949), vii, https://babel.hathitrust.org/cgi/pt?id=mdp.39015056996500&view=1up&seq=13.

16. Whitehill, *The East India Marine Society.*

17. Daniel Trilling, "What National Museums Tell Us About National Identities," *Apollo*, February 26, 2018, https://www.apollo-magazine.com/what-national-museums-tell-us-about-national-identities.

18. Trilling, "What National Museums Tell Us."

19. Trilling.

20. Ann Pamela Cunningham, "To the Ladies of the South," *Charleston Mercury*, December 2, 1853. And quoted in https://muse-jhu-edu.proxy.lib.umich.edu/chapter/2203675/pdf.

21. "The Birth of the Mount Vernon Ladies' Association," George Washington's Mount Vernon, accessed June 4, 2021, https://www.mountvernon.org/preservation/mount-vernon-ladies-association/early-history/birth-of-the-mount-vernon-ladies-association.

22. Carol Borchert Cadou, Luke J. Pecoraro, Thomas A. Reinhart, eds., *Stewards of Memory: The Past, Present, and Future of Historic Preservation at George Washington's Mount Vernon* (Charlottesville, VA: University of Virginia Press, 2018).

23. "The Birth of the Mount Vernon Ladies' Association."

24. Mount Vernon Ladies Association of the Union, *An Illustrated Handbook of Mount Vernon, the Home of Washington* (Philadelphia: Beck Engraving Co., 1932), https://babel.hathitrust.org/cgi/pt?id=hvd.hx4k9t&view=1up&seq=4.

25. Mount Vernon Ladies Association, *An Illustrated Handbook.*

26. Kate Haulman, "'George Washington's Mount Vernon.'"

27. Kate Haulman.

28. Michael Kammen, *Mystic Chords of Memory: The Transformation of Tradition in American Culture* (New York: Vintage Books, 1991), 154.

29. Bonnie Pitman, "Muses, Museums, and Memories," *Daedalus* 128, no. 3 (1999): 1, https://www.jstor.org/stable/20027565.

30. Steven Conn as quoted in Pitman, "Muses, Museums, and Memories."

31. Pitman.

32. Metropolitan Museum of Art, "Making the Met: 1870–2020," accessed June 4, 2021, https://www.metmuseum.org/-/media/files/exhibitions/2020/making-the-met-large-print-labels.pdf.

33. Thanks to Elizabeth Harmon, "From Public Trust to Private Foundation: American Philanthropy and the Politics of Surplus Wealth, 1826–1929" (PhD dissertation, University of Michigan, 2017).

34. Ingrid A. Steffensen-Bruce, *Marble Palaces: Temples of Art* (Lewisburg, PA: Bucknell University Press, 1998), 11.

35. Steffensen-Bruce, *Marble Palaces, Temples of Art.*

36. Conn, *Museums and American Intellectual Life*, 9.

37. Conn, 13.

38. Tony Bennett, *The Birth of the Museum: History, Theory, Politics* (New York: Routledge, 1995), 95.

39. Colin Davey, *The American Museum of Natural History and How It Got That Way* (New York: Fordham University Press, 2019), 3.

40. Donna Haraway, "Teddy Bear Patriarchy: Taxidermy in the Garden of Eden, New York City, 1908–1936," *Social Text* no. 11 (Winter, 1984–1985): 20, https://doi.org/10.2307/466593.

41. Michael Yudell, *Race Unmasked: Biology and Race in the Twentieth Century* (New York: Columbia University Press, 2014), 45.

42. Robert W. Rydell, "The Proximity of the Past: Eugenics in American Culture," *Modern Intellectual History* 7, no. 3: 667, https://doi.org/10.1017/S1479244310000296.

43. Michael Yudell, *Race Unmasked*.

44. As quoted in Yudell, *Race Unmasked*, 47.

45. Yudell, 15.

46. Phillips Verner Bradford and Harvey Blume, *Ota Benga: The Pygmy in the Zoo* (New York: St. Martin's Press, 1992), 121.

47. "Man and Monkey Show Disapproved by Clergy," *New York Times*, September 10, 1906, https://timesmachine.nytimes.com/timesmachine/1906/09/10/101797010.pdf?pdf_redirect=true&ip=0.

48. "Man and Monkey Show Disapproved by Clergy."

49. "Brain of Last Yahi Indian Found at Smithsonian," *New York Times*, February 21, 1999, https://www.nytimes.com/1999/02/21/us/brain-of-last-yahi-indian-found-at-smithsonian.html.

50. Kevin L. Cook, "Reckoning with the West at the Centennial," March 27, 2018, https://www.historynet.com/reckoning-west-centennial/.

51. Henry Sockbeson, "Repatriation Act Protects Native Burial Remains and Artifacts," *Native American Rights Fund Legal Review* 16, no. 1 (1991): 1, https://www.narf.org/nill/documents/nlr/nlr16-1.pdf.

52. Sockbeson, "Repatriation Act," 2.

53. Goode, *Museum-History and Museums of History*.

54. Mary Jo Arnoldi, "From the Diorama to the Dialogic: A Century of Exhibiting Africa at the Smithsonian's Museum of Natural History," *Cahiers d'Études Africaines*, vol. 39, Cahier 155/156, Prélever, exhiber. La mise en musées (1999), 701–726.

55. Daniel Larkin, "The Met Misses the Mark in Recounting Its Own Complicated History," Hyperallergic, November 11, 2020, https://hyperallergic.com/598105/making-the-met-review-metropolitan-museum-of-art.

56. For more on this, see Mabel O. Wilson, *Negro Building: Black Americans in the World of Fairs and Museums* (Oakland: University of California Press, 2021).

57. "1901–1925," Library of Congress, accessed June 7, 2021, https://www.loc.gov/collections/african-american-perspectives-rare-books/articles-and-essays/timeline-of-african-american-history/1901-to-1925.

58. Sumaya Kassim, "The Museum Will Not Be Decolonised," Media Diversified, November 15, 2017, https://mediadiversified.org/2017/11/15/the-museum-will-not-be-decolonised.

59. Kassim, "The Museum Will Not Be Decolonised."
60. Kassim.

CHAPTER 4. WHITE TEMPLES RESHAPED?

1. Melani McAlister, *Epic Encounters: Culture, Media, and U.S. Interests in the Middle East Since 1945* (Berkeley: University of California Press, 2005), 126.

2. McAlister, *Epic Encounters*, 127

3. As quoted in McAlister, 142.

4. McAlister, 142.

5. McAlister, 140

6. Wilson, *Negro Building*, 244.

7. Wilson, 245.

8. "Flewellen, Icabod," Encyclopedia of Cleveland History, accessed June 8, 2021, https://case.edu/ech/articles/f/flewellen-icabod.

9. As quoted in Wilson, *Negro Building*, 247.

10. "About the Wright," The Charles H. Wright Museum of African American History, accessed Jun 8, 2021, https://www.thewright.org/about -wright.

11. "About the Wright."

12. Fath Davis Ruffins, "Mythos, Memory, and History: African American Preservation Efforts, 1820–1990," *Museums and Communities: The Politics of Public Culture*, eds. Ivan Karp, Christine Mullen Kreamer, and Steven D. Lavine (Washington, D.C.: Smithsonian Institution Press, 1992), 557.

13. Ruffins, "Mythos, Memory, and History," 565.

14. Wilson, *Negro Building*, 266.

15. Wilson, 294.

16. Wilson, 294.

17. Le Han, "Our Home Is Here: History, Memory, and Identity in the Museum of Chinese in America," *Communication, Culture, and Critique* 6 (2013): 161.

18. Peter C. Marzio, *A Nation of Nations: The People Who Came to America as Seen Through Objects and Documents Exhibited at the Smithsonian Institution* (New York: Harper & Row, 1976), 306.

19. Marzio, *A Nation of Nations*.

20. Elizabeth Kastor, "Remembrance of Sorrows Past," *Washington Post*, October 1, 1987, https://www.washingtonpost.com/archive/lifestyle/1987/10 /01/remembrance-of-sorrows-past/b2e20e28-d5bd-4309-bde8-6e8cc8fb34a4.

21. Kastor, "Remembrance of Sorrows Past."

22. Sandra C. Taylor, "A More Perfect Union, by Thomas Crouch," *Public Historian* 10, no. 3 (1988): 92–93, https://doi.org/10.2307/3378533.

23. "Senate Resolution 257—Relating to the 'Enola Gay' Exhibit," *The Journal of American History* 82, no. 3 (1995): 1136–144, https://doi.org/10.2307/2945120.

24. "About the Museum," National Museum of the American Indian, https://americanindian.si.edu/about.

25. 101st Congress, National Museum of the American Indian Act, S.978, 101st Cong. (1989), https://americanindian.si.edu/sites/1/files/pdf/about/NMAIAct.pdf.

26. C. Joseph Genetin-Pilawa, "Exhibit Review: *Nation to Nation: Treaties Between the United States and American Indian Nations*, National Museum of the American Indian, Smithsonian Institution, Washington, DC," *The Public Historian* 38, no. 2 (2016): 72–79, https://doi.org/10.1525/tph.2016.38.2.72.

27. Scott Boehm, "Privatizing Public Memory: The Price of Patriotic Philanthropy and the Post 9/11 Politics of Display," *American Quarterly* 58, no. 4 (2006): 1147–1166, https://www.jstor.org/stable/40068409.

28. Michael A. Fletcher, "Helms Vows to Block African-American Museum Senate Filibuster Could Kill Measure the Create Smithsonian Facility on Mall," *Baltimore Sun*, October 4, 1994, https://www.baltimoresun.com/news/bs-xpm-1994-10-04-1994277046-story.html.

29. Fletcher, "Helms Vows to Block African-American Museum."

30. Lonnie Bunch, *A Fool's Errand: Creating the National Museum of African American History and Culture in the Age of Bush, Obama, and Trump* (Washington, D.C.: Smithsonian Books, 2019), 158.

31. "The Building," *National Museum of African American History and Culture*, accessed June 9, 2021, https://nmaahc.si.edu/explore/building.

32. "James Madison's Montpelier Reveals Groundbreaking Exhibition, The Mere Distinction of Colour," *Cision PR Newswire*, June 5, 2017, https://www.prnewswire.com/news-releases/james-madisons-montpelier-unveils-groundbreaking-exhibition-the-mere-distinction-of-colour-300468158.html.

33. Silvia Dominguez, Simón E. Weffer, and David Embrick, "White Sanctuaries: White Supremacy, Racism, Space, and Fine Arts in Two Metropolitan Museums," *American Behavioral Scientist* 64, no. 14 (2020): 2028–2043, https://doi.org/10.1177/0002764220975077.

34. Dominguez, Weffer, and Embrick, "White Sanctuaries."

35. Dominguez, Weffer, and Embrick.

36. Maurice Berger, "Are Art Museums Racist?" *Art in America*, March 31, 2020, https://www.artnews.com/art-in-america/features/maurice-berger-are-art-museums-racist-1202682524.

37. Robert Coles, "Whose Museums?" *American Art* 6, no. 1 (Winter, 1992), 6–11.

SECTION III. PATRIOTIC PRACTICES

1. Gladys Hansen, "Dorothea Lange at Raphael Weill School—1942," The Museum of the City of San Francisco, March 1999, http://www.sfmuseum .org/hist10/lange2.html.

2. William A. Galston, "In Defense of a Reasonable Patriotism," Brookings, July 23, 2018, https://www.brookings.edu/research/in-defense-of -a-reasonable-patriotism.

3. Cody Dodge Ewert, "Lessons in Loyalty: American Patriotism and Education in the Progressive Era" (master's thesis, University of Montana, 2012), https://scholarworks.umt.edu/cgi/viewcontent.cgi?article=1639&context=etd.

4. Patricia Yollin, "A Photographer's Quest: Japanese-American Internment Then and Now," KQED, April 8, 2015, https://www.kqed.org/news/1048 2521/a-photographers-quest-japanese-american-internment-then-and-now.

5. Wilfred M. McClay, "How to Think About Patriotism," *National Affairs*, no. 35 (Spring 2018), https://www.nationalaffairs.com/publications/detail/how -to-think-about-patriotism.

6. Andrew Ujifusa, "'Trump Commission Says Identity Politics and 'Bitterness' Have Warped History Classes," *Education Week*, January 18, 2021, https://www.edweek.org/policy-politics/trump-commission-says-identity -politics-and-bitterness-have-warped-history-classes/2021/01.

7. Ujifusa, "Trump Commission."

8. Ujifusa.

9. David Aldridge, "National Anthem Is Inseparable from Politics," NBA, May 28, 2018, https://www.nba.com/news/morning-tip-national-anthem -history-first-amendment.

CHAPTER 5. ALLEGIENCE GOT PLEDGED

1. Cecilia Elizabeth O'Leary, *To Die For: The Paradox of American Patriotism* (Princeton: Princeton University Press, 2000), 11.

2. Thomas Paine, *Common Sense* (Philadelphia: R. Bell, 1776), https://www .loc.gov/item/2006681076.

3. O'Leary, *To Die For*, 12.

4. O'Leary.

5. O'Leary, 15.

6. "Madison Debates: June 29," The Avalon Project: Documents in Law, History and Diplomacy, accessed June 9, 2021, https://avalon.law.yale.edu/18 th_century/debates_629.asp.

7. O'Leary, *To Die For*, 18.

8. O'Leary, 19.

9. O'Leary, 20.

10. Peter Ansoff, "The Flag on Prospect Hill," *Raven* 13 (2006): 77–100, https://web.archive.org/web/20150205121402/http://www.nava.org/sites/de fault/files/NAVA_Raven_v13_2006_p077-100.pdf.

11. "Journals of the Continental Congress Vol. 8," *A Century of Lawmaking for a New Nation: U.S. Congressional Documents and Debates, 1774–1875*, accessed June 9, 2021, http://memory.loc.gov/cgi-bin/ampage?collId=lljc&file Name=008/lljc008.db&recNum=90.

12. Matthew Dennis, "New Nationalism in an 'Era of Good Feelings,'" National Park Service, accessed June 9, 2021, https://www.nps.gov/articles/ new-nationalism-in-an-era-of-good-feelings.htm.

13. Dennis, "New Nationalism."

14. Jefferson Morley, "Even Republicans Should Care About the Racist History of 'The Star-Spangled Banner,'" *Washington Post*, August 28, 2020, https://www.washingtonpost.com/outlook/2020/08/28/even-republicans -should-care-about-racist-history-star-spangled-banner.

15. As quoted in Jefferson Morley, *Snow-Storm in August: The Struggle for American Freedom and Washington's Race Riot of 1835* (New York: Knopf Doubleday, 2013), 40. My colleague Mark Clague contests this quote.

16. Morley, "Even Republicans Should Care."

17. David Clark Scott, "Is the US National Anthem a Racist Song?" *The Christian Science Monitor Daily*, June 30, 2020, https://www.csmonitor.com/ Daily/2020/20200630/Is-the-US-national-anthem-a-racist-song.

18. Adam Forgie, "Petition to Remove 'Star-Spangled Banner' as Anthem Calls It 'Racist, Elitist, Sexist,'" KUTV, June 26, 2020, https://kutv.com/news /nation-world/petition-to-remove-star-spangled-banner-as-anthem-calls-it -racist-elitist-sexist.

19. Forgie, "Petition to Remove 'Star-Spangled Banner.'"

20. O'Leary, *To Die For*, 21.

21. As quoted in Sally Jenkins, "How the Flag Came to Be Called Old Glory: New Research May Settle a Family Feud Over the Origins of an American Icon," *Smithsonian Magazine*, October 2013, https://www.smithsonianmag .com/history/how-the-flag-came-to-be-called-old-glory-18396. I should add that this is often quoted and always without a source.

22. "Walt Whitman Writes His Mother About a Regimental Flag," *Civil*

War Book of Days 5, no. 14 (2014), https://civilwarbookofdays.org/2014/04/04/walt-whitman-writes-his-mother-about-a-regimental-flag.

23. "Walt Whitman Writes His Mother About a Regimental Flag," *Civil War Book of Days* 5, no. 14 (2014), https://civilwarbookofdays.org/2014/04/04/walt-whitman-writes-his-mother-about-a-regimental-flag.

24. John M. Coski, *The Confederate Flag: America's Most Embattled Emblem* (Cambridge: Belknap Press, 2005), 3. https://web-p-ebscohost-com.proxy.lib.umich.edu/ehost/ebookviewer/ebook/ZTcwMHhuYV9fMjgyMjcwX19BTg2?sid=04569915c-4e0c-473e-b57f-264f1df648a5@redis&vid=0&format=EB&rid=1.

25. Miles, as quoted in Coski, *The Confederate Flag*, 4.

26. Thomas, as quoted in Kyle Kim and Priya Krishnakumar, "What You Should Know About the Confederate Flag," *LA Times*, July 9, 2015, https://web.archive.org/web/20150712023515/http://www.latimes.com/visuals/graphics/la-na-g-confederate-flag-history-20150623-htmlstory.html.

27. "'Are We a Nation?' Address of Hon. Charles Sumner before the New York Young Men's Republican Union, at the Cooper Institute, Tuesday evening, Nov. 19, 1867," Making of America, https://quod.lib.umich.edu/m/moa/ABJ1723.0001.001?rgn=main;view=fulltext.

28. "'Are We a Nation?'"

29. John M. Coski, "Embattled Banner: The True History of the Confederate Flag," HistoryNet, accessed June 10, 2021, https://www.historynet.com/embattled-banner-the-true-history-of-the-confederate-flag.htm.

30. Coski, "Embattled Banner."

31. Coski.

32. As quoted in "Civil War Soldiers: Information and Articles About Soldiers from the Civil War," HistoryNet, accessed June 10, 2021, https://www.historynet.com/civil-war-soldiers.

33. Peter Levine, "Draft Evasion in the North During the Civil War, 1863–1865," *The Journal of American History* 67, no. 4 (1981), https://www.oah.org/site/assets/files/8710/08_jah_1981_levine.pdf.

34. Jessie Campisi and A. J. Willingham, "Behind the Lyrics of the 'Star-Spangled Banner,'" CNN, accessed June 10, 2021, https://www.cnn.com/interactive/2018/07/us/national-anthem-annotated/.

35. "Grand Army of the Republic History," Sons of Union Veterans of the Civil War, accessed June 10, 2021, http://www.suvcw.org/?page_id=167.

36. "Grand Army of the Republic History."

37. "Grand Army of the Republic History,"

38. O'Leary, *To Die For*, 33.

39. O'Leary, 30.

40. O'Leary, 40.

41. Barbara A. Gannon, *The Won Cause: Black and White Comradeship in the Grand Army of the Republic* (Chapel Hill: University of North Carolina Press, 2011), 5.

42. O'Leary, *To Die For*, 103.

43. Richard J. Ellis, *To the Flag: An Unlikely History of the Pledge of Allegiance* (Lawrence, Kansas: University of Kansas Press, 2005), 1.

44. Ellis, *To the Flag*, 4.

45. As quoted in Ellis, 4.

46. Ellis, 5.

47. As quoted in Ellis, 7.

48. As quoted in Ewert, "Lessons in Loyalty," 13.

49. "National School Celebration of Columbus: The Official Programe," *The Youth's Companion*, 65 (September 8, 1892), 446.

50. Ewert, "Lessons in Loyalty," 11.

51. Ewert, 8.

52. Ewert, 27.

53. M. B. C. True, "School Libraries," *Education* 12, no. 4 (December 1891), 216.

54. O'Leary, *To Die For*, 109.

55. "Citizenship Syllabus Now Being Distributed; Textbook Will Be Used by National Americanization Committee to Teach Immigrants," *New York Times*, Apr 2, 1916, https://www.nytimes.com/1916/04/02/archives/citizenship -syllabus-now-being-distributed-textbook-will-be-used-by.html.

56. O'Leary, *To Die For*, 220.

CHAPTER 6. ALLEGIENCE GOT PAID FOR

1. "Creel to Direct Nation's Publicity," *New York Times*, April 15, 1917, https://timesmachine.nytimes.com/timesmachine/1917/04/15/102333118 .html?zoom=14.51&pageNumber=1.

2. "Creel to Direct Nation's Publicity."

3. Christopher Capozzola, *Uncle Sam Wants You: World War I and the Making of the Modern American Citizen* (New York: Oxford University Press, 2008), 7.

4. Capozzola, *Uncle Sam Wants You*, 9.

5. Capozzola, 11.

6. Capozzola, 8.

7. Capozzola, 11.

8. Cody Dodge Ewert, "Lessons in Loyalty: American Patriotism and

Education in the Progressive Era," (master's thesis, University of Montana, 2012), 3.

9. Ewert, "Lessons in Loyalty," 4.

10. Sarah Boxer, "Whitewashing the Great Depression: How the Preeminent Photographic Record of the Period Excluded People of Color from the Nation's Self-Image," *The Atlantic*, December , 2020, https://www.theatlantic.com/magazine/archive/2020/12/whitewashing-the-great-depression/616936.

11. Franklin D. Roosevelt, "Executive Order 9182 Establishing the Office of War Information," *The American Presidency Project*, accessed June 10, 2021, https://www.presidency.ucsb.edu/documents/executive-order-9182-establishing-the-office-war-information.

12. Linda Gordon and Gary Y. Okihiro, *Impounded: Dorothea Lange and the Censored Images of Japanese American Internment* (New York: W. W. Norton & Company, 2006), 17.

13. Gordon and Okihiro, *Impounded*, 5.

14. Torsten Bell, "We Feel More Patriotic When the Government Splashes the Cash," *Guardian*, March 1, 2020, https://www.theguardian.com/commentisfree/2020/mar/01/we-feel-more-patriotic-when-the-government-splashes-the-cash.

15. Felicia R. Lee, "Questioning U.S. Identity in the Aftermath of 9/11," *New York Times*, November 4, 2006, https://www.nytimes.com/2006/11/04/theater/04sund.html.

16. John Bodnar, "Belligerent Patriotism, or Why Donald Trump Cannot Mourn the Dead," History News Network, August 23, 2020, https://historynewsnetwork.org/article/177007.

17. Bodnar, "Belligerent Patriotism."

18. Olivia B. Waxman, "Here's How Standing for the National Anthem Became Part of U.S. Sports Tradition," *Time*, September 25, 2017, https://time.com/4955623/history-national-anthem-sports-nfl.

19. "One Run Gives Red Sox First Game of Series," *New York Times*, September 6, 1918, https://timesmachine.nytimes.com/timesmachine/1918/09/06/97025138.html?pageNumber=14.

20. "Pro Football Pass for the President," *New York Times*, August 23, 1945, https://timesmachine.nytimes.com/timesmachine/1945/08/23/1131282 22.html?pageNumber=19.

21. "Pro Football Pass for the President."

22. John McCain and Jeff Flake, *Tackling Paid Patriotism: A Joint Oversight Report*, accessed June 10, 2021, https://static.politico.com/98/a4/d61b3cae45f0 a7b79256cf1da1e0/flake-report.45am.pdf, 1.

23. McCain and Flake, *Tackling Paid Patriotism*, 1.

24. McCain and Flake.

25. McCain and Flake.

26. Chris Isidore, "NFL Revenue: Here Comes Another Record Season," CNN Business, September 10, 2015, https://money.cnn.com/2015/09/10/news/companies/nfl-revenue-profits.

27. McCain and Flake, *Tackling Paid Patriotism*.

28. Dave Hogg, "The Military Paid Pro Sports Teams $10.4 Million for Patriotic Displays, Troop Tributes," SBNation, November 4, 2015, https://www.sbnation.com/2015/11/4/9670302/nfl-paid-patriotism-troops-mcain-flake-report-million.

29. "Blumenthal, McCain, Flake File Amendment to Stop NFL 'Patriotism for Profit' Practices," Richard Blumenthal, June 5, 2015, https://www.blumenthal.senate.gov/newsroom/press/release/blumenthal-mccain-flake-file-amendment-to-stop-nfl-patriotism-for-profit-practices.

30. Corky Siemaszko, "NFL Agrees to Reimburse U.S. Taxpayers $720K for 'Paid Patriotism,'" NBC News, May 19, 2016, https://www.nbcnews.com/news/us-news/nfl-agrees-reimburse-u-s-taxpayers-720k-paid-patriotism-n577031.

31. Roger Goodell, "Dear Senators McClain and Flake" (letter), November 2, 2015, https://nflcommunications.com/Documents/2015%20Releases/11022015%20--%20McCain%20Flake%20Letter.pdf.

32. Goodell, "Dear Senators McClain and Flake."

33. Siemaszko, "NFL Agrees to Reimburse U.S. Taxpayers."

34. Michael McCann, "Can the NFL or Its Teams Legally Require Players to Stand for the Anthem? NFLPA Doesn't Think So," *Sports Illustrated*, May 8, 2018, https://www.si.com/nfl/2018/05/08/nflpa-grievance-eric-reid-national-anthem.

35. NFL Sports Boston, August 29, 2016, https://www.nbcsports.com/boston/new-england-patriots/nfl-teams-being-field-anthem-relatively-new-practice.

36. Melanie Schmitz, "How the NFL Sold Patriotism to the Military for Millions," *Think Progress*, September 25, 2017, https://archive.thinkprogress.org/nfl-dod-national-anthem-6f682cebc7cd/.

37. Patrick Sauer, "Stephen A. Smith Points Out NFL's Paid Patriotism Problem," Vice, September 14, 2016, https://www.vice.com/en/article/yp89dj/stephen-a-smith-points-out-nfls-paid-patriotism-problem.

38. Paula Reed Ward, "DOD Paid $53 Million of Taxpayers' Money to Pro Sports for Military Tributes, Report Says," *Pittsburgh Post-Gazette*, November 6, 2015, https://www.post-gazette.com/news/nation/2015/11/06/

Department-of-Defense-paid-53-million-to-pro-sports-for-military-tributes
-report-says/stories/201511060140.

39. "Blumenthal, McCain, Flake File Amendment."

40. "Blumenthal, McCain, Flake File Amendment."

41. Cindy Boren, "A Timeline of Colin Kaepernick's Protests Against
the Police, Four Years After They Began," *Washington Post*, August 26, 2020,
https://www.washingtonpost.com/sports/2020/06/01/colin-kaepernick
-kneeling-history.

42. Tadd Haislop, "Colin Kaepernick Kneeling Timeline: How Protests
During the National Anthem Started a Movement in the NFL," *Sporting
News*, September 13, 2020, https://www.sportingnews.com/us/nfl/news/colin
-kaepernick-kneeling-protest-timeline/xktu6ka4diva1s5jxaylrcsse.

43. Boren, "A Timeline."

44. Boren.

45. "Trump: NFL Kneelers 'Maybe Shouldn't Be in Country,'" *BBC News*,
May 24, 2018, https://www.bbc.com/news/world-us-canada-44232979.

46. Washington Examiner (@dcexaminer), "Trump wishes NFL owners
would tell anthem protesters 'get that son of a bitch off the field right now,'"
Twitter, September 22, 2017, https://twitter.com/dcexaminer/status/911139176
1070731264.

47. Jemele Hill, "The War on Black Athletes," *The Atlantic*, January 13,
2019, https://www.theatlantic.com/politics/archive/2019/01/why-trump
-targeted-colin-kaepernick/579628.

48. *Today*, "NFL Apologizes to Players for Dismissing Racism Concerns,"
June 6, 2020, video, https://www.youtube.com/watch?v=H1egx6tz5wo.

49. Nick Selbe, "Roger Goodell Offers Apology to Colin Kaepernick,"
Sports Illustrated, August 23, 2020, https://www.si.com/nfl/2020/08/24/roger
-goodell-apologizes-colin-kaepernick-national-anthem-protest.

50. Jason Reid, "NFL to Stencil 'End Racism' on End Zone Borders as
Part of Social Justice Rollout for Kickoff Week," ESPN, July 27, 2020, https://
www.espn.com/nfl/story/_/id/29549338/nfl-stencil-end-racism-takes-all-us
-end-zone-borders-kickoff-week.

51. "Remembering George Floyd, One Year Later," NFL, accessed June
10, 2021, video, https://www.nfl.com/causes/inspire-change.

IMAGE CREDITS

Introduction   Figure 1, page 2: White Lies Matter, Inc.

Section I   Figure 2, page 30: Alamy Images.
Figure 3, page 31: Ranee Saunders.

Chapter 1   Figure 4, page 41: Kieran O'Keefe.
Figure 5, page 53: Alamy Images.

Chapter 2   Figure 6, page 68: Alamy Images.

Section II   Figure 7, page 92: Alamy Images.

Chapter 4   Figure 8, page 145: Alamy Images.
Figure 9, page 148: Courtesy of The Montpelier
Foundation.

Section III   Figure 10, page 154: Dorothea Lange.

Conclusion   Figure 11, page 208: Travis Fullerton. Virginia Museum
of Fine Arts, Richmond. Purchased with funds provided
by Virginia Sargeant Reynolds, in memory of her
husband, Richard S. Reynolds, Jr., by exchange, Arthur
and Margaret Glasgow Endowment, Pamela K. and
William A. Royall, Jr., Angel and Tom Papa, Katherine
and Steven Markel, and additional private donors,
2019.39.

INDEX

ABOUT THE AUTHOR

KRISTIN ANN HASS teaches in the Department of American Culture at the University of Michigan. She is the author of *Sacrificing Soldiers on the National Mall*, a study of militarism, race, and US war memorials, and *Carried to the Wall: American Memory and the Vietnam Veterans Memorial*, an exploration of public memorial practices and the legacies of the Vietnam War. She holds a PhD in American studies and has worked in several historical museums, including the National Museum of American History. She was also the cofounder of *Imagining America: Artists and Scholars in Public Life*, a national consortium of educators and activists dedicated to campus-community collaborations, and she is currently the faculty coordinator for the University of Michigan Humanities Collaboratory.